Helping and Being Helped

The Claremont Symposium on Applied Social Psychology

This series of volumes highlights important new developments on the leading edge of applied social psychology. Each volume concentrates on one area where social psychological knowledge is being applied to the resolution of social problems. Within that area, a distinguished group of authorities present chapters summarizing recent theoretical views and empirical findings, including the results of their own research and applied activities. An introductory chapter integrates this material, pointing out common themes and varied areas of practical applications. Thus each volume brings together trenchant new social psychological ideas, research results, and fruitful applications bearing on an area of current social interest. The volumes will be of value not only to practitioners and researchers, but also to students and lay people interested in this vital and expanding area of psychology.

Books in the Series

Interpersonal Processes, *Stuart Oskamp and Shirlynn Spacapan, Editors*

The Social Psychology of Health, *Shirlynn Spacapan and Stuart Oskamp, Editors*

The Social Psychology of Aging, *Shirlynn Spacapan and Stuart Oskamp, Editors*

People's Reactions to Technology, *Stuart Oskamp and Shirlynn Spacapan, Editors*

Helping and Being Helped, *Shirlynn Spacapan and Stuart Oskamp, Editors*

Helping and Being Helped

Naturalistic Studies

Shirlynn Spacapan
Stuart Oskamp
Editors

 **The Claremont Symposium on Applied Social Psychology**

 **SAGE** PUBLICATIONS
The International Professional Publishers
Newbury Park   London   New Delhi

For information address:

SAGE Publications, Inc.
2455 Teller Road
Newbury Park, California 91320

SAGE Publications Ltd.
6 Bonhill Street
London EC2A 4PU
United Kingdom

SAGE Publications India Pvt. Ltd.
M-32 Market
Greater Kailash I
New Delhi 110 048 India

Printed in the United States of America

Library of Congress Cataloging-in-Publication Data

Main entry under title:

Helping and being helped : naturalistic studies / Shirlynn Spacapan,
    Stuart Oskamp, editors.
        p.   cm. — (The Claremont Symposium on Applied Social Psychology)
    Revised papers presented at the 7th symposium held Feb 3, 1990.
    Includes bibliographical references and index.
    ISBN 0-8039-4327-X. — ISBN 0-8039-4328-8 (pbk.)
    1. Helping behavior—Congresses.   I. Spacapan, Shirlynn.
    II. Oskamp, Stuart.   III. Series: Claremont Symposium on Applied
Social Psychology (Series)
    BF637.H4H45 1992   91-10711
    158'.3—dc20   CIP

FIRST PRINTING, 1992

Sage Production Editor: Diane S. Foster

Contents

Preface

The group of behaviors that are variously labeled as helping behavior, altruism, or prosocial acts comprises a classic area of inquiry within social psychology. Recent years have seen a rapidly increasing number of studies in this area and publication of several books on the topic. A unique contribution of the present volume, however, is its emphasis on helping "in the real world"—that is, helping behavior as it naturally occurs in our daily lives, rather than that captured in an artificial social laboratory. In addition, many of the *types* of helping discussed in the following pages represent situations unique to these last two decades of the twentieth century. For example, volunteering one's services as a helper to someone with AIDS is clearly an opportunity that was unheard of even a decade ago. Similarly, recent medical advances that prolong human life have created opportunities to help by donating a kidney, or caring for an elderly person with Alzheimer's disease. Each of these forms of help is among those covered in the chapters to follow.

These chapters are based on presentations given at the seventh Claremont Symposium on Applied Social Psychology on February 3, 1990. Although various areas of psychology have annual conferences dedicated to presenting new developments within their specified fields, only the Claremont group has sponsored an annual conference on applied social psychology. These symposia bring distinguished psychologists from various parts of North America to join in discussion and analysis of important issues in applied social psychology. The Claremont Symposium has focused on social psychological applications to organizational settings, public policy issues, interpersonal processes, health, aging, and new technologies in robots and aerospace.

This series of symposia has been made possible through the generous financial support of all six of the Claremont Colleges—Claremont Graduate School, Claremont McKenna College, Harvey Mudd College, Pitzer College, Pomona College, and Scripps College. This year, additional thanks are due Harvey Mudd College for faculty research funds that covered expenses involved in the preparation of this volume and enabled the first editor to work on the book. We are also grateful to Gail M. Williamson, now of the University of Georgia at Athens, for serving as a discussant of the presentations at the conference. Finally, our personal thanks go to Shawn Okuda and Steve Yukawa for their help with indexing, and to Catherine Cameron and Mike Nichol for their social support.

In preparing this volume, the contributors have expanded their conference presentations and addressed some of the issues raised by the audience discussion. We have encouraged them to maintain a somewhat informal style and a personalized tone by including anecdotal information to illustrate their research findings and theoretical material. Our initial chapter introduces each of the substantive chapters and summarizes common themes that several of them touch on.

Because of the thoroughness with which each topic is covered, we believe this volume will be accessible and interesting to students and others who may be unfamiliar with the field. Because of the new, previously unpublished work in the following pages, we believe the volume will be important for scholars interested in cutting-edge research. In addition, the authors' cogent discussions of the implications of their work will be valuable to practitioners and policymakers who must apply social psychology in the real world.

Shirlynn Spacapan
Stuart Oskamp
Claremont, California

1

An Introduction to Naturalistic Studies of Helping

SHIRLYNN SPACAPAN
STUART OSKAMP

In 1964, Kitty Genovese was knifed to death as 38 of her neighbors watched from the safety of their own apartments (see Latané & Darley, 1970). When her screams caused someone to turn on a light or open a window, the killer would leave, only to return when the lights went out. It took her attacker over 35 minutes to kill her—yet, even with all that time and her clear cries for help, none of Ms. Genovese's neighbors called the police. Numerous similar stories in the media have suggested that if we were ever in need of help—say, with a stalled car on the freeway, or perhaps just needing change in order to use a public telephone—we would be unlikely to receive much aid from bystanders. Although the media have attributed this to the "apathy" in our society, social psychologists have demonstrated otherwise. In many cases where help is not given, it is not the result of "apathetic" or "inhumane" bystanders, but rather of human errors in social judgment, lack of communication, or faulty group dynamics. Regardless of its causes, the failure to help has implications that extend beyond injury to the person in need, for several authors have suggested that bystander passivity sows the seeds of group violence and other social ills (see Adler, 1990; Staub, 1989).

The Genovese incident resulted in a veritable explosion of work on bystander intervention in particular, and helping behavior in general, aimed at answering the question, "Why don't people help?" After that first wave of research, other important issues have arisen. A related set of questions is posed by the authors of the following chapters: How do offers of assistance affect the *help-seeker? Who* is likely to help? What are the *negative* aspects, or costs, of helping relationships?

In addition to posing a somewhat different set of questions, a unique contribution of this volume is its emphasis on helping "in the real world"—that is, helping behavior as it naturally occurs in people's daily lives, not just the sort captured in the confines of an artificial social laboratory. As Wills points out (in Chapter 2), controlled laboratory experimentation is invaluable for identifying constructs, and we do not dispute that. One value of the present volume, however, is that the contributors are testing classic laboratory-derived social psychological constructs for their relevance and generalizability to the real world. The kinds of settings and populations that are explored include volunteers who assist AIDS patients, spouses supporting diabetics and recent stroke patients, family caregivers of relatives with Alzheimer's disease (AD), living kidney donors, and self-help groups like Alcoholics Anonymous or less formal arrangements such as peer helping. These situations differ from those studied in the typical, early laboratory studies in that the helping behavior probably results from a deliberate decision to help, is of longer duration, and may be risky or costly.

In answer to the earlier question of "who helps," the examples in the last paragraph hint that much helping behavior in our society occurs within family or friendship circles. But what about other cases, such as people who have volunteered to work in AIDS clinics, or those non-family members who have offered to be living kidney donors? Are certain people more likely to be altruistic or helpful? London's (1970) study of Christians who saved Jews from the Nazis suggested that those helpers were characterized by a spirit of adventurousness and an intense identification with a parental model of high moral standards. One wonders if these characteristics are common to other helpers, as well. A few studies have explored this question to date, and the present volume is noteworthy for its acknowledgement of this aspect of helping behavior.

Another contribution of this volume pertains to its coverage of the often-neglected negative side of helping behavior: What are the emotional costs of caring for a person with a terminal disease? Do caregivers develop resentment of their charges? Why do some attempts to provide social support fail? What are the emotional costs of being a recipient of care and support?

A host of relatively ignored questions about help-seekers are also addressed in this volume: Precisely what do help-seekers expect to gain from self-help groups or other forms of assistance? What kinds of attempts to help are viewed as unnecessary overprotection by the recipient? Work oñ each of these questions is very new and sheds light on how attempts to help, or provide social support, go awry. This information enhances our understanding of the dynamics of helping, and may also provide clues as to why some people are unwilling to be involved in a helping relationship.

The distinguished contributors to this volume provide coverage of necessary background information in each of these areas and describe recent theory, research, and applications. This first chapter presents an overview of the volume, summarizes the substantive chapters, and highlights important issues that are common to several of the chapters.

Overview of the Book

The following chapters begin with a review of the helping process in the context of personal relationships, presented by Thomas Ashby Wills in Chapter 2. This "context of personal relationships" is dealt with more specifically in Chapter 3, where Louis Medvene discusses peer helping and self-help groups. In both of these chapters, as in the research reported in Chapter 4 by Christine Dunkel-Schetter, David E. Blasband, Lawrence G. Feinstein, and Tracy Bennett Herbert, the focus is on the help-seeker or the recipient of a supportive interaction. Dunkel-Schetter and her colleagues also suggest a conceptual framework for studying social support that includes the perspectives of the support provider, the recipient, and an outside "third party." More than one perspective is acknowledged in Chapter 5, where Suzanne C. Thompson and Jennifer S. Pitts examine the effects of chronic illness on the help-seeker (the ill person), his or her helper or caregiver (the well spouse), and the couple's marriage.

The remaining three chapters emphasize the perspective of the help provider. In Chapter 6, Richard Schulz, Gail M. Williamson, Richard K. Morycz, and David E. Biegel study the care*givers* of people with Alzheimer's disease, as well as considering the patient's status and functioning. The research reported in Chapter 7 by Eugene Borgida, Cynthia Conner, and Laurie Manteufel centers on a little-studied group of helpers—those who donate a kidney to save another person's life. In the last chapter, Mark Snyder and Allen M. Omoto present results from their program of cross-sectional and longitudinal lab and field studies on volunteers who work with people with AIDS. Each of these seven chapters is briefly summarized here.

The Helping Process

In Chapter 2, Thomas Ashby Wills points out that laboratory studies of helping behavior suggest that people do not seek help very often, whereas the opposite conclusion is reached when help-seeking is studied in the field. Aiming to reconcile these different conclusions from lab and field settings, he provides an overview of pertinent research in each setting. In reviewing the lab work, Wills suggests a number of factors (such as threats to self-esteem) that may be behind the low frequency of help-seeking. Other factors that increase help-seeking in the lab (e.g., friendship between the seeker and provider, the opportunity to reciprocate the help) appear to be relevant in explaining the high frequency of help-seeking in field studies (particularly the preference for informal sources like friends and family). Though lab and field studies typically differ in the type of problem for which help is sought (i.e., lab problems are usually less serious, or less relevant to the self, than are the real-world problems of field studies), Wills emphasizes the importance of the context of personal relationships in understanding differences in helping between settings. He elucidates one contextual factor—the existence of multiple support networks in real-world field settings—by presenting brief results of three previously unpublished studies. He concludes by noting the primacy of emotional support as a key difference between the context of ongoing personal relationships and that of the laboratory.

Self-Help Groups and Peer Helping

Following Wills's overview of the help-seeking literature, Louis Medvene focuses on specific ways in which people seek help through self-help groups and peer counseling, and he provides an overview of the diversity and commonality among self-help groups and peer counseling relationships. This sets the stage for a discussion of the role of similarity between parties in a helping relationship, emphasizing the importance of social comparison theory in understanding self-help groups. Here Medvene explains the "paradox of help-seeking" (Wills, 1983)—laboratory findings that people prefer "downward" comparisons with those less well-off, in contrast to field studies suggesting that "upward" comparisons with better-off friends and family lead to more help-seeking. Attempting to understand this paradox in a study of help-seeking preferences of undergraduates, Medvene found that students preferred contact with an upward-comparison, experientially similar peer over contact with a variety of other potential helpers (e.g., another student who was worse off than they were, or a mental health professional) in dealing with both academic or relationship problems. Such upward comparisons were preferred for their potential for self-improvement of the help-seeker, whereas motives of self-evaluation and self-enhancement did not appear to be driving students' choice of helpers (contrary to the extant literature).

When Is Support Effective?

Chapter 4 is noteworthy for its presentation of a conceptual framework for studying social support. Christine Dunkel-Schetter, David E. Blasband, Lawrence G. Feinstein, and Tracy Bennett Herbert incorporate two key dimensions together with three different perspectives in their framework: Both the intentions behind the helpful attempt and the immediate effects on the recipient should be considered from the perspectives of the provider, the recipient, and an outside observer. Examining the recipient's perspective, this chapter features the results of two new studies—one related to Blasband's dissertation work with 40 gay and bisexual men with AIDS, the other from Feinstein's dissertation on 40 diabetic patients and their spouses. The authors are interested in the quantity of support received by a given individual and factors that increase or decrease the probability that a helpful, support-ive act will be attempted, but here they also address the more qualitative question of mediators of the effects of support. That is, why do some attempts to help succeed whereas others fail? Both of their studies employ a naturalistic paradigm involving semistructured interviews, and both uphold Wills's previous claim that emotional forms of support seem uniformly helpful. Unhelpful types of "support" include advice that implies failure or blame on the part of the recipient and behaviors that convey overinvolvement, oversolicitousness, or overconcern. This chapter closes with a helpful section suggesting directions for future research on support provider characteristics.

Chronic Illness and Marriage

Chapter 5, by Suzanne C. Thompson and Jennifer S. Pitts, begins with an overview of three types of theoretical perspectives on family relationships: social exchange theories (e.g., equity, interdependence), family dynamic theories (e.g., family systems, role theory), and family resource or coping theories. Two themes that emerge from these theo-ries are that chronic illness could create inequities or a dependence that negatively affects a marriage and, as Dunkel-Schetter and her col-leagues point out, that caregiving spouses may overprotect their ill partners. However, Thompson and Pitts's review of past research leads them to conclude that dramatic, consistent effects of illness on marital satisfaction are not observed, even though both spouses are under great stress and the illness creates inequities in the relationship. Thompson and Pitts then discuss the "dilemma of caregiving"—the fact that caregiving indicates not only the love and concern of the well spouse but also the dependence and helplessness of the ill spouse. Two studies of stroke patients by Thompson and her colleagues have examined this dilemma in terms of spousal styles of caregiving. Results revealed a positive relationship between patients' depression and the extent to which their spouses overprotected them and criticized or held them to unrealistic expectations. Moreover, a third study revealed that feeling overprotected was not related to objective factors like the patient's functioning or even the number of things that the well spouse did for him or her, but rather to the caregiver's negative attitudes and tendency to withhold upsetting news.

Alzheimer's Caregivers

Depression is also an outcome variable of interest and patient status is also viewed as an objective stressor in Chapter 6, by Richard Schulz, Gail M. Williamson, Richard K. Morycz, and David E. Biegel. Here, however, the caregiver's (rather than the help-seeker's) depression is examined. Like other contributors to this volume, the authors consider both the person being helped and the help provider as they offer a social psychological approach for studying the costs and benefits of helping disabled individuals. Their approach is a stress-coping model encompassing objective stressors (e.g., patient characteristics like functional disability, or prognosis), the caregiver's perceived stress or burden, enduring outcomes (e.g., caregiver depression or health), and "conditioning" variables (e.g., caregiver age, income, or support available) that may affect how the other three sets of variables interact. Schulz and his colleagues provide a detailed account of new longitudinal research that focuses on objective stressors and conditioning variables as predictors of caregiver depression. Results revealed that caregiver depression was related to the amount of assistance the patient needed and the frequency of the patient's problem behaviors (objective stressors), as well as to conditioning variables concerning the caregiver's support network. Over the 18 months of the study, patients' conditions declined, yet overall caregiver depression did not increase significantly. Dividing caregivers into groups of those who became more depressed, became less depressed, and did not change enabled further examination of predictors of caregiver depression. In conclusion, the authors reevaluate their stress-coping model and consider the relevance of temporal response models like the wear-and-tear hypothesis, the adaptation hypothesis, and the trait hypothesis in accounting for their data.

Living Kidney Donation

Whereas Schulz and his colleagues reported that research on Alzheimer's caregivers is plentiful but systematic studies of the disease's impact on patients are virtually nonexistent, the opposite is true of living kidney donation—here there are very few studies on the helper, or kidney donor. In Chapter 7, Eugene Borgida, Cynthia Conner, and Laurie Manteufel acknowledge that research on the one-time, risky behavior of kidney donation may not generalize to the more usual forms of helping practiced in everyday life or studied by social psychologists (e.g., blood donation). However, social psychological theory and research—particularly Ajzen's (1985) theory of planned behavior—can serve as a base for studying this unusual prosocial act, and the results can inform and enrich our understanding of basic decision-making processes.

The authors review research that hints at donor ambivalence about donation (not unlike the complex feelings that Thompson and Pitts find are held by some caregivers), and yet conclude that the decision to donate a kidney is usually made quickly and spontaneously. The theories of planned behavior and reasoned action are used in a new study aimed at predicting kidney donation. Because there are factors in kidney donation that are beyond the potential donor's control (e.g., his or her blood type may not be compatible with that of the person in need), the more general theory of planned behavior, with its component of perceived behavioral control, was expected and found to have greater explanatory power than the theory of reasoned action. In discussing these findings, the authors emphasize the careful, deliberate process of decision making in this context—in contrast to previous reports that the decision to donate is typically a snap decision.

AIDS Volunteerism

In the final chapter, Mark Snyder and Allen M. Omoto investigate *who* volunteers to help people with AIDS (PWAs) and present a three-stage model of the volunteer process (antecedents, experiences, and consequences) that acknowledges the deliberate, long-term, and costly nature of this help. The focus of this chapter is on antecedents at the individual level of analysis, particularly on what motivates people to volunteer. Here the authors revive and employ a functional approach, which suggests that similar acts of volunteerism serve quite different functions for different individuals: For some people volunteer work may meet social needs, for others it may fulfill a desire for knowledge, or be a way to express personal values, and so on.

Results from Snyder and Omoto's earlier studies demonstrated that people generally see AIDS volunteer work as a very different kind of helping from other forms of volunteer work; even volunteers in non-AIDS programs reported that though they themselves volunteered for rather selfish reasons, it would take selfless reasons to motivate them to do AIDS volunteer work. What does motivate actual AIDS volunteers? Those in training to be AIDS volunteers appeared mainly to be fulfilling needs for knowledge and value expression. Those who were already active in AIDS-related work were a heterogeneous group in demographic terms and in terms of their motivation for volunteering, although the value-expressive function was their most frequently cited reason. When Snyder and Omoto's research moved from antecedents to experiences of volunteerism, they found that different motivations for serving were associated with differing choices of volunteer tasks (e.g., office tasks versus direct contact with a PWA as a buddy), and that initial motivations predicted later attrition of volunteers. This chapter closes with an overview of the tradition of action research, which emphasizes research as a key aspect of social action—a fitting conclusion for this volume of studies that have such important implications for practice and public policy.

Key Themes in the Volume

The theory and research in these chapters converge on a number of key themes that are prominent in the psychology of helping and being helped. Five of these recurring themes are discussed in the following sections.

A Context of Personal Relationships

From the outset, this volume emphasizes the importance of the context of personal relationships in understanding helping behavior. As noted earlier, it is primarily the contextual difference in personal relationships to which Wills's attributes the observed differences in helping between lab and field settings. In Chapter 2, he discusses five processes or contextual differences between paradigms that may result in greater help-seeking in field settings: the ability of the seeker to reciprocate; the history of sharing, intimacy, or self-disclosure between seeker and provider; the balance that must be struck regarding similarity of the seeker and provider versus threats to the self-esteem of the seeker; the existence of communal norms as opposed to a competitive or exchange orientation; and the existence of multiple support networks in field settings.

These factors not only may affect whether or not one seeks help in a given setting, but also may determine some of the outcomes of the helping relationship. For example, a communal orientation and the closeness of the relationship between the caregiver and an Alzheimer's victim (prior to the onset of AD) have been linked to caregiver outcomes such as depression and to patient outcomes like mortality and likelihood of being placed in an institution (see Chapter 6 by Schulz et al.). In research by Thompson and her colleagues (Chapter 5), the quality of the relationship between a stroke patient and his or her caregiver (usually the spouse) was a powerful predictor of patient depression, even after objective circumstances such as the severity of the stroke were controlled. Some aspects of the quality of the marital relationship determined the support received by diabetics from their spouses, according to research reported by Dunkel-Schetter et al. in Chapter 4. And Snyder and Omoto (Chapter 8) are investigating the relationships that develop between PWAs and volunteers to determine the forms of these relationships and their consequent effects on both parties. In various ways, then, the contributors to this volume incorporate personal relationships as part of their consideration of helping behavior.

Complex Conceptualizations of Helping

As Thompson and Pitts point out in Chapter 5, one criticism that is frequently leveled at this field is that there are no simple, universally accepted definitions of concepts like helping and social support. To illustrate some of the definitional complexities in this field, note the terminology used in Chapter 4, where Dunkel-Schetter and her colleagues clearly outline the type of support that they are studying. They define social support in terms of support that is *received* rather than that which is perceived as *available,* and they employ a three-category classification scheme of emotional, informational, and instrumental support. The typical conceptualization of helping behavior in social psychological research is similar to the instrumental type of support, but the other kinds may be equally or more important in some situations.

These authors' review of relevant research further emphasizes the complexity of support, for they point out that not only does the *type* of support determine its effectiveness, but also some *sources* of support are more helpful than others. Moreover, source and type of support may interact such that a given source may be more appropriate for providing a given type of support, and type of support may interact with types of stressful situations (e.g., cancer versus bereavement versus diabetes).

Similarly, in Chapter 3, Medvene points out that people will seek help from different types of individuals depending on the sort of problem they are facing. The complexity of these relationships among types and sources of support is in evidence throughout this volume, as many contributors note that there will be no simple answers to simple questions like "Who helps?" and "Why do they help?"

Helping Without Being Altruistic

Chapter 6, in which Schulz and his colleagues report on the positive aspects of caring for a relative with AD, is the only one that features an extended section on the benefits that one may realize from helping another person. Nevertheless, each chapter acknowledges the fact that the helper may also profit from a helpful act, and several note that we do not necessarily help our fellow human beings for purely altruistic reasons. In reviewing the effects of a partner's illness on the well spouse, Thompson and Pitts (Chapter 5) note that caregiving can increase the caregiver's sense of self-efficacy and enhance his or her self-image. In discussing the "intention" dimension of their model for studying social support, Dunkel-Schetter and her colleagues (Chapter 4) provide examples of support attempts motivated by self-interest. As another example, among the behavioral beliefs on the questionnaire constructed by Borgida, Conner, and Manteufel (Chapter 7), prospective kidney donors could indicate the extent to which the donation would "make me feel better about myself," "result in a closer personal relationship between [the person in need] and me," and "make me feel more satisfied about my life." And Medvene (Chapter 3) tells us that some long-term participants in self-help groups like Alcoholics Anonymous insist that their support of newer members should not be taken as selfless, for the "old-timers" obtain enhanced self-esteem from comparing themselves to worse-off newcomers.

Similarly, some of the respondents in research by Snyder and Omoto (Chapter 8) revealed that they actually volunteered their services for selfish reasons such as résumé building and gaining experience. Then, too, it is important to remember that the nature of functional approaches (like that taken by Snyder and Omoto) implies that a given behavior serves some function for the actor—in this case, that the helping behavior serves some need for the helper. Thus the old debate over whether any behavior can truly be altruistic, or whether a behavior is altruistic only if we can't observe what the helper gains from the act (see Skinner, 1971), seems irrelevant in light of these contributors' views that a helpful act can aid the helper as well as the help-seeker.

Classic Social Psychological Theories Employed

The preceding summaries of each chapter in this volume mentioned the theories that guided each investigation. It is noteworthy that each of these applied contributions is rooted in classic theoretical views that are at the core of social psychology. For example, Snyder and Omoto revive functional theories, which were important in the early years of social psychology but have been long neglected. Their work, combined with that of other current investigators (e.g., Pratkanis, Breckler, & Greenwald, 1988), promises to develop further and extend the functional approach. Borgida and his colleagues test two theories that have been important in exploring the attitude-behavior relationship: the theory of reasoned action and its offshoot, the theory of planned behavior. Both Wills's chapter and that of Dunkel-Schetter and her colleagues focus on theories of social support, attempting to refine and clarify them in addition to investigating how they apply in the area of helping relationships. In addition, Wills's review bears on theories of self-esteem, and his emphasis on the importance of reciprocal relationships hints at the importance of equity theory.

Thompson and Pitts's theoretical overview explicitly considers the applicability to caregiving relationships of social exchange theories such as equity theory, family dynamics theories such as role theory and family systems theory, and resource and coping theories. On the latter topic, their chapter overlaps with Schulz et al.'s, which utilizes a stress-coping model to analyze the costs and benefits of helping and being helped. Finally, Medvene's discussion of self-help groups and peer helping relationships emphasizes the importance of social comparison theory, as well as of Schachter's fear-affiliation hypothesis and of Byrne's similarity-attraction paradigm. Not only do these authors rely on established social psychological theories in structuring their research, but in many cases their findings also contribute to extending and refining the coverage of these theories.

Implications for Policy and Practice

Each of the following chapters has much to offer practitioners who must apply social psychology in the real world. Many of the chapters contain sections devoted exclusively to the practical implications of the reviewed research and theory. As examples, Medvene (Chapter 3) offers specific applications of his research findings to the design of self-help groups, and Schulz and his colleagues (Chapter 6) conclude with a section on identifying characteristics of caregivers who may be particularly vulnerable to the stresses of caregiving. In other chapters, ideas on applying the reported findings are integrated throughout the material, as in Chapter 4, where Dunkel-Schetter and her colleagues provide ideas on how their research results can be applied to help people become good support providers.

In either form of presentation, the authors have taken pains to be explicit about the translation of their research or theory into practice. For example, in discussing the results of research with stroke patients, Thompson and Pitts (Chapter 5) tie in their earlier review of theory and provide a helpful section suggesting adaptive interaction styles for caregiving situations. They suggest that adaptive styles must allow for the *reciprocity* emphasized in Wills's chapter, demonstrate caring and love in the sort of *emotional support* stressed by both Wills and Dunkel-Schetter et al., and encourage *open communication* without shielding or withholding information or feelings. As another example, Wills (Chapter 2) suggests that the applied implications of the reviewed research bear crucially on ways to increase the "help resources" of people with limited social support—for example, teaching them to seek help with an opportunity for reciprocity built into the request. In sum, many of the findings and theories reported in this volume are eminently useful in people's daily lives, and the contributors have taken explicit steps in the direction of ensuring that readers have a clear understanding of how their work may be applied.

In addition to their utility in people's usual day-to-day activity, many of the issues raised in the following pages have valuable and far-reaching implications for organizational or public policy. For example, an understanding of the decision to donate an organ is especially critical from a health care policy standpoint, given the inefficiencies in the organ procurement system, the increasing success of transplantation, and evidence that one third of those people who need a kidney die before one is obtained. Thus the research reported in Chapter 7 by Borgida and his colleagues is important not only for its contribution to our academic knowledge of helping behavior and the process of making consequential, psychologically involving decisions, but also for its possible application by organ transplant center personnel. Similarly, the series of findings in Snyder and Omoto's (Chapter 8) program has implications for recruiting and retaining more volunteers to help PWAs, thus easing the load on our inefficient and overburdened health care system. Their findings also testify to many people's kindness and concern for their fellow humans, and thus such applied research may inform and refine existing social psychological theories on helping and relationships.

References

Adler, T. (1990, October). Passivity of bystanders encourages social evil. *APA Monitor,* pp. 36-37.

Ajzen, I. (1985). From intentions to actions: A theory of planned behavior. In J. Kuhl & J. Beckman (Eds.), *Action-control: From cognition to behavior* (pp. 11-39). Heidelberg, Germany: Springer.

Latané, B., & Darley, J. M. (1970). *The unresponsive bystander: Why doesn't he help?* New York: Appleton-Century-Crofts.

London, P. (1970). The rescuers: Motivational hypotheses about Christians who saved Jews from the Nazis. In J. Macaulay & L. Berkowitz (Eds.), *Altruism and helping behavior: Social psychological studies of some antecedents and consequences.* New York: Academic Press.

Pratkanis, A. R., Breckler, S. J., & Greenwald, A. G. (Eds.). (1988). *Attitude structure and function.* Hillsdale, NJ: Lawrence Erlbaum.

Skinner, B. F. (1971). *Beyond freedom and dignity.* New York: Knopf.

Staub, E. (1989). *The roots of evil: The psychological and cultural origins of genocide.* Cambridge, UK: Cambridge University Press.

Wills, T. A. (1983). Social comparison in coping and help-seeking. In B. M. DePaulo, A. Nadler, & J. D. Fisher (Eds.), *New directions in helping* (Vol. 2, pp. 109-142). New York: Academic Press.

2

The Helping Process in the Context of Personal Relationships

THOMAS ASHBY WILLS

This chapter provides an overview of the helping process by considering how helping operates in the context of ongoing personal relationships. At present there are two bodies of research on helping and help-seeking. One is the laboratory research on help-seeking and reactions to receiving aid, conducted with sophisticated designs and experimental control of variables (see DePaulo, Nadler, & Fisher, 1983; Fisher, Nadler, & DePaulo, 1983; Nadler, 1986). The other is the field research on social support, using correlational designs, often with representative community samples (Cohen & Wills, 1985; House, Landis, & Umberson, 1988; Sarason, Sarason, & Pierce, 1989). These areas of research have engaged the attention of investigators in social psychology and epidemiology because they bear on important questions of how social relationships contribute to health and well-being (e.g., Cohen, 1988; Diener, 1984; Wills, 1991).

I became involved in this topic initially through a convergence of two interests. One was research on the factors that influence how a helping relationship influences the helper's perceptions of the recipient, both in laboratory paradigms (Wills, 1976) and in profes-

AUTHOR'S NOTE: Preparation of this chapter was supported in part by Grant #1-R01-DA05950 from the National Institute on Drug Abuse.

sional helping relationships (Wills, 1978). Another was an interest in social comparison theory and the question of how favorable or unfavorable comparisons affect self-perceptions and behavior (Wills, 1981). These interests converged in a paper considering how person-perception factors influence help-seeking (Wills, 1983). Since then my interest in social support and family relationships has led to epidemiologic research on the supportive aspects of help-seeking and helping, with a focus on adolescents (Wills, 1990; Wills & DePaulo, 1991; Wills & Vaughan, 1989).

In surveying the literature on helping, it is evident that a number of variables show replicated results for helping as studied in laboratory settings. These include similarity between the helper and the recipient, the cost of helping, and the centrality of the task for the recipient's self-esteem. These variables typically produce comparable results for help-seeking behavior and for reactions to receiving help (see DePaulo et al., 1983; Fisher et al., 1983). However, the findings for these variables as obtained in laboratory settings seem, on the face of it, to be the opposite of the typical data from field settings. This poses a question as to how these two types of findings can be reconciled.

The purpose of this chapter is to address this question and consider the current state of laboratory and field research on helping and help-seeking. Its goal is to delineate processes that contribute to the difference between laboratory and field data. The approach is not to assert that one is right and the other wrong, but to consider how the *context of helping* differs in the two settings. By trying to understand the difference between laboratory and field results, we may achieve a better understanding of helping and help-seeking in the real world. Toward this end, the chapter first considers some basic data on the prevalence of help-seeking in laboratory and field settings, and then discusses five processes that are relevant to understanding helping in the context of personal relationships.

This chapter focuses on the process of help-seeking for relatively discrete life stressors, because the correspondence between laboratory and field data is more tractable. It does not give detailed attention to factors that influence the helper's behavior, because there is little evidence from epidemiological studies that bears on that question. An exemplary start is being made by examining reactions to support behaviors in real settings (see, for example, other chapters in this volume) and by studying how chronic strains and rejection of help may affect the helper (Rook, 1990; Rosen, Mickler, & Collins, 1987; Schulz &

Tompkins, 1990). Further development of this work should broaden our knowledge of the positive and negative functions of interpersonal relationships.

Data on Help-Seeking

Some data on help-seeking will serve to introduce what we know about the basic parameters of helping as it occurs in various contexts. These data also set some boundaries on how the helping process can be understood.

Help-Seeking in Laboratory Settings

First, consider the rate of help-seeking in laboratory paradigms. In the typical laboratory study the subject is presented with a task requirement, is informed that another subject is participating who could potentially provide help with the task, and then is given an opportunity to ask the other person (or the experimenter) for help. In these types of studies, the probability of help-seeking is generally low (see DePaulo, 1982; Nadler, 1986). A representative sample of laboratory studies that exemplify relevant processes, and in which it was possible to determine the absolute percentage of subjects who seek help, is summarized in Table 2.1. (In many studies, the investigators report differences in mean levels for a composite score of help-seeking or help-seeking delay, so it is not possible to determine the absolute frequency of help-seeking.) The table shows the percentage of subjects who sought help in the lowest-probability condition, and contrasts this with the percentage who sought help in the highest-probability condition. (Usually these represent two cells from a 2 × 2 design, with the other rates intermediate.) This summary shows that rates of help-seeking are variable. The lowest rates are in the single digits; the highest rates can be in the 80s and 90s. The following section discusses these studies, giving attention to details of the experimental designs and noting sources of variability in this literature.

It is not difficult to design a paradigm where none of the subjects asks for help. For example, Miller and McFarland (1987) gave college

Table 2.1
Percentage Rates of Help-Seeking Under Various Conditions in Selected Laboratory Studies

Study	Lower cell and condition	Higher cell and condition	Notes
DePaulo (1978)	9 Child helper	29 Adult helper	
Stokes & Bickman (1974)	10 Attractive/ nonrole helper	70 In-role helper	
Morris & Rosen (1973)	14 Inadequate/ no reciprocity	84 Adequate	Physical-handicap setting
Nadler, Shapiro, & Ben-Itzhak (1982)	6 Female/ attractive helper	63 Unattractive helper	Male subjects
" "	17 Female	92 Male/attractive	Female subjects
Shapiro (1980)	25 Stranger/ high cost	80 Friend/any cost	
Shapiro (1978)	33 Public help-seeking/public performance	87 Private help-seeking	Helping encouraged
Greenberg & Shapiro (1971)	37 No reciprocation	71 Reciprocation	Physical-handicap setting

student subjects an article on the self-concept, written (especially for this study) in an obtuse and incomprehensible manner. The subjects were told that the experimenter (a faculty member) was busy working in her office but that they could ask her for help if they had "any really serious problems in understanding the paper." In several studies using this basic paradigm, the investigators found that none of the subjects asked for help (Miller & McFarland, 1987, 1990); these studies are not shown in Table 2.1 because the rate of help-seeking was 0% in all conditions. The helping context in these studies probably maximized embarrassment because the subject had to go to some effort in help-seeking, and had to ask a prestigious stranger for help in a manner that clearly implied intellectual inferiority.

Another example of a low rate of help-seeking is provided in a study by DePaulo (1978). In a telephone survey, community residents were asked whether they would be interested in receiving free art lessons given either by a child (reputed in some conditions to have a good capacity for teaching) or by an adult. Results indicated that when the potential helper was a child, only 9% of subjects were interested in receiving lessons, compared with 29% when the teacher was an adult. These data are consistent with previous results from Druian and De-Paulo (1977), which showed that subjects (Vassar College students) were disinterested in receiving help from a 10-year-old child on a word-spelling task, even when the potential helper's performance was excellent and could improve the subject's own performance.

A study by Morris and Rosen (1973) exemplifies the range of rates observed in laboratory settings. Pairs of subjects participated in a purported study of disability where they were asked to simulate a visual or motor handicap by wearing an eye patch or arm sling, respectively. After a practice task, subjects were informed privately that their performance was either adequate or inadequate in comparison to norms. They then performed an experimental task (making paper boxes) on which they had to meet a numerical quota in order to receive compensation for the study. Subjects were told they could ask the other subject for help on the task, and that they would or would not have an opportunity to reciprocate any help received. The lowest rate of help-seeking (14%) was observed when the subject felt inadequate and had no opportunity to reciprocate; the highest rate (84%) occurred when the subject felt adequate and did anticipate an opportunity to reciprocate help received. This study demonstrates that feelings of threat to self-esteem (from perceived inadequacy) are a barrier to help-seeking in the laboratory setting, but an opportunity to reciprocate may serve to counter this process.

Another interesting difference was shown in a study by Stokes and Bickman (1974). In a purported perception experiment, subjects were placed in a situation where they had to ask for help from another person in order to complete the experimental task. The independent variable was whether the other person was presented as an experimenter (thus being in a normative role as a potential help provider) or as another subject who had already completed the study and was filling out a questionnaire (thus being in a nonrole position). The physical attractiveness of the other person was also varied. In this study, the nonrole condition produced a low rate of help-seeking when the helper was attractive (10%), but when the person was unattractive the rate was high (70%). For the in-role condition, help-seeking was high regardless of attractiveness (60% and 65%). Here the variable of attractiveness apparently created self-esteem concerns, as subjects might feel inadequate when asking for help from a person they judged as more attractive than themselves. The role position of the helper, however, served to reduce these esteem concerns.

Another variable of interest concerns the visibility of the help-seeking request. Shapiro (1978) examined this in a laboratory study presented as a clinical judgment task, where female subjects made judgments of neuroticism from TAT cards. The subject was made to feel incompetent through feedback on a pretest, and then was told that she could consult a set of guidelines that were available because "some people need help in increasing their accuracy." Visibility of help-seeking was manipulated by introducing a confederate who, in the public help-seeking condition, sat in the room and observed whether the subject consulted the guidelines. Visibility of task performance was manipulated by informing the subject that she would receive feedback on performance in a face-to-face interview with a staff member (public performance) or that her performance would be scored months later by a computer (private performance). Results indicated that when performance was public, help-seeking was relatively infrequent (33%) under public conditions but relatively frequent (87%) under private conditions.[1] This study suggests that making a visible help-seeking request in front of a stranger carries a threat to self-esteem, which acts as a barrier to help-seeking.

Finally, the nature of the relationship between helper and recipient was studied by Shapiro (1980). Subjects participating in pairs worked on novel motor tasks, and tasks were arranged so that the subject needed help. The pairs of subjects were either friends or strangers, and the experiment was arranged so that the cost to the helper of providing help was either minimal or substantial. In the high-cost condition, the rate of help-seeking was 25% when the other was a stranger but was 80% when the other was a friend. Thus friendship acts to increase the rate of help-seeking.

In summary, the laboratory studies have shown that rates of help-seeking in laboratory settings tend to be low, implying that certain barriers to help-seeking are operative there. The identified barriers are perceived inadequacy or threat to self-esteem (Rosen, 1983), inability to reciprocate (Greenberg & Westcott, 1983), and the visibility and embarrassment potential of the help-seeking request (Shapiro, 1983). Some factors, however, seem to reduce these barriers; specifically, a friendship relationship, an opportunity to reciprocate, and the normative role of the helper.

Help-Seeking in Field Settings

In the typical field study of help-seeking, a representative sample of a community is drawn (usually by random sampling from residence lists) and subjects are assessed (either through mail surveys or through direct interviews in homes) to determine their recent experiences with psychological distress and help-seeking (for reviews, see Gourash, 1978; McKinlay, 1972; Wills, 1987; Wills & DePaulo, 1991). The usual procedure is to ask subjects whether in a recent period (usually a year) they had a personal problem for which they considered seeking help; if so, whether they did seek help; and, if so, what type of help was sought. The nature of the problem is usually defined as one that involves a major life crisis or an extended period of worry and unhappiness.

For example, in an epidemiologic study by Veroff, Kulka, and Douvan (1981), a sample of 2,267 adults was drawn from the 48 coterminous states through a multistage probability area design so as to be representative of the U.S. population. Respondents were interviewed in homes by a trained interviewer using a lengthy semistructured protocol that included sections on subjective well-being, social networks, life events, and help-seeking patterns. The lead-in question suggested to subjects that problems sometimes come up in life and then continued: "Let's suppose you had a lot of personal problems and you're very unhappy all the time. Let's suppose you've been that way for a long time and it isn't getting any better. What do you think you'd do about it?" After a spontaneous response from the subject, a series of questions and probes were used to determine the occurrence of major negative life crises and periods of unhappiness in his or her life, and to determine whom (if anyone) the subject had turned to in coping with that event.

The subject was given lists of potential helpers that included formal help sources (psychiatrist, psychologist, social worker, counselor, doctor, etc.) and informal sources (husband, wife, son, daughter, brother, sister, friend, relative, etc.).

Data from this community sample indicated a high level of help-seeking, with a preference for informal sources of help. For coping with major life crises, 3% of the respondents used formal help only, 45% used informal help only, and 39% used a combination of informal and formal help; only 13% of the subjects reported not having had any kind of help. When asked about the number of informal sources they had talked to in the last crisis, 28% indicated having one resource person, 22% two persons, and 34% three or more persons; only 16% indicated having used no informal help resource. Thus in this study there was a strong differential of informal:formal help-seeking (a 15:1 ratio by one criterion), and the data suggested that most subjects had sought help from several persons.[2]

Similar results were obtained in an epidemiologic study by Brown (1978) with a sample of 1,106 Chicago-area adults. Across 26 types of life problems examined, 68% of subjects had sought some type of help (again as opposed to alternative modes of coping with the problem). The overall distribution of help resources indicated a 4:1 ratio of informal:formal help. Neighbors and Jackson (1984) found similar results in a representative sample of Afro-Americans. In all studies, there were some interactions with problem type (for example, professionals were used more for problems with achievement or health), but for the typical life stressors encountered in the general population, the data indicate that help from informal social networks is a major coping resource.

The results of these large-scale studies have limitations in that the definitions of help-seeking are somewhat general and the time frame over which helping is assessed can be considerable. Nonetheless, findings are consistent across these and studies of help-seeking for more discrete events and populations, as summarized in Table 2.2. Two conclusions are supported by these data. First, the rate of help-seeking is high; depending on the criterion, data usually show 80% to 90% of subjects seeking some kind of help. Second, the ratio of informal:formal help-seeking holds up across studies; typically there is a ratio of 5:1 or greater. The difference narrows somewhat for major life crises (McCrae, 1984; Norcross & Prochaska, 1986; Wilcox & Birkel, 1983), but it still remains even at the highest level of problem severity. There

Table 2.2
Percentage Rates of Use of Formal and Informal Help in Community Studies of Help-Seeking

Study	Problem type and time frame	Formal help only	Informal help only	Formal plus informal help
Brown (1978)	Troublesome event, last 4 years	12	48	40
Dooley & Catalano (1984)	Emotional problem, last 3 months	29	46	n/a
Neighbors & Jackson (1984)	Significant event	4	43	44
Veroff, Kulka, & Douvan (1981)	Major life crisis	3	45	39
Wilcox & Birkel (1983)	Minor worries	9	38	n/a
" "	Persistent depression	27	40	n/a
Young, Giles, & Plantz (1982)	Common problems of living, last year	17	56	n/a

NOTE: n/a = not available.

is the suggestion in the data of a consistent progression in help-seeking, with minor problems dealt with primarily by informal networks, more persistent problems taken to formal helping agents such as clergy and medical practitioners, and serious problems eventually referred to mental health specialists (Wills & DePaulo, 1991). Because of the lack of true longitudinal data, however, this model is still speculative.

A relevant study of a general-population sample with an intermediate time span was conducted in Los Angeles by Dooley and Catalano (1984). This study was based on 12 quarterly telephone surveys in which respondents were asked whether they had had "an emotional problem" in the last three months and whether they had sought help for it. Data indicated that, of the respondents experiencing a problem, 75% had sought help, primarily from informal sources (friends and family) rather than from formal sources (psychotherapists, doctors, or self-help groups). Here the use of alternative coping was not assessed.

Some of the results have additional interest. For example, Wilcox and Birkel (1983), in a study of divorced women, supplemented retrospective reports of help-seeking with data from journals kept by subjects over four 1-week periods, in which subjects reported any problems they confronted. These data indicated that respondents listed an average of 5.3 problems encountered per week and sought help an average of 3.2 times per week, for an average proportion of 60%. In a general-population sample, Stone and Neale (1984) obtained daily data on coping with "the most bothersome problem of the day" over a 3-month period. Their data, which included eight alternative coping mechanisms, indicated that seeking emotional support was used for 15% of the problems encountered. These data, together, suggest the frequency of help-seeking may be higher than the figures obtained from retrospective reports, considering that these data represent 1- to 3-month periods compared with the 1- to 4-year periods assessed retrospectively in survey studies.

Studies on perceived support from informal sources provide another stream of evidence. In this research, subjects complete an inventory on the extent to which they perceive certain supportive functions as being available from their network. These data show a high level of perceived functional support. For example, on the scales for emotional and instrumental support from the Interpersonal Support Evaluation List, mean scores approximate 10 to 11 on a 12-point scale (Brookings & Boulton, 1988; Cohen, Mermelstein, Kamarck, & Hoberman, 1985); on the Social Provisions Scale, subscale means approximate 12 to 13 on a 16-point scale (Cutrona & Russell, 1987); and on the Social Support Questionnaire, mean support satisfaction scores are about 145 on a 162-point scale (Sarason, Levine, Basham, & Sarason, 1983; Sarason, Sarason, & Pierce, 1990; Sarason, Sarason, & Shearin, 1986). These data are consistent with other evidence showing that persons perceive informal sources as being highly supportive.

A quantitative estimate of the level of help-seeking is provided by studies that have used rigorous criteria to determine rates of seeking professional treatment for mental health problems. The typical study of this type determines the presence of psychological disorder through either a symptom screening scale or a diagnostic interview. Persons are considered psychologically impaired if they have high symptomatology scores on the screening scale or are rated as meeting the criteria for a psychiatric diagnosis. Each respondent's history of treatment seeking is determined, and analyses aim to determine what proportion of impaired persons have received professional treatment. Again, results are consistent. When psychological distress is indexed by screening scales, the median treatment rate is 27% (Neugebauer, Dohrenwend, & Dohrenwend, 1980). When disorder is indexed by DSM-III diagnoses, the typical six-month treatment rate is 19% (Weissman, 1987); that is, 81% of persons with diagnosable disorders do not seek professional help.

That these results are not attributable simply to financial considerations is suggested by studies in health maintenance organization (HMO) settings, where mental health care does not incur additional expense. Ware, Manning, Duan, Wells, and Newhouse (1984) followed a sample of 4,444 HMO enrollees over a total of 12,435 person-years of observation. Psychological status was determined through a mental health inventory administered at the baseline period, and subjects' use of mental health services was determined from HMO records. Service utilization was classified as mental health related if it included a mental health procedure or diagnosis, irrespective of whether this was from general medical providers or from formally trained mental health specialists; an index of formal treatment was obtained by considering only procedures delivered by a mental health specialist (i.e., a psychologist or psychiatrist). In this study, the statistically estimated 1-year treatment rate among persons in the upper third of symptomatology was 11% for any mental health treatment and 6% for formal treatment; that is, 94% did not seek formal treatment. Thus in this prospective study, conducted in a setting where professional treatment was available without cost, the great majority of persons with elevated psychological distress did not seek help.

To summarize, data from studies of community samples indicate that among persons in the general population, help-seeking for psychological problems is a relatively frequent experience. This general conclusion is qualified by the fact that there is a marked preference for informal sources of help (i.e., spouse, friends, and family), so the most frequent help-seeking occurs within informal social networks. Also, persons are discriminating about help-seeking, and when personal problems are serious they are more willing to seek help from professionals, though the most frequent pattern involves combining formal and informal help.

How, then, do these data compare with findings from laboratory settings? Of course this is not a simple question because there are other substantial differences between the settings. In field studies the problems are probably more serious than in laboratory settings, the potential helpers are often friends rather than strangers, and the problems are more self-relevant than are the intellectual or motor tasks used in typical laboratory studies. Yet one could argue that help-seeking should be less likely when there is more esteem threat and when the potential helper is similar rather than dissimilar. In sum, one could conclude from laboratory studies that help-seeking is a relatively infrequent occurrence (i.e., there are considerable barriers to seeking help), but data from field studies indicate that help-seeking is a relatively frequent occurrence. How are these differences to be understood?

Processes Affecting Laboratory and Field Data on Help-Seeking

What processes are relevant for understanding the overall differences in helping between settings? The following sections discuss some processes that seem relevant for this issue, and note some questions that are unresolved in either laboratory or field research.

Reciprocity

A factor that differs between typical laboratory paradigms and the conditions of ongoing personal relationships is the level of reciprocity. Reciprocity processes have been demonstrated in laboratory studies, which show persons are much more likely to seek help when they perceive that they will be able to reciprocate (Greenberg & Westcott, 1983). For example, in the Morris and Rosen (1973) study, the situation was arranged so that if the subject asked for help from the other person, he or she either would or would not have an opportunity subsequently to make some boxes that would be counted toward the other person's experimental quota. Results showed that subjects were more likely to ask for help when they expected an opportunity to return the help received, an effect that was particularly strong when subjects felt inadequate (43% help-seeking in the reciprocation condition, compared with 14% in the nonreciprocation condition). Similar effects for reciprocity have been found in other laboratory studies (e.g., Clark,

Gotay, & Mills, 1974; Greenberg & Shapiro, 1971; Nadler, Mayseless, Peri, & Chemerinski, 1985).

One could hypothesize that the high rates of help-seeking observed for informal help in field studies occur because such relationships are reciprocal. In an ongoing relationship, helping actions are occurring frequently, and it is likely that if help is sought for one situation there will be an opportunity to provide help to the former help-giver in another (possibly unrelated) situation. Although this seems an important aspect of helping in the real world, there is surprisingly little evidence from field studies on this issue. Antonucci and Israel (1986), in a representative sample of elderly, found that respondents did perceive a high degree of reciprocity in their support relationships; and Rook (1987) found that persons were more satisfied with a relationship when it was perceived as reciprocal. However, there is little evidence directly linking reciprocity of helping to perceived support, or showing whether persons are more likely to provide help in a relationship that is perceived as reciprocal. This is an area where a process identified in laboratory research has received relatively little attention in field research, and more data from field studies would be useful for understanding reciprocity in help from informal sources.

There is also a question how reciprocity would operate in the decision to seek formal help (e.g., from a psychologist). There, one has no opportunity to reciprocate directly the type of help received (i.e., counseling for personal problems), but there is a repayment in monetary terms. At the same time, the psychotherapist is normatively labeled as being in a helping role—a factor that increases help-seeking in laboratory studies. Thus one might expect a high level of help-seeking from professionals, but the observed rate is low; hence other factors must be operative. What these other factors are is unknown—effort, cost, stigma, and visibility are all plausible candidates. This represents another interesting question for field research (see Fischer, Winer, & Abramowitz, 1983).

Intimacy and Self-Disclosure

Another important aspect of ongoing personal relationships is intimacy and self-disclosure. In laboratory studies, this component of relationships is almost necessarily absent because the paradigms usually involve short-term interactions between strangers. By contrast, in an enduring relationship there is a history of sharing worries and confiding about problems, talking about failures as well as successes, and showing concern and support for the other's worth in times of difficulty. This aspect of personal relationships has been variously termed confidant support, esteem support, or emotional support validation (Wills, 1985).

Field studies have shown the central role of intimacy in the supportive effects of relationships. In the social support literature, measures of confidant relationships or emotional support appear to be the primary factors in buffering the impact of negative life events (Cohen & Wills, 1985; Wills, 1991). Where specific effects have been tested, it has been found that the buffering effect of marital relationships is primarily accounted for by the intimacy and quality of communication in the relationship (Husaini, Neff, Newbrough, & Moore, 1982; Stemp, Turner, & Noh, 1986). Kessler and Essex (1982) showed in multiple regression analyses that the buffering effect of social support for chronic life strains was primarily mediated by the degree of intimacy in the relationship. Another interesting fact about this effect is that emotional support and intimacy are implicated in buffering effects for a variety of stressors including economic hardship, household strains, and parenting problems (Kessler & Essex, 1982; Krause, 1987a). Furthermore, emotional support seems to be just as important for adolescents as it is for adults (see Greenberg, Siegel, & Leitch, 1983; Wills & Vaughan, 1989; Wills & Vaccaro, 1990).

Why is intimacy important? There is actually little evidence from field research that bears directly on this question (see Reis, 1990). Several possible mechanisms are suggested. The presence of intimacy in a relationship makes it easier to bring up problems, so that others are aware of one's needs. A history of self-disclosure in a relationship may also provide more accurate perceptions of the other's needs, so that the timing or nature of helping efforts will be more appropriate. Also, in intimate relationships, instrumental assistance or advice and guidance may have more impact because they are perceived as motivated by caring and concern. At present, though, the field research has provided little understanding of exactly how intimacy shapes coping and adaptation.

Here is where constructs and theories of intimacy derived from laboratory research (see Clark & Reis, 1988) may be useful for testing how helping operates in field settings. For example, what kinds of interactions lead to the sense of being understood and cared for that forms the basis for perceived intimacy (see Melamed & Brenner, 1990; Reis & Shaver, 1988)? What kinds of self-disclosure lead to perceived intimacy in ongoing relationships (see Fitzpatrick, 1987)? And how do personality characteristics influence the development of attachment and intimacy (Cohen, Sherrod, & Clark, 1986; McAdams & Constantian, 1983; McAdams, Healy, & Krause, 1984; Sarason et al., 1990)? These kinds of constructs may be useful for understanding how intimacy influences helping in ongoing personal relationships.

Similarity and Esteem Threat

In laboratory studies, the role of similarity in help-seeking and reactions to aid has been extensively studied. Similarity is typically defined by manipulated information about the attitudinal or personality characteristics of a coparticipant. It is found that persons are less likely to seek help from a similar other, and they react more negatively if they do receive help from a similar other (e.g., Fisher, Nadler, & Whitcher-Alagna, 1982; Nadler & Fisher, 1988). This contrasts with other findings in social psychological research, which show that similar others are perceived as more likable and more credible. Similarity is believed to have a deterrent effect on help-seeking in these studies because it arouses threats to self-esteem through unfavorable social comparison, which is particularly strong when the other is highly similar to the self (see Tesser, 1990; Wills, 1983).

In field studies, however, there is a marked preference for help from friends, spouse, and family, who almost by definition are similar others (e.g., similarity is one of the strongest determinants of marital satisfaction; Spanier & Lewis, 1980). A preference for receiving help from friends and peers is consistently found in college student samples, and this is true for academic and vocational problems as well as personal/emotional problems (Christensen & Magoon, 1974; Tinsley, Brown, de St. Aubin, & Lucek, 1984; Tinsley, de St. Aubin, & Brown, 1982). In epidemiological studies, as previously noted, there is also a strong differential between formal and informal help-seeking (Brown, 1978; Dooley & Catalano, 1984; Veroff et al., 1981). Even among persons formally seeking help, there is a preference for peer self-help groups over formal psychotherapy (Toro, Rappaport, & Seidman, 1987). In studies of social support there has been little attention to similarity of help sources, but one study (Lin, Woelfel, & Light, 1985) demonstrated that respondents had more favorable reactions when support persons were similar to the self. Moreover, Medvene (see Chapter 3) has shown that college students who contemplate seeking help have a strong preference for a peer helper who has had a similar problem.

In this area, there is a large discrepancy between results from laboratory and field paradigms, and this may occur for several reasons. One has already been suggested in laboratory studies, which show much more help-seeking from friends than from strangers (DePaulo, 1982; Nadler, Fisher, & Ben-Itzhak, 1983; Shapiro, 1980). In one sense this finding seems trivial—people could say, "Of course I prefer to seek help from a friend." Yet the question remains, considering underlying principles: Why does this difference exist? One possible explanation again is reciprocity, given that friends probably have a history of reciprocal helping that is lacking in contact with a stranger. This history shows that the other person is reliable and responsive in dealing with one's problems, and it might by itself make persons less concerned about seeking help from a friend. However, this linkage has never been explicitly made, even in laboratory studies.

But there seems to be more involved than just reciprocity. Another factor is that the helping indexed in field studies of close relationships is primarily emotional support, which involves reciprocal self-disclosure (see Hays, 1984, 1985). This aspect of helping is more characteristic of friend relationships and informal social networks, and it probably serves to reduce esteem concerns because one's weak points and limitations are already known to (and accepted by) the other person. This factor may make the context of helping fundamentally different, because the esteem threat experienced in laboratory settings is reduced or eliminated.

At present there is little evidence on how esteem threat is experienced in field settings. Do people experience any esteem threat in ongoing personal relationships, or is the amount of esteem concern inversely related to the supportiveness of the relationship? The work of Tesser has shown that persons are sensitive to superior performance by a close other on a central dimension (e.g., Tesser, 1990), so one could say that esteem concerns are not absent in close relationships. But beyond this there is little knowledge of the perceived esteem threat associated with various help sources (or types of help) in ongoing personal relationships.

Relationship Norms

Another difference between studies of helping in laboratory and field settings is that ongoing personal relationships may be guided by different norms than short-term encounters. Laboratory paradigms tend to emphasize situations where achievement motives are dominant, whereas personal relationships may be guided by quite different types of norms. Specifically, typical laboratory interactions may be guided by the norms of competition and direct exchange, whereas personal relationships are guided by what Clark and Mills (1979) have termed *communal norms.* In a communal relationship context, there is increased concern for the other's welfare, in contrast to exchange situations where the goal is strict maximization of one's own gains. In an exchange situation one's well-being is linked directly to one's own gains, whereas in communal situations one's subjective well-being is linked to satisfaction of the other's needs and affective states. Under these two different sets of norms, one would expect substantial differences in how persons react to helping and help-seeking.

The direct evidence for this comes from laboratory research. For example, Clark and Mills (1979) had subjects work at the same time as another person on a task, and induced the expectation that they would be able to interact with the person subsequently. Relationship orientation was varied by informing subjects either that the partner was interested in meeting people (communal orientation) or very occupied in his or her personal life and not interested in meeting new people (exchange orientation). Subjects provided help to the other person, and either did or did not receive a direct benefit (repayment) from the other person. Results showed that under the communal orientation, subjects liked the partner *less* when they received a repayment for their help, whereas under the exchange orientation subjects liked the other person *more* when they received a repayment. (Recall that the latter finding is typical in laboratory studies of reciprocity.) Later studies showed that under a communal orientation, people do not keep track of joint inputs to a task, whereas under an exchange orientation people do keep close track of each other's inputs (Clark, 1984); and under a communal orientation, people keep track of the other's needs even when there is no opportunity to help or reciprocate (Clark, Mills, & Powell, 1986). Under a communal orientation, help provided and positive reactions to helping increase with the other's instrumental needs or affective need state, whereas under an exchange orientation these decrease (Clark, Ouellette, Powell, & Milberg, 1987; Williamson & Clark, 1989). Thus it is evident that in close or communal relationships, people have very different reactions to helping than they do in an exchange relationship.

In field studies this issue has been largely unexamined. We know that in their significant relationships, persons perceive high levels of support and concern and are willing to expend considerable energy in helping. Yet there has been little examination in field research of the types of relationship orientations (exchange versus communal) that people hold, how these orientations relate to help-seeking and perceived support, and so on. More research is needed to investigate how properties of communal relationships, as indicated in laboratory settings, apply to supportive processes in ongoing personal relationships.

One complexity of this issue should be noted. I previously suggested that reciprocity (of instrumental help and emotional support) is an important component of personal relationships in field settings, and also that in the communal relationship model, people are theoretically insensitive to reciprocity, at least on a short-term basis. There is probably not a real contradiction here, as close relationships must have some degree of reciprocation in order to be satisfying (Hatfield, Traupmann, Sprecher, Utne, & Hay, 1985; Sabatelli & Cecil-Pigo, 1985). But one question is whether a communal orientation tends to arise because of emotional support and self-disclosure (which shows that the other cares and is concerned), or whether the basic communal orientation tends to influence the course of the relationship. This question requires longitudinal research on relationship development in order to learn how emotional support and communal orientations develop (Clark & Reis, 1988; Reis, 1990).

Multiple Networks

The issue of multiple network involvements has not been examined in most studies because support is construed in terms of overall available support (from any source). This is not unreasonable, but in the real world, persons may be members of multiple networks. For adolescents this issue has particular importance because teenagers participate in several networks, notably the networks of same-age peers and the network of family members (parents and siblings). These respective networks may have quite different effects on adolescents' emotions and behavior.

The focus of our recent research has been on the differential effects of family and peer support. This phenomenon first appeared in survey studies of social support as a coping mechanism among seventh-grade students. These studies included measures of the extent to which the subject talked to peers and to parents, respectively, when he or she had a problem. The items for peer and parent support were worded to tap the seeking of general emotional support (i.e., confiding and caring). These measures were then related in multiple regression analyses (with demographic controls) to criterion variables of cigarette smoking and alcohol use. The findings showed that peer and parental support had opposite effects. In terms of main effects, peer support was positively related to substance use, whereas parental support was inversely related to substance use (Wills & Vaughan, 1989).

The other striking aspect of these data was that support variables interacted with substance use cues in the social network. For example, peer support had no relationship to smoking when there were no friends who smoked, but it had an increasingly stronger effect as the number of smoking peers increased. Conversely, parental support was unrelated to substance use when there was little substance use in the peer network, but it had an increasingly stronger (protective) effect as the level of use in the peer network increased. Thus there seem to be interacting effects of networks, such that emotional support from parents has repercussions for particular types of interpersonal transactions within the peer network (Wills, 1990).

Some recent dissertations at the Ferkauf Graduate School have pursued this question with respect to the functioning of drug users who are in methadone maintenance treatment. Robert Zielony was concerned with the determinants of AIDS-risk behavior in this population. He interviewed a sample of 130 clients with measures that included an inventory of functional social support (the ISEL; Cohen & Hoberman, 1983) and a scale that indexes social integration (i.e., multiple roles and memberships in the community). The criterion measure in this study was a composite index of behaviors that could place the client at risk for AIDS. Zielony (1989) employed multiple regression analyses with demographic controls and found that functional support and social integration were independently related to AIDS risk; that is, there is something about having good social integration that provides a different effect from having good emotional support. Moreover, Zielony found that indices of functional support bore different implications for the risk measure. Notably, emotional (appraisal) support was related to lower risk, whereas companionship (belongingness) support was positively related to greater risk. It appears that in this context, emotional support from a significant other may help to counteract the potentially adverse influence of frequent social interaction with a drug-using social group (Zielony & Wills, 1990).

Another study specifically considered illicit drug use, measured in this case through biochemical analyses that were a standard part of the treatment program. Asher Pakier (1989) interviewed a sample of 100 clients and included measures of social integration and recent life stress (the LES; Sarason, Johnson, & Siegel, 1978). Pakier employed multiple regression analyses with a statistical control for employment status, a potential confounder for these types of data. He found there was a stress-buffering effect of social integration with respect to drug use; that is, among persons with low social integration there was a strong relationship between greater life stress and more illicit drug use, whereas among persons with high social integration the effect of life stress on drug use was minimal. A path analysis of the data indicated that the contributions of social integration and life stress on drug use were direct effects, not mediated through an index of trait anxiety (Pakier & Wills, 1990). Together with Zielony's data, these findings suggest that having a variety of social roles is protective against undesirable behaviors, possibly because it increases self-control ability.

To investigate the effect of support on substance use at an earlier phase, a colleague and I recently completed a study of family support and competence dimensions as predictors of adolescent substance use. This study (Wills & Vaccaro, 1990) surveyed a sample of children in the sixth, seventh, and eighth grades in parochial schools in New York City. The schools draw from areas of the city that are of lower to middle socioeconomic status. The sample was 51% Hispanic, 25% Black, and 17% White. The total sample size for the survey was 1,289 students. Students were administered a questionnaire that included scales for life events, three perceived competence measures (academic competence, social competence with peers, and social competence with adults), and measures of positive and negative affect. We also designed and included a 15-item scale of family support based on the functional model, designed to index emotional support and instrumental support from parents as perceived by the child. This new measure proved to have good internal consistency within scales, and factor analyses showed that the two subscales measured different dimensions of social support. The criterion variables in this study were self-report items asking about the frequency of cigarette smoking, alcohol consumption, and marijuana use; these items were combined to provide a composite index of substance use.

The results provided evidence for a theoretical model of how family support influences adolescent drug use. Analyses used multiple regression with the composite substance use score as the criterion, and predictor variables were entered together with complete demographic controls for age, sex, and race. The following effects were significant at the $p < .0001$ level, unless noted otherwise. The components of the model, and the findings, were as follows:

(1) Family support was inversely related to substance use, and the scales for emotional support and instrumental support ($p < .001$) predicted independently of each other. This shows that both aspects of social support have a role in protective processes.

(2) Family support had a symmetric influence on affect; that is, it was related to increased positive affect and decreased negative affect. Again, emotional and instrumental support each made unique contributions in these analyses.

(3) Family support was related to increased competence. The unique contributions of emotional support and instrumental support, respectively, were $p < .01$ and $p < .0001$ for academic competence; $p < .05$ and $p < .0001$ for peer social competence; and $p < .0001$ (both effects) for adult social competence. Thus social support was demonstrated to have an effect on actual competence dimensions.

(4) Substance use was predicted by affect measures and by competence measures. Substance use was related to greater negative affect and less positive affect ($p < .0001$ for main effects), and a significant interaction ($p < .01$) was obtained, such that substance use was disproportionately elevated among children with high negative affect and low positive affect. The competence measures also were related to drug use, with substance use elevated among children with low academic competence ($p < .0001$) and low adult competence ($p < .0001$); whereas peer social competence was positively related to drug use ($p < .01$). Again, these were independent effects.

So we know from these data something about how family support works. It is related to more favorable affective states and to greater competence. These in turn are related to lower drug use.

There are still unanswered questions with this research. We know that social integration is effective for reducing what may be termed deviant behaviors (e.g., illicit drug use), but it is not clear whether this influence operates through normative/attitudinal factors, improving self-control and coping ability, or explicit social pressure (see House et al., 1988; Umberson, 1987). In the complex net of parent and peer relationships, it is not clear what parts are providing emotionally supportive functions, and what parts are serving to promote undesirable behavior (cf. Wills, 1990). The data serve to illustrate the complex nature of helping in real-world settings and the number of questions that remain to be answered.

Conclusions

This chapter has outlined some findings from laboratory and field research on helping and help-seeking, noted that there is a discrepancy, and suggested some processes that may aid in understanding the differing properties of helping in laboratory and field settings. The generally high rate of help-seeking observed in field studies seems to be attributable to several factors that characterize the context of helping as it occurs in ongoing personal relationships. These are a history of reciprocity in helping, a relationship with a substantial degree of intimacy, a context of emotional support where esteem threats in helping are minimized, and relationship norms that operate to minimize some of the barriers to helping encountered in laboratory settings (e.g., costs of helping). Additionally, in personal relationships the visibility of help-seeking is low, normative considerations encourage helping as a role activity, and people have multiple networks available as sources of help.

The variables discussed above have for the most part been identified in laboratory studies, so this exemplifies the value of controlled experimentation for identifying constructs. At the same time, prevalence data from field studies indicate a very different frequency of help-seeking than is found in laboratory studies, suggesting that the context of helping in ongoing relationships is quite different. This exemplifies the value of epidemiological data for providing a cross-check on the external validity of conclusions from laboratory studies (see Cohen, Evans, Krantz, & Stokols, 1980). Additionally, the epidemiologic research has produced concepts such as social integration and emotional support, which appear to have value for understanding close relationships as they occur in real-world settings. Thus continued research on helping and help-seeking in naturalistic settings has value for building the theory base of social psychology (see Nadler, Fisher, & DePaulo, 1983). More research of this type is greatly needed.

One general conclusion to be derived from this discussion is the primary role of emotional support in ongoing personal relationships. This dimension, indexed in social support studies by functional measures, appears to be an important element for the stress-buffering property of social relationships (Wills, 1991). The perception of emotional support seems to be contributed by the development of intimacy and confiding in a relationship, and this aspect makes seeking help for a personal problem from a spouse or friend a quite different matter than asking a stranger for assistance. This aspect of seeking help in the context of a close relationship is, I think, the main difference between laboratory and field studies. What I have tried to do here is to show *how* it makes a difference.

This said, it should also be noted that in real-world settings, there is little understanding of how emotional support works. Does it improve well-being through perception and appraisal mechanisms, or through influences on coping behavior (Cohen & Wills, 1985; Thoits, 1986)? Does emotional support act primarily through influence on affective states, self-efficacy, or self-esteem (Krause, 1987b; Wills, 1991)? What kinds of interpersonal transactions and specific behaviors lead to the perception of intimacy and emotional support (Dunkel-Schetter et al., Chapter 4 of this volume; Melamed & Brenner, 1990)? How does emotional support influence the operation of other supportive functions? These questions all remain to be addressed through studies of intimacy and support in real-world settings.

Looking at another side of the question, what functions do people want from supportive relationships? There is actually little evidence on how persons in the general population perceive their desired sources of support. There are findings in the literature on marital satisfaction, for example, showing that concepts such as communication and affection are desired properties of marital relationships (Spanier & Lewis, 1980).

Laboratory research on intimacy has suggested that feeling validated and feeling cared for are essential parts of the construct (Clark & Reis, 1988). There is also an extensive body of literature on formal psychotherapy that emphasizes the importance of acceptance and trustworthiness for clients' perceptions of supportive psychotherapists (e.g., Elliott et al., 1982; Wills, 1982). Yet little of this work has been applied to derive a better understanding of the desired functions of helping relationships in the real world. It seems clear that an interdisciplinary approach would help to inform and advance this work.

In considering these issues, we should maintain a stance of theoretical caution. Helping situations differ markedly in their psychological demands, so we should not posit any necessarily invariant findings in real-world settings. Consider the examples of an 8-year-old needing math tutoring in a classroom setting, a 16-year-old needing support for problems of adolescent adjustment, a 30-year-old needing help with problems of parenting, a 40-year-old experiencing job difficulties and midlife crisis, and a 70-year-old caring for a spouse with a chronic disease. These persons have very different support needs, and their decisions to seek (or not seek) help will probably differ according to these needs and the type of help potentially available (Cohen & McKay, 1984; Cutrona, 1990). Clearly there is a need to study how the setting and the stage of the life cycle affect helping and help-seeking (Cohen & Wills, 1985; Wills, 1987).

Implications

Finally, let me note some applied implications of work on helping and help-seeking. One implication is that basic research has provided some evidence on the dimensions of close relationships, and these can provide goals for interventions to improve or restore functioning in relationships under strain. Complete development of this idea is beyond the scope of the present chapter, but the implications are evident (see Reis, 1990).

There is another implication, in a different direction. This pertains to the question of how to increase helping resources for persons with support limitations, for example the isolated elderly (Cutrona, 1990) or parents with limited social networks (Wahler, 1990). It seems that some of the findings from laboratory studies that identify barriers to help-seeking could be used to design training programs that would enable persons to become better help-seekers. For example, role-play situations could be used to teach help-seeking—initially in less visible ways, on less ego-central tasks, with low cost for the helper and reciprocity built into the initial agreement, and from persons having some acquaintance rather than complete strangers. Issues of timing may be important, and persons could be taught to seek help when feeling more adequate rather than at times when self-esteem is depressed. Precise issues of the wording of help-seeking requests, and attention to both verbal and nonverbal behavior, could also be addressed on the basis of laboratory research (see DePaulo, 1982; Wills & DePaulo, 1991). Help-seeking does not have to be pursued in a direct manner, but can also be approached in a more indirect manner (Glidewell, Tucker, Todt, & Cox, 1983).

There is also a rich body of descriptive literature on how help-seeking behavior is shaped by social networks and social integration. For example, several studies have examined helpseeking for psychological distress in college populations (Tracey, Sherry, & Keitel, 1986) and in the community (Horwitz, 1977; Neighbors & Jackson, 1984). In addition, an interesting literature demonstrates the value of social integration for instrumental needs (Birkel & Repucci, 1983; Powell & Eisenstadt, 1983; Young, Giles, & Plantz, 1982). This work also has implications for suggesting how social integration can be increased through utilizing untapped network connections and building formal organizational memberships (see Gottlieb, 1988; Hall & Wellman, 1985).

Notes

1. In this study, subjects in the public help-seeking condition perceived their pretest performance as poorer than in the private condition, so the 33% rate may actually be somewhat inflated.

2. In this study the use of alternative coping responses (passive acceptance, religious coping, self-help coping) was assessed in addition to help-seeking. These alternative responses were used with some frequency for minor worries but not for major life crises.

References

Antonucci, T. C., & Israel, B. A. (1986). Veridicality of social support. *Journal of Consulting and Clinical Psychology, 54*, 432-437.

Birkel, R. C., & Repucci, N. D. (1983). Social networks, information seeking, and the utilization of services. *American Journal of Community Psychology, 11*, 185-205.

Brookings, S. B., & Boulton, B. (1988). Confirmatory factor analysis of the Interpersonal Support Evaluation List. *American Journal of Community Psychology, 16*, 137-147.

Brown, B. B. (1978). Social and psychological correlates of help-seeking behavior among urban adults. *American Journal of Community Psychology, 6*, 425-439.

Christensen, K. C., & Magoon, T. M. (1974). Perceived hierarchy of help-giving sources for two categories of student problems. *Journal of Counseling Psychology, 21*, 311-314.

Clark, M. S. (1984). Record-keeping in two types of relationships. *Journal of Personality and Social Psychology, 47*, 549-557.

Clark, M. S., Gotay, C. C., & Mills, J. (1974). Acceptance of help as a function of similarity of the potential helper and opportunity to repay. *Journal of Applied Social Psychology, 4*, 224-229.

Clark, M. S., & Mills, J. (1979). Interpersonal attraction in exchange and communal relationships. *Journal of Personality and Social Psychology, 37*, 12-24.

Clark, M. S., Mills, J., & Powell, M. C. (1986). Keeping track of needs in communal and exchange relationships. *Journal of Personality and Social Psychology, 51*, 333-338.

Clark, M. S., Ouellette, R., Powell, M. C., & Milberg, S. (1987). Recipient's mood, relationship type, and helping. *Journal of Personality and Social Psychology, 53*, 94-103.

Clark, M. S., & Reis, H. T. (1988). Interpersonal processes in close relationships. *Annual Review of Psychology, 39*, 609-672.

Cohen, S. (1988). Psychosocial models of the role of social support in the etiology of physical disease. *Health Psychology, 7*, 269-297.

Cohen, S., Evans, G. W., Krantz, D. S., & Stokols, D. (1980). Effects of aircraft noise on children: Moving from the laboratory to the field. *American Psychologist, 35*, 231-243.

Cohen, S., & Hoberman, H. M. (1983). Positive events and social supports as buffers of life change stress. *Journal of Applied Social Psychology, 13*, 99-125.

Cohen, S., & McKay, G. (1984). Social support, stress, and the buffering hypothesis: A theoretical analysis. In A. Baum, S. E. Taylor, & J. E. Singer (Eds.), *Handbook of psychology and health* (Vol. 4, pp. 253-267). Hillsdale, NJ: Lawrence Erlbaum.

Cohen, S., Mermelstein, R., Kamarck, T., & Hoberman, H. M. (1985). Measuring the functional components of social support. In I. G. Sarason & B. R. Sarason (Eds.), *Social support: Theory, research and applications* (pp. 73-94). The Hague, Netherlands: Martinus Nijhoff.

Cohen, S., Sherrod, D. R., & Clark, M. S. (1986). Social skills and the stress-protective role of social support. *Journal of Personality and Social Psychology, 50*, 963-973.

Cohen, S., & Wills, T. A. (1985). Stress, social support, and the buffering hypothesis. *Psychological Bulletin, 98*, 310-357.

Cutrona, C. E. (1990). Stress and social support—In search of optimal matching. *Journal of Social and Clinical Psychology*, 12, 3-14.

Cutrona, C. E., & Russell, D. W. (1987). The provisions of social relationships and adaptation to stress. In W. H. Jones & D. Perlman (Eds.), *Advances in personal relationships* (Vol. 1, pp. 37-67). Greenwich, CT: JAI.

DePaulo, B. M. (1978). Accepting help from teachers—When the teachers are children. *Human Relations, 31,* 459-474.

DePaulo, B. M. (1982). Social-psychological processes in informal help-seeking. In T. A. Wills (Ed.), *Basic processes in helping relationships* (pp. 255-279). New York: Academic Press.

DePaulo, B. M., Nadler, A., & Fisher, J. D. (Eds.). (1983). *New directions in helping: Help-seeking* (Vol. 2). New York: Academic Press.

Diener, E. (1984). Subjective well-being. *Psychological Bulletin, 95,* 542-575.

Dooley, D., & Catalano, R. (1984). Why the economy predicts help-seeking: A test of competing explanations. *Journal of Health and Social Behavior, 25,* 160-176.

Druian, P. R., & DePaulo, B. M. (1977). Asking a child for help. *Social Behavior and Personality, 5,* 33-39.

Elliott, R., Stiles, W. B., Shiffman, S., Barker, C. B., Burstein, B., & Goodman, G. (1982). The empirical analysis of help-intended communications. In T. A. Wills (Ed.), *Basic processes in helping relationships* (pp. 333-356). New York: Academic Press.

Fischer, E. H., Winer, D., & Abramowitz, S. I. (1983). Seeking professional help for psychological problems. In A. Nadler, J. D. Fisher, & B. M. DePaulo (Eds.), *New directions in helping* (Vol. 3, pp. 163-185). New York: Academic Press.

Fisher, J. D., Nadler, A., & DePaulo, B. M. (Eds.). (1983). *New directions in helping: Recipient reactions to aid* (Vol. 1). New York: Academic Press.

Fisher, J. D., Nadler, A., & Whitcher-Alagna, S. (1982). Recipient reactions to aid. *Psychological Bulletin, 91,* 27-54.

Fitzpatrick, M. A. (1987). Marriage and verbal intimacy. In V. J. Derlega & J. Berg (Eds.), *Self-disclosure: Theory, research and therapy.* New York: Plenum.

Glidewell, J. C., Tucker, S., Todt, M., & Cox, S. (1983). Professional support systems: The teaching profession. In A. Nadler, J. D. Fisher, & B. M. DePaulo (Eds.), *New directions in helping* (Vol. 3, pp. 189-212). New York: Academic Press.

Gottlieb, B. H. (Ed.). (1988). *Marshalling social support: Formats, processes, and effects.* Newbury Park, CA: Sage.

Gourash, N. (1978). Help-seeking: A review of the literature. *American Journal of Community Psychology, 6,* 413-423.

Greenberg, M. S., & Shapiro, S. P. (1971). Indebtedness: An adverse aspect of asking for and receiving help. *Sociometry, 34,* 290-301.

Greenberg, M. S., & Westcott, D. R. (1983). Indebtedness as a mediator of reactions to aid. In J. D. Fisher, A. Nadler, & B. M. DePaulo (Eds.), *New directions in helping* (Vol. 1, pp. 85-112). New York: Academic Press.

Greenberg, M. T., Siegel, J. M., & Leitch, C. J. (1983). The nature and importance of attachment relationships to parents and peers during adolescence. *Journal of Youth and Adolescence, 12,* 373-386.

Hall, A., & Wellman, B. (1985). Social networks and social support. In S. Cohen & L. Syme (Eds.), *Social support and health* (pp. 23-42). New York: Academic Press.

Hatfield, E., Traupmann, J., Sprecher, S., Utne, M. K., & Hay, J. (1985). Equity and intimate relations. In W. Ickes (Eds.), *Compatible and incompatible relationships* (pp. 91-117). New York: Springer-Verlag.

Hays, R. B. (1984). The development and maintenance of friendship. *Journal of Social and Personal Relationships, 1,* 75-98.

Hays, R. B. (1985). A longitudinal study of friendship development. *Journal of Personality and Social Psychology, 48,* 909-924.

Horwitz, A. (1977). Family, kin, and friend networks in psychiatric help-seeking. *Social Science and Medicine: Medical Psychology and Sociology, 12,* 297-304.

House, J. S., Landis, K. R., & Umberson, D. (1988). Social relationships and health. *Science, 241,* 540-545.

Husaini, B. A., Neff, J. A., Newbrough, J. R., & Moore, M. C. (1982). The stress-buffering role of social support and personal competence among the rural married. *Journal of Community Psychology, 10,* 409-426.

Kessler, R. C., & Essex, M. (1982). Marital status and depression: The role of coping resources. *Social Forces, 61,* 484-507.

Krause, N. (1987a). Chronic financial strain, social support, and depressive symptoms among older adults. *Psychology and Aging, 2,* 185-192.

Krause, N. (1987b). Life stress, social support, and self-esteem in elderly populations. *Psychology and Aging, 2,* 349-356.

Lin, N., Woelfel, M. W., & Light, S. C. (1985). The buffering effect of social support consequent to an important life event. *Journal of Health and Social Behavior, 26,* 247-263.

McAdams, D. P., & Constantian, C. A. (1983). Intimacy and affiliation motives in daily living: An experience sampling analysis. *Journal of Personality and Social Psychology, 45,* 851-861.

McAdams, D. P., Healy, S., & Krause, S. (1984). Social motives and patterns of friendship. *Journal of Personality and Social Psychology, 47,* 828-838.

McCrae, R. R. (1984). Situational determinants of coping responses. *Journal of Personality and Social Psychology, 46,* 919-928.

McKinlay, J. B. (1972). Some approaches and problems in the use of services. *Journal of Health and Social Behavior, 13,* 115-152.

Melamed, B. G., & Brenner, G. F. (1990). Social support and chronic medical stress: An interaction-based approach. *Journal of Social and Clinical Psychology, 12,* 104-117.

Miller, D. T., & McFarland, C. (1987). Pluralistic ignorance: When similarity is interpreted as dissimilarity. *Journal of Personality and Social Psychology, 53,* 298-305.

Miller, D. T., & McFarland, C. (1990). When social comparison goes awry: The case of pluralistic ignorance. In J. Suls & T. A. Wills (Eds.), *Social comparison: Contemporary theory and research* (pp. 287-313). Hillsdale, NJ: Lawrence Erlbaum.

Morris, S. C., & Rosen, S. (1973). Effects of felt adequacy and opportunity to reciprocate on help seeking. *Journal of Experimental Social Psychology, 9,* 265-276.

Nadler, A. (1986). Self-esteem and the seeking and receiving of help. In B. Maher & W. Maher (Eds.), *Progress in experimental personality research* (Vol. 14, pp. 115-163). New York: Academic Press.

Nadler, A., & Fisher, J. D. (1988). The role of threat to self-esteem and perceived control in recipient reactions to aid. In L. Berkowitz (Ed.), *Advances in experimental social psychology* (Vol. 19, pp. 81-83). New York: Academic Press.

Nadler, A., Fisher, J. D., & Ben-Itzhak, S. (1983). Effects of single or multiple act aid as a function of donor and task characteristics. *Journal of Personality and Social Psychology, 44*, 310-321.

Nadler, A., Fisher, J. D., & DePaulo, B. M. (Eds.). (1983). *New directions in helping: Applied perspectives on help-seeking and receiving* (Vol. 3). New York: Academic Press.

Nadler, A., Mayseless, O., Peri, N., & Chemerinski, A. (1985). Effects of opportunity to reciprocate and self-esteem on help-seeking behavior. *Journal of Personality, 53*, 23-35.

Nadler, A., Shapiro, R., & Ben-Itzhak, S. (1982). Effects of helper's physical attractiveness and sex of helper on males' and females' help-seeking behavior. *Journal of Personality and Social Psychology, 42*, 90-99.

Neighbors, H. W., & Jackson, J. S. (1984). The use of informal and formal help: Four patterns of illness behavior in the Black community. *American Journal of Community Psychology, 12*, 629-644.

Neugebauer, R., Dohrenwend, B. P., & Dohrenwend, B. S. (1980). Formulation of hypotheses about the true prevalence of functional psychiatric disorders among adults. In B. P. Dohrenwend, B. S. Dohrenwend, M. S. Gould, B. Link, R. Neugebauer, & R. Wunsch-Hitzig (Eds.), *Mental illness in the United States* (pp. 45-94). New York: Praeger.

Norcross, J. C., & Prochaska, J. O. (1986). The psychological distress and self-change of psychologists, counselors, and laypersons. *Psychotherapy, 23*, 102-114.

Pakier, A. (1989). *Predictors of drug abuse in a methadone maintenance sample*. Unpublished doctoral dissertation, Ferkauf Graduate School of Psychology, New York.

Pakier, A., & Wills, T. A. (1990, August). *Life stress and social support predict illicit drug use among methadone clients*. Paper presented at the meeting of the American Psychological Association, Boston.

Powell, D. R., & Eisenstadt, J. W. (1983). Predictors of help-seeking in an urban setting: The search for child care. *American Journal of Community Psychology, 11*, 401-422.

Reis, H. T. (1990). The role of intimacy in interpersonal relations. *Journal of Social and Clinical Psychology, 12*, 15-30.

Reis, H. T., & Shaver, P. (1988). Intimacy as an interpersonal process. In S. Duck (Ed.), *Handbook of personal relationships* (pp. 367-389). Chichester, UK: John Wiley.

Rook, K. S. (1987). Reciprocity of social exchange and social satisfaction among older women. *Journal of Personality and Social Psychology, 52*, 145-154.

Rook, K. S. (1990). Parallels in the study of social support and social strain. *Journal of Social and Clinical Psychology, 12*, 118-132.

Rosen, S. (1983). Perceived inadequacy and help-seeking. In B. M. DePaulo, A. Nadler, & J. D. Fisher (Eds.), *New directions in helping: Help-seeking* (Vol. 2, pp. 73-107). New York: Academic Press.

Rosen, S., Mickler, S. E., & Collins, J. E. (1987). Reactions of would-be helpers whose offer of help is spurned. *Journal of Personality and Social Psychology, 53*, 288-297.

Sabatelli, R. M., & Cecil-Pigo, E. F. (1985). Relationship interdependence and commitment in marriage. *Journal of Marriage and the Family, 47*, 931-937.

Sarason, I. G., Johnson, J. H., & Siegel, J. M. (1978). Assessing the impact of life changes: The Life Experiences Survey. *Journal of Consulting and Clinical Psychology, 46*, 932-946.

Sarason, I. G., Levine, H. M., Basham, R. B., & Sarason, B. R. (1983). Assessing social support: The Social Support Questionnaire. *Journal of Personality and Social Psychology, 44*, 127-139.

Sarason, I. G., Sarason, B. R., & Pierce, G. R. (Eds.). (1989). *Social support: An interactional view*. New York: John Wiley.

Sarason, I. G., Sarason, B. R., & Pierce, G. R. (1990). Social support: The search for theory. *Journal of Social and Clinical Psychology, 12*, 133-147.

Sarason, I. G., Sarason, B. R., & Shearin, E. N. (1986). Social support as an individual difference variable. *Journal of Personality and Social Psychology, 50*, 845-855.

Schulz, R., & Tompkins, C. A. (1990). Life events and changes in social relationships: Examples, mechanisms, and measurement. *Journal of Social and Clinical Psychology, 12*, 69-77.

Shapiro, E. G. (1978). Effects of visibility of task performance and seeking help. *Journal of Applied Social Psychology, 8*, 163-173.

Shapiro, E. G. (1980). Is seeking help from a friend like seeking help from a stranger? *Social Psychology Quarterly, 43*, 259-263.

Shapiro, E. G. (1983). Embarrassment and help-seeking. In B. M. DePaulo, A. Nadler, & J. D. Fisher (Eds.), *New directions in helping: Help-seeking* (Vol. 2, pp. 143-163). New York: Academic Press.

Spanier, G. B., & Lewis, R. A. (1980). Marital quality: A review of the seventies. *Journal of Marriage and the Family, 42*, 825-840.

Stemp, P. S., Turner, R. J., & Noh, S. (1986). Psychological distress in the postpartum period: The significance of social support. *Journal of Marriage and the Family, 48*, 271-277.

Stokes, S. J., & Bickman, L. (1974). The effect of the physical attractiveness and role of the helper on help-seeking. *Journal of Applied Social Psychology, 4*, 286-294.

Stone, A. A., & Neale, J. M. (1984). A new measure of daily coping. *Journal of Personality and Social Psychology, 46*, 892-906.

Tesser, A. (1990). Emotion in social comparison and reflection processes. In J. Suls & T. A. Wills (Eds.), *Social comparison: Contemporary theory and research* (pp. 115-145). Hillsdale, NJ: Lawrence Erlbaum.

Thoits, P. A. (1986). Social support as coping assistance. *Journal of Consulting and Clinical Psychology, 54*, 416-423.

Tinsley, H. E. A., Brown, M. T., de St. Aubin, T. M., & Lucek, J. (1984). Relation between expectancies for a helping relationship and tendency to seek help from a campus help provider. *Journal of Counseling Psychology, 31*, 149-160.

Tinsley, H. E. A., de St. Aubin, T. M., & Brown, M. T. (1982). College students' help-seeking preferences. *Journal of Counseling Psychology, 29*, 523-533.

Toro, P. A., Rappaport, J., & Seidman, E. (1987). Social climate comparison of mutual help and psychotherapy groups. *Journal of Consulting and Clinical Psychology, 55*, 430-431.

Tracey, T. J., Sherry, P., & Keitel, M. (1986). Distress and help-seeking as a function of person-environment fit and self-efficacy. *American Journal of Community Psychology, 14*, 657-676.

Umberson, D. (1987). Family status and health behaviors: Social control as a dimension of social integration. *Journal of Health and Social Behavior, 28*, 306-319.

Veroff, J. B., Kulka, R. A., & Douvan, E. (1981). *Mental health in America: Patterns of help-seeking 1957-1976*. New York: Basic Books.

Wahler, R. G. (1990). Some perceptual functions of social networks in coercive mother-child interactions. *Journal of Social and Clinical Psychology, 9*, 43-53.

Ware, J. E., Jr., Manning, W. G., Jr., Duan, N., Wells, K. B., & Newhouse, J. P. (1984). Health status and the use of outpatient mental health services. *American Psychologist, 39*, 1090-1100.

Weissman, M. M. (1987). Advances in psychiatric epidemiology: Rates and risks for major depression. *American Journal of Public Health, 77*, 445-451.

Wilcox, B. L., & Birkel, R. C. (1983). Social networks and the help-seeking process: A structural perspective. In A. Nadler, J. D. Fisher, & B. M. DePaulo (Eds.), *New directions in helping* (Vol. 3, pp. 235-255). New York: Academic Press.

Williamson, G. M., & Clark, M. S. (1989). Providing help and desired relationship type as determinants of changes in moods and self-evaluations. *Journal of Personality and Social Psychology, 56*, 722-734.

Wills, T. A. (1976, August). *Perceptual consequences of helping another person.* Paper presented at the meeting of the American Psychological Association, Washington, DC.

Wills, T. A. (1978). Perceptions of clients by professional helpers. *Psychological Bulletin, 85*, 968-1000.

Wills, T. A. (1981). Downward comparison principles in social psychology. *Psychological Bulletin, 90*, 245-271.

Wills, T. A. (1982). Nonspecific factors in helping relationships. In T. A. Wills (Ed.), *Basic processes in helping relationships* (pp. 381-404). New York: Academic Press.

Wills, T. A. (1983). Social comparison in coping and help-seeking. In B. M. DePaulo, A. Nadler, & J. D. Fisher (Eds.), *New directions in helping* (Vol. 2, pp. 109-142). New York: Academic Press.

Wills, T. A. (1985). Supportive functions of interpersonal relationships. In S. Cohen & L. Syme (Eds.), *Social support and health* (pp. 61-82). New York: Academic Press.

Wills, T. A. (1987). Help-seeking as a coping mechanism. In C. R. Snyder & C. Ford (Eds.), *Coping with negative life events: Clinical and social psychological perspectives* (pp. 19-50). New York: Plenum.

Wills, T. A. (1990). Multiple networks and substance use. *Journal of Social and Clinical Psychology, 9*, 78-90.

Wills, T. A. (1990). Social support and the family. In E. Blechman & M. McEnroe (Eds.), *Emotions and the family* (pp. 75-98). Hillsdale, NJ: Lawrence Erlbaum.

Wills, T. A. (1991). Social support and interpersonal relationships. *Review of Personality and Social Psychology, 12,* 265-289.

Wills, T. A., & DePaulo, B. M. (1991). Interpersonal analysis of the help-seeking process. In C. R. Snyder & D. R. Forsyth (Eds.), *Handbook of social and clinical psychology* (pp. 350-375). Elmsford, NY: Pergamon.

Wills, T. A., & Vaccaro, D. (1990). *The role of family support and competence in adolescent substance use.* Unpublished manuscript, Albert Einstein College of Medicine, New York.

Wills, T. A., & Vaughan, R. (1989). Social support and substance use in early adolescence. *Journal of Behavioral Medicine, 12*, 321-339.

Young, C. E., Giles, D. E., Jr., & Plantz, M. C., (1982). Natural networks: Help-giving and help-seeking in two rural communities. *American Journal of Community Psychology, 10*, 457-469.

Zielony, R. D. (1989). *Psychosocial predictors of AIDS risk behavior in methadone maintenance patients.* Unpublished doctoral dissertation, Ferkauf Graduate School of Psychology, New York.

Zielony, R. D., & Wills, T. A. (1990, August). *Predictors of AIDS risk in methadone patients.* Paper presented at the meeting of the American Psychological Association, Boston.

3

Self-Help Groups, Peer Helping, and Social Comparison

LOUIS MEDVENE

The public press, as well as psychologists, have been giving increasing attention to self-help groups. In a recent cover story, *Newsweek* (Leerhsen, Lewis, Pomper, Davenport, & Nelson, 1990) estimated that 15 million Americans were participating in such groups. In the *American Psychologist*, Jacobs and Goodman (1989) estimated that 6 to 8 million adults are participating at any one time. If these estimates are anywhere near accurate, they suggest there are almost as many people participating in self-help groups as in psychotherapy. Estimates from the national Epidemiologic Catchment Area study are that 6% to 7% of the population use mental health services during any 6-month period (Hough et al., 1987).

Although most people are aware of Alcoholics Anonymous (AA), they may be less aware of the thousands of new groups that have been organized during the past 20 years by people concerned with a variety of mental health, other health, and life transition problems. Some of the better known examples are the Compassionate Friends for bereaved parents and the National Alliance for the Mentally Ill for families with mentally ill members. Local and statewide clearinghouses for information and referral have promoted the growth of these new groups, as was recommended by the President's Commission on Mental Health (1978).

In 1978, a national clearinghouse was created, and since that time more than 40 local and statewide clearinghouses have been organized around the country. More recently, C. Everett Koop sponsored a Surgeon General's Workshop on Self-Help and Public Health (1988). Since the workshop, health and mental health professionals, along with leaders of self-help groups, have organized a National Council on Self-Help and Public Health. In a separate development, self-help group leaders have organized a National Self-Help Alliance (SHALL). Most recently, the National Institute of Mental Health funded a multiyear, national center for Self-Help Research and Knowledge Dissemination at the University of Michigan.

These developments make the self-help movement an interesting social phenomenon worthy of study in its own right. Additionally, given that self-help groups have the potential for helping large numbers of people, it is important to know the answers to questions like: What is self-help? How does it work? Is it effective? Should it be supported?

Such questions raise the larger conceptual issue of what theory or set of theories will be useful guides for understanding and working with self-help groups. Social comparison theory is a logical choice because of its emphasis on interpersonal similarity as a basis for understanding the processes involved in self-evaluation, self-improvement, and affiliation. As originally stated (Festinger, 1954), the theory focused on the human tendency to choose people who were similar with respect to ability level or skill as comparative others. More recently, attention has shifted to social comparison processes under conditions of threat, with interest focusing on the question of whether people prefer to compare themselves to better-off others (upward comparison) versus worse-off others (downward comparison; Wills, 1981, 1983). The main goal of this chapter is to explore the usefulness of social comparison theory in raising a set of questions that promise to be of heuristic value in increasing our understanding of self-help groups. The initial questions of interest are as follows: (a) How widespread are preferences for contact with others who have similar problems? (b) Do preferences for contact with experientially similar others vary with their comparative status—upward, lateral, or downward? and (c) What motivates people to seek contact with experientially similar others?

As a first step toward answering these questions, an exploratory study of the help-seeking preferences of UCLA college undergraduates was carried out, and it is reported later in this chapter.

As background for this research, a brief summary follows of some previous applications of social comparison theory to research on coping and help-seeking, particularly Wills's (1983) work on downward comparison theory. Brief overviews are also included of the research stimulated by Schachter's (1959) fear-affiliation hypothesis and Byrne's (1971) similarity-attraction paradigm. This literature provides the basis for the two exploratory research hypotheses that guided the study, the results of which are presented in the second section. The discussion of the results in the third section cites the recent social psychological literature on social comparison processes and self-esteem.

My interest in self-help groups grows out of experiences I had as a community organizer during the late 1960s and early 1970s. During this time, I worked with both the National Welfare Rights Organization (a grass-roots organization of welfare recipients) and the federal anti-poverty program as a VISTA (Volunteers In Service To America) volunteer. These experiences gave me an appreciation of the difficulties of organizing, as well as the benefits of participation. I see self-help groups as a continuation of this grass-roots community organizing tradition. My previous research has focused on process and outcome in community-based groups, including both the National Alliance for the Mentally Ill and groups for middle-aged divorcing women (Medvene, in press; Medvene & Krauss, 1989).

Diversity and Commonality Among Self-Help Groups

At first blush, self-help groups seem best characterized by their diversity. They are diverse with respect to (a) problem type—for example, there are groups for people with chronic health problems, with psychiatric problems, and with life transition problems; (b) leadership type—for example, groups that are led by laypersons, others that are professionally led (hybrid self-help groups), and still others that are co-led by professionals and peers; (c) process or group format—for example, some follow extremely rigid formats, whereas others allow for spontaneity; (d) goals—for example, some groups exist to provide support, others to promote advocacy, and still others for both goals; and

(e) organizational structure—for example, in some groups members rotate in and out of the leadership role, whereas other groups have formally elected officers.

If there is a generic, underlying commonality, it is the core belief that people who have the shared experience of a common problem have unique resources to offer one another. By virtue of their experiential similarity, others are believed to be uniquely capable of providing resources such as understanding, acceptance, information, and knowledge. As the saying goes, "Only someone who has walked in my shoes can truly understand me."

Several concepts in the social science literature on self-help groups articulate these sentiments. Borkman's (1976) concept of "experiential knowledge" denotes the value placed on expertise that can be gained only from living with a problem, as opposed to learning about it indirectly. Riessman's (1965) "helper-therapy principle" states the axiom that people benefit and gain support from the act of helping others.

A working definition of a self-help group would include the following elements: (a) homogeneity of members with respect to problem type; (b) leadership provided by lay members, or by professionals who are working with the consent of the members; (c) opportunities for members to play the roles of both helper and help-seeker; (d) minimal or no fee; and (e) voluntary participation (Katz & Bender, 1976; Powell, 1987).

Research on the effectiveness of self-help groups is at a stage of development comparable to outcome research on psychotherapy in the 1950s. Global questions about effectiveness are being asked, rather than more specific questions such as for whom are they effective, and under what conditions. In addition, research designs that involve random assignment to treatment and comparison groups are relatively rare. Nonetheless, there are some encouraging research findings (Medvene, 1990). Most encouraging are the results of a study (Spiegel, Bloom, Kraemer, & Gottheil, 1989) of a professionally led (hybrid) support group for mastectomized cancer patients. Women who participated in the group lived an average of 1½ years longer than similarly ill women in a control condition. Interestingly, the group was co-led by a woman whose cancer was in remission, as well as by a therapist.

Self-help groups are also sources of social support, and it would be a mistake to study them as if they were simply alternate service delivery systems. Research is also needed that views self-help groups as intrinsically interesting and socially innovative sources of community.

Peer Counseling

Like members of self-help groups, clients in peer counseling relationships are presumably attracted to the counselors because of their similarities. Peer counselors are similar to their clients in status, and they also often share certain demographic characteristics—especially age, in the case of student counselors. Nationally, peer counselors provide a variety of services on college campuses, including (a) health services—for example, with peer health counselors; (b) counseling for academic problems, provided by students who are working or volunteering in counseling offices; (c) general counseling, as provided by dorm counselors; and (d) crisis intervention, via mental health hotlines handled by students (Giddan, 1988).

In a review of the extensive literature regarding the effectiveness of college-based peer helpers, Giddan (1988) noted that a number of studies have demonstrated the effectiveness of trained peer (student) helpers. In several studies, trained peer helpers were as effective or more effective than professional helpers. Giddan hypothesized that attitudinal and experiential similarities between counselor and client were critically important, and he called for more research on the role of experiential similarities in helping relationships.

Giddan's call for more research was based, in part, on the literature regarding the positive effects of client-counselor experiential similarities in professional counseling relationships. For example, Atkinson and Schein (1986) concluded that experiential similarity (e.g., matching counselors having a history of alcoholism with alcoholic clients, and counselors with a history of psychological treatment with delinquents) was attractive to clients. Clients rated experientially similar counselors as having more positive regard for them and being more unconditionally accepting. Thus the counseling literature reinforces the idea that experiential similarity can enhance the attractiveness of potential helpers, and can also influence process (e.g., increasing rates of self-disclosure) and outcomes.

Seeking Help from
Experientially Similar Others

The question of why people with a problem seek help from others with the same problem should be at the heart of research on self-help groups. Yet we know little about why, for example, a cancer patient seeks help from another cancer patient, or a bereaved parent from another bereaved parent. For what purposes and under what conditions do people seek help from experientially similar others?

This question has rarely been addressed in the self-help literature. There are virtually no prospective data regarding what people hope to gain by joining self-help groups. Most studies involve samples of people who are already participating in established groups. These studies indicate that the great majority of participants in self-help groups are white, female, college educated, and in the 30- to 50-year-old age range (Powell, 1987). With regard to outcomes, the most frequently reported testimonials are "no longer feeling alone" and gaining information about how to cope with problems (Medvene, 1990; Powell, 1987). Insofar as the reported benefits can suggest initial motivations, it may be speculated that participants are seeking to reduce their sense of social isolation, and want to gain information helpful in problem-focused coping.

This chapter now turns to a brief review of social comparison theory as it has been applied to research on coping and help-seeking.

The Relevance of Social Comparison Theory

Social comparison theory and the related work of Schachter (1959) and Byrne (1971) provide theoretical bases for expecting that help-seekers would prefer contact with experientially similar helpers. Experientially similar others might be preferred because they would be expected to provide information that could be used for purposes of self-evaluation, self-enhancement, and self-improvement, and they might be expected to satisfy affiliative needs. It would also be expected that preferences would vary with the comparative status of experientially similar others: For example, goals of self-improvement would be expected to be associated with preferences for contact with upward-comparison others (i.e., people who are currently better off than oneself).

Festinger (1954) emphasized the motive of objective self-evaluation in his original statement of social comparison theory. In this formulation, comparative others were chosen who were similar with respect to ability level—in order to get more accurate information—and they were always slightly better, as an expression of a unidirectional drive upward in ability or skill. Schachter (1959) applied the theory to different circumstances, social comparison under conditions of threat. The theme of Schachter's work with the fear-affiliation hypothesis is suggested by his reformulation of the familiar cliché about misery into "misery loves miserable company."

More recently, Wills (1981, 1983) has applied social comparison theory to the stress and coping area and has shown the role played by social comparison processes, more broadly conceived to include downward comparisons. Wills cited evidence that under conditions of threat people seek to compare themselves to others who are worse off. These downward comparisons are motivated by needs for self-enhancement rather than objective self-evaluation. In support of the downward-comparison hypothesis, Wills cited findings from a number of laboratory studies (Fisher & Nadler, 1982; Hakmiller, 1966). Evidence for the downward-comparison hypothesis also comes from field studies of cancer patients (Collins, Dakof, & Taylor, 1988; Taylor, Falke, Shoptaw, & Lichtman, 1986; Wood, Taylor, & Lichtman, 1985). In these studies, patients spontaneously compared themselves to worse-off experientially similar others, and regularly judged themselves to be coping better than most of their peers.

Findings from laboratory studies of helping are also consistent with the downward-comparison hypothesis. Subjects are likely to refuse help from similar-status others (Fisher & Nadler, 1982; Wills & DePaulo, 1991), presumably because this threatens their self-esteem. Help from more successful similar others is assumed to imply an upward comparison and to be threatening to self-esteem (Nadler, 1987).

However, other data from field studies of helping relationships are consistent with the upward-comparison hypothesis. Epidemiologic studies of help-seeking consistently report that people seek help most frequently from friends and family members (Norcross & Prochaska, 1986; Veroff, Kulka, & Douvan, 1981). Presumably, seeking help from others who are not currently troubled exposes people to the risks of upward comparisons. Yet field studies of cancer patients also report preferences for contact with patients who are better off or as well-off (Molleman, Pruyn, & van Knippenberg, 1986; Taylor, Aspinwall, Dakof, & Reardon, 1988).

Wills (1983) has labeled these conflicting sets of findings as *the paradox of help-seeking*. In posing this paradox, Wills contrasted two sets of motives and comparative processes: needs for self-enhancement, in the interest of maintaining self-esteem, versus needs for objective self-evaluation, in the interest of self-improvement. The paradox is that people frequently seek help from sources that theory and research indicate would be expected to jeopardize self-esteem and lead to self-devaluations.

Taylor and Lobel (1989) offered a partial resolution of this paradox. They suggested that people prefer *information about* downward-comparison others for purposes of self-enhancement, but seek *contact with* upward-comparison others for purposes of self-improvement. In Taylor and Lobel's analysis, these preferences for information versus contact with distinctive comparative others serve different needs and may exist simultaneously. For example, upward contact can satisfy informational needs related to problem-focused coping efforts, whereas downward comparisons can satisfy emotion-focused coping needs and be purely comparative.

Taylor and Lobel's analysis illustrates the ways in which the processes of social comparison and coping can be closely intertwined. When behavior under threat is examined, needs for information (associated with problem-focused coping) and needs for affiliation (associated with emotion-focused coping) can be difficult to distinguish from social comparison motives. It may be that the relative importance of these two sets of needs varies throughout the coping process, such that each is primary at different points in time. In past research, distinctions between these two sets of processes and social comparison motives have often been unclear.

Taylor and Lobel's analysis is also useful because it suggests a both-and rather than an either-or solution to the paradox of help-seeking. A both-and solution with reference to self-help groups suggests that participants make upward, downward, and lateral comparisons during various phases of their involvement with groups. That is, participants engage in social comparison processes in making decisions about joining, in the course of participating, and in relation to outcome. Anecdotal observations of AA groups suggest how introducing a social comparison perspective promises to offer insight into the motives of participants.

At every AA meeting, members testify about how much better off they are now than they were before joining AA—clearly a downward comparison to the former self. And every new AA member develops a relationship with a sponsor, an old-timer, someone who knows the program—clearly an upward comparison. Continuing members, in turn, come to sponsor newcomers, offering AA's program to others—clearly a downward comparison. Known as "12-stepping," this phase is the last step in AA's 12-step program and implies sufficient mastery of the previous 11 steps so that members are ready to teach the program to others. AA members often insist that 12-stepping shouldn't be understood as purely altruistic, and social comparison theory suggests some of the ways in which 12-stepping can be self-enhancing. Additionally, members frequently talk about the bonds of fellowship—bonds formed among equals, which involve lateral comparisons. Given that feelings of alienation and isolation seem to be prevalent among AA members, feelings of fellowship may be one of the primary rewards of participation.

The extent to which each of these processes is characteristic of an individual's experiences within AA or in other self-help groups is an empirical question. For example, few other self-help organizations seem to teach their members to make specific kinds of social comparisons as didactically as AA does. Additionally, social comparisons can have negative consequences, as when newcomers learn about old-timers whose condition is significantly worse than their own. Such worse-off comparative others can suggest threatening prognoses for new members (Coates & Winston, 1983). Whatever the consequences in particular cases, social comparison theory promises to increase our understanding of the motives that initially attract people, as well as of the potential rewards and costs of participation in self-help groups.

Schachter's and Byrne's Research on Similarity

Schachter's (1959) fear-affiliation hypothesis and Byrne's (1971) similarity-attraction paradigm both suggest that affiliative needs also account for some portion of the attractiveness of others with similar problems. However, the picture that emerges from reviews of this literature is that there are specifiable limiting conditions to the principle that similarity attracts—especially when the similarity is based on shared experience of a common problem.

Schachter's fear-affiliation hypothesis suggests that people who share common problems might seek the company of others who are similarly threatened in order to evaluate the appropriateness of their emotional reactions, and/or to reduce their fear. Subsequent research has specified a number of limiting conditions including the following: (a) Attraction is minimized when the threat arouses socially embarrassing anxiety (Sarnoff & Zimbardo, 1961) or profoundly upsetting emotions (Dabbs & Helmreich, 1972); and (b) affiliation only reduces fear when the companion models a calming response (Cottrell & Epley, 1977).

Kulik and Mahler's (1989) study of the preferences for hospital roommates of patients about to undergo cardiac surgery illustrates some of the limiting conditions of the fear-affiliation hypothesis. In their study, patients preferred to room with others who had already undergone surgery, rather than to be with patients who were more similar to themselves in that they were also about to undergo surgery. Kulik and Mahler speculated that patients wanted to gain useful information from more experienced roommates, and had little need to evaluate the appropriateness of their emotional reactions. Remarkably, Kulik and Mahler (1987) reported in an earlier article on the same study that patients who roomed with postoperative patients were less anxious preoperatively, were more ambulatory postoperatively, and were released more quickly from the hospital.

Byrne's (1971) work demonstrates that attraction is associated with perceived similarities in attitudes and personality traits that are of central importance to oneself. The bulk of the evidence suggests that similarity leads to attraction, which leads to liking. Subsequent research has identified some limiting conditions, whereby similarity can lead to rejection. For example, in a laboratory study, Taylor and Mettee (1971) demonstrated that similar others who behaved obnoxiously were more disliked than dissimilar others who also behaved obnoxiously. Such findings are clearly relevant to self-help groups where the basis of similarity is often a highly stigmatizing condition (e.g., alcoholism, drug addiction, or mental illness).

Exploratory Research Hypotheses

This overview of social comparison suggests a variety of motives that might lead people to seek help from experientially similar others, as well as some motives for avoiding contact. If we assume that their problems are not highly stigmatized or discomforting, it would be expected that students would have stronger preferences for contact with upward- or lateral-comparison peers who are experientially similar, rather than with downward-comparison peers. It would also be expected that students' motives for contact with upward-comparison peers would involve self-improvement. Other motives for seeking help from experientially similar others would include self-evaluation, self-enhancement, and meeting affiliative needs.

On the basis of the theories of social comparison and affiliation, two exploratory hypotheses were developed for the present study:

(1) Preferences for contact with experientially similar peers will vary as a function of peers' comparative standing. Respondents will have higher preferences for contact with their upward-comparison experientially similar peers than for their downward-comparison peers.

(2) Gains anticipated from contact with experientially similar peers will include self-evaluation, self-improvement, self-enhancement, and meeting affiliative needs.

The literature on help-seeking has demonstrated the relevance of several additional variables:

(1) Stress levels and severity of threat (Wills, 1983)—Stress has been found to be positively related to seeking help from mental health professionals.

(2) Self-esteem (Nadler, 1987)—Self-esteem has been found to be negatively related to help-seeking, with people low in self-esteem seeking help more often than people who have high levels of esteem (Wills & DePaulo, 1991).

(3) Need for affiliation (Lieberman & Videka-Sherman, 1986)—People high in need for affiliation would be expected to seek more social contact with peers.

(4) Locus of control (Lefcourt, Martin, & Saleh, 1984)—Internals are more likely to seek help than externals (Fischer & Turner, 1970).

(5) Demographic variables such as gender and ethnicity (Veroff et al., 1981)—Females would be expected to seek help more frequently than males, and Asians are less likely than Caucasians to seek help from mental health professionals (Lin, Inui, Kleinman, & Womack, 1982).

Measures of each of these variables were included in the following study in order to assess their relationship to help-seeking. Hypotheses were not developed about the relationship of these variables to help-seeking because they seem to be interrelated in complex ways and because their effects seem to be highly contextual. For example, help-seeking for academic problems is more likely when internal attributions of controllability for problem cause and solution are made (Ames & Lau, 1982). Moreover, internal attributions are likely to be associated with lower self-esteem, which is also associated with help-seeking in academic as well as work settings (Burke & Weir, 1976; Harris, Tessler, & Potter, 1977). However, gender differences in attributional style are well established in academic achievement contexts. Males are more likely to attribute academic failure to external causes (e.g., lack of effort), whereas females are likely to attribute failures to internal causes (e.g., lack of ability; Weiner, 1986).

Variables that would need to be considered if complete hypotheses about interacting factors were stated would include the nature of the problem (i.e., academic or social), gender, causal attributions, and initial level of self-esteem. Additionally, it might be expected that need for affiliation would be associated with preferences for seeking help from peers. Because of this complexity, an exploratory approach was taken toward the impact of each of these variables, rather than developing detailed hypotheses.

Method

Respondents and Types of Problems

Convenience sampling was used to recruit research participants. Members of an undergraduate class at UCLA on laboratory methods in social psychology recruited research participants using a variety of techniques. They approached students and asked them to fill out questionnaires (a) after other classes; (b) on campus in other locations, such as in dining halls or coffeehouses; and (c) in apartments and dormitories. Additionally, respondents were recruited from the introductory psychology class, and from a relevant undergraduate class for students training to become peer health counselors. Research participants ($N = 175$) responded anonymously to the questionnaire.

Respondents were told that the purpose of the research was to learn more about coping with stress. Toward this end, the first questionnaire item was open-ended and asked respondents to identify and describe a serious problem they had had while they were at UCLA. Respondents were encouraged to describe a current problem, but were given the option of describing a problem that they had already resolved. They were asked to answer all of the remaining questionnaire items with reference to this problem.

Respondents' answers to the open-ended question regarding problem type were coded and classified into the following categories: (a) academic problems ($n = 88$)—these included being dismissed from UCLA for poor academic performance, being placed on "subject to dismissal" status, being placed on academic probation, failing a class, and doing poorly in a class; (b) relationship problems ($n = 39$)—these included the breakup of a long-term relationship, parental divorce or separation, and extreme shyness; (c) being an adult child of an alcoholic (ACOA, $n = 24$); (d) concerns with life after graduation ($n = 8$); and (e) miscellaneous others ($n = 16$). The results of the data analyses reported here are confined to respondents with either academic or relationship problems, because the numbers of respondents with other problems were too small for meaningful analysis. These results were virtually identical to the analyses carried out with the full data set.

Table 3.1 presents the sex, race, and year-in-school status of the respondents. As it shows, the majority of respondents were upper division students. There were statistically significant differences between the sexual and racial composition of respondents who identified themselves as having academic versus relationship problems. Respondents who answered the questionnaire with reference to academic problems were significantly more likely to be (a) Asian rather than the other racial categories, $\chi^2 (6) = 13.68$, $n = 123$, $p < .02$; and (b) third-year students rather than first-, second-, or fourth-year students, $\chi^2 (3) = 9.8$, $n = 74$, $p < .02$.

Fifty-three percent of the respondents completed the questionnaire with reference to problems that were current. Respondents who

Table 3.1
Demographic Characteristics of Respondents
by Problem Type (in Percentages)

	Problem Type	
Characteristic	*Academic* *(n = 88)*	*Relationship* *(n = 39)*
Sex		
Female	67	50
Male	33	50
Race		
Asian	44	21
White	26	37
Hispanic	17	16
Mideastern	4	16
Black	4	5
Pacific islander/other	7	5
Year in school		
First	13	0
Second	13	11
Third	54	33
Fourth	21	57

answered the questionnaire with reference to problems that had already been resolved, on average, were describing problems that had been resolved within the past 9 months.

Questionnaire

The questionnaire was a 60-item instrument. Respondents answered items concerning (a) level of stress (using a 100-degree stress thermometer); (b) use of and satisfaction with sources of social support (Sarason, Sarason, Shearin, & Pierce, 1987); (c) one open-ended and several closed-ended questions regarding causal attributions; (d) a four-item need for affiliation scale (Lieberman & Videka-Sherman, 1986); (e) five items measuring locus of control over behaviorally relevant outcomes (Mirels, 1970); (f) a 10-item self-esteem scale (Rosenberg, 1965); (g) a four-item loneliness scale (Russell, Peplau, & Cutrona, 1980); and (h) demographic characteristics.

Preferences for Contact

This report is primarily concerned with the respondents' preferences for contact with potential helpers. They indicated their interest in having contact with six different sources of help after reading the following instruction:

Assume that it would be possible for you to have contact with various sources of help. Assume that it would be possible for you to have contact with any of the types of people listed below.

The six possible helpers were described in the following ways:

(1) Another UCLA student who is also having problems like mine and who is having a harder time than I am.
(2) Another UCLA student who is also having problems like mine and is coping about as well as I am with things.
(3) Another UCLA student who is also having problems like mine and who has learned some ways of coping that have enabled him/her to significantly lessen discomfort and improve.
(4) Another UCLA student who does not have problems like mine, but has general expertise in counseling skills and in coping skills.
(5) A mental health professional who has never had problems like mine, but has general expertise in counseling skills and in coping skills.
(6) A set of educational materials concerning ways to deal with my kinds of problems.

Respondents first indicated how interested they were in having contact with each source by answering on a scale that ranged from 1 (*not at all*) to 5 (*quite a bit*). Respondents then ranked each potential source of help in terms of their preference, by placing the rank number next to each potential source. The ranks ranged from 1 (*most preferable*) to 6 (*least preferable*).

Respondents then answered an open-ended item regarding what they hoped to gain from contact with their first-ranked source of help. The instructions were:

Please indicate, for the first ranking only, what you would hope to gain from this source of help. Please be as specific as possible in terms of what you would like to gain.

Categories were derived, a priori, from social comparison theory to code students' responses to this open-ended question. The categories were (a) self-evaluation—for example, "wanting to know how well I was doing"; (b) self-improvement—for example, "wanting to learn new strategies for dealing with my problem"; and (c) self-enhancement—for example, "I would be relieved to know that someone was doing worse than I was." Additional categories had to be developed to include all the types of answers given. These were: (d) affiliation—for example, "knowing someone else who had the same problem would make me feel less alone"; (e) self-understanding—for example, "wanting to understand myself better"; and (f) helping others—for example, "wanting to help someone else."

Three psychology graduate students coded the responses. After criteria were developed, there were no cases of disagreement between coders.

Results

Analyses of respondents' preferences for and rankings of potential helpers supported the first exploratory hypothesis, that respondents would prefer contact with upward-comparison, experientially similar peers than with downward-comparison peers. A MANOVA analysis of respondents' preferences for each of the six potential helpers was highly significant: $F(5, 117) = 30.52$, $p < .0001$. Table 3.2 shows the results of a series of post hoc Scheffé contrasts, and indicates that respondents had significantly higher preferences for contact with their experientially similar upward-comparison peers than for each of the other potential helpers.

Respondents also preferred contact with their lateral-comparison experientially similar peers to contact with mental health professionals and educational materials. Additionally, respondents preferred contact with their downward-comparison experientially similar peers to contact with mental health professionals. Finally, respondents preferred contact with an expert peer to contact with a mental health professional.

Table 3.3 shows that the same pattern of ranking of potential sources of help held both for respondents with academic and for those with relationship problems.

Table 3.2
Preferences for Potential Sources of Help

Source of help	Mean preference (n = 117)	Standard deviation	Percentage ranked first (n = 100)
Upward peer	3.87	1.13	52
Lateral peer	3.20[a]	1.22	15
Downward peer	2.97[a]	1.26	8
Expert peer	2.87[a]	1.17	4
Educational materials	2.68[ab]	1.29	12
Professional	2.38[abcd]	1.16	9

NOTE: Only respondents with academic or relationship problems are included here. Ns are less than 127 because of missing data.
a. Means significantly lower than upward peer, Scheffé, $p < .05$.
b. Means significantly lower than lateral peer, Scheffé, $p < .05$.
c. Means significantly lower than downward peer, Scheffé, $p < .05$.
d. Means significantly lower than expert peer, Scheffé, $p < .05$.

Gains Expected From Contact With Helper

Analyses of the gains respondents expected from contact with their first-ranked sources of help gave some support to the second exploratory hypothesis, that the motives of self-evaluation, self-improvement, affiliation, and self-enhancement would be primary. Table 3.4 shows that most respondents were hoping to gain information that would lead

Table 3.3
First-Ranked Sources of Help and Problem Type

Type of problem	Source of Help					
	Downward peer	Lateral peer	Upward peer	Expert peer	Professional	Educational materials
Academic (n = 74)	8	15	50	4	9	14
Relationship (n = 26)	8	15	58	4	8	8

NOTE: Numbers are percentages of students who ranked each helping source first. Ns are reduced because of missing data.

Table 3.4
Gains Expected from Contact with All
First-Ranked Sources of Help

Type of gain expected	n	%
Self-improvement	33	49
Affiliation	18	26
Self-understanding	10	15
Help others	2	4
Self-enhancement	1	1
Self-evaluation	0	0
Nothing	2	3
Uncodeable	1	1

NOTE: Only respondents with academic or relationship problems are included here. N is less than 100 because 32 respondents did not list any expectations.

to self-improvement. The second largest number of respondents was hoping to satisfy affiliative needs; for example, they wanted to "feel less alone" or to "talk to someone who could really understand."

There was an association between respondents' preferences for contact with potential helpers and what they hoped to gain from contact with their most-preferred source of help. As Table 3.5 shows, 65% of the respondents who ranked their experientially similar upward-comparison peers as their first choice hoped to gain information that would lead to self-improvement. In contrast, 82% of the respondents who ranked their lateral-comparison experientially similar peers as their first choice hoped to satisfy affiliative needs.

These same patterns of association between expected gains and rankings of potential helpers held true for both groups of respondents, those with academic problems as well as those with relationship problems.

Stress and Preferences for
Mental Health Professionals

In an effort to assess the meaningfulness of respondents' expressed preferences for contact with mental health professionals, the self-reports of use of professional help were analyzed. Respondents who

Table 3.5
Gains Expected from Contact with
First-Ranked Sources of Help

Expected gains	Down-ward peer (n = 6)	Lateral peer (n = 11)	Upward peer (n = 34)	Expert peer (n = 3)	Profes-sional (n = 7)	Educa-tional materials (n = 7)	Total (n = 68)
Self-improvement	33	9	65	33	43	57	49
Affiliation	17	82	18	33	14	–	26
Self–understanding	–	9	12	33	43	15	15
Help others	17	–	3	–	–	–	4
Self–enhancement	17	–	–	–	–	–	1
Self–evaluation	–	–	–	–	–	–	–
Nothing	17	–	–	–	–	28	3
Uncodeable	–	–	3	–	–	–	1

NOTE: Numbers are percentages based on the answers of people ranking each source of help first. Only respondents with academic or relationship problems are included.

reported having sought help from a mental health professional expressed a higher preference for the professional (when responding to the questions about preferences for contact with the six helpers) than did respondents who had not sought professional help: $M = 2.8$ versus $M = 2.4$; $t(147) = 2.52$, two-tailed; $p < .04$.

For respondents with relationship problems, there was a statistically significant positive relationship between level of stress and preference for contact with a mental health professional: $r(37) = .31, p < .04$. This replicates the findings in the literature of a positive relationship between stress and help-seeking from professionals (Wills, 1983). A contrasting relationship was found for students who were responding with reference to academic problems. They were less likely to prefer contact with a mental health professional as their reported stress level increased: $r(87) = -.19, p < .04$.

Effects of Personality and
Demographic Variables

There was a statistically significant negative relationship between self-esteem and preference for educational materials. For students who reported academic problems, the relationship was $r(83) = -.20, p < .03$. For respondents with relationship problems, the correlation was $r(34) = -.31, p < .04$. There were no other significant relationships among preferences for any of the potential helpers and the variables measuring stress, need for affiliation, loneliness, or locus of control.

With regard to gender, females had a significantly greater preference for professionals than did males: $M = 2.76$ versus $M = 2.00$; $t(33) = 2.19$, two-tailed; $p < .03$. However, this only held true when the problems were concerned with relationships.

Discussion

The findings support the usefulness of social comparison theory as a conceptual framework for understanding self-help groups. They indicate that respondents preferred helpers who were experientially similar, and that the comparative status of these helpers mattered. However, respondents' motives for seeking initial contact with similar helpers did not involve needs for self-evaluation or for self-enhancement, as would be expected from the literature. Respondents' motivations were more directly associated with stress and coping behaviors; the most frequently cited motive for contact was the desire to gain information that would be useful in problem solving.

The findings suggest that preferences for contact with experientially similar others are highly specific, both with respect to motives and with respect to the comparative status of the other. The implications are that people participate in self-help groups for very specific reasons (e.g., to gain problem-solving information). It can be speculated that different patterns of participation are associated with these motivations: People may attend only one or two meetings if they are only seeking information, but they may participate regularly if they are seeking to satisfy affiliative needs. It would be expected that information seeking would be a motive for participation when the desired information is difficult to obtain from other sources, such as family, friends, or professionals. Examples might include the case of a rare disease, or of a highly stigmatized disease that is rarely talked about, or situations where professional norms discourage the sharing of technical information with laypeople (e.g., sharing diagnostic information about mental illness with parents). Data from a variety of studies (Medvene, 1990; Powell, 1987) indicate that these patterns of participation that correspond to different motivations are common in self-help groups—many of which are organized by people suffering from rare or stigmatized diseases—although there is currently an absence of explanatory hypotheses.

The findings here also suggest that experiential similarity reduces the threatening aspects of receiving help from peers. For evidence, note that the three experientially similar peers were all preferred to the expert peer, but even the expert peer was preferred to a professional helper or to educational materials. Perhaps help-seekers attribute special expertise or understanding to experientially similar helpers. Perhaps experientially similar others are viewed as being in some ways like friends, whom people are much more likely to approach for help than professionals.

The Paradox of Help-Seeking and Experiential Similarity

Respondents' markedly different responses to the two upward-comparison peers—the experientially similar UCLA student versus the peer expert—are of great interest because they mirror the paradox of help-seeking (Wills, 1983). The respondents here expressed relatively little desire for contact with peer experts, just as subjects in lab studies were not inclined to accept help from peers. At the same time, respondents here expressed a preference for contact with their experientially similar upward-comparison peers, just as people in field studies report seeking help most frequently from friends and family.

A reasonable explanation for the students' comparative lack of interest in the peer expert is that such contact would be a threat to self-esteem. Nadler and Fisher (1986; Nadler, 1987) hypothesized that aspects of helping interactions that underscore the self-threatening implications of receiving help produce negative and defensive recipient reactions. In contrast, respondents' preferences in this study for contact with their upward-comparison experientially similar peers suggest that there are some aspects of experiential similarity that ameliorate threats to self-esteem. It is also possible that experiential similarity increases the benefits that are anticipated from contact with upward-comparison peers.

Two hypotheses can be offered to account for these findings. First, in terms of threats to self-esteem, experiential similarity may reduce help-seekers' evaluation apprehension that peers will judge them negatively. This hypothesis is similar to Wills and DePaulo's (1991) explanation for the findings from epidemiologic studies that people seek help most frequently from friends and family members. They argue that there is much self-disclosure in friendships, and that disclosures of distress would be expected to elicit offers of help within such relationships. This argument can be extended in the following way: If one presumes a history of personal self-disclosures within friendships, one can assume that friends have engaged in a series of reciprocal disclosures of negative information. In such a relationship, the self-disclosure of one additional piece of negative information will be minimally threatening. Similarly, the act of seeking help from an experientially similar peer may be like a reciprocal disclosure, for the help-seeker can anticipate that the helper will say, "Oh, yes, I've had the same problem too."

A second hypothesis, concerning benefits, is that experiential similarity suggests a closeness such that the goal of reaching the same level of functioning as the helper seems more attainable. Also, such perceived closeness may suggest cooperative relations between the help-seeker and the helper. A plausible explanation for refusals of peers' offers of help in laboratory settings is that competitive relationships have been created in these settings (e.g., DePaulo et al., 1989). Such competitive relationships would increase the threatening aspects of receiving help.

Expected Gains and Motives for Contact

The respondents' most frequently stated motive for seeking contact was the desire to gain information that would be useful for problem-focused coping efforts (e.g., "learning new techniques for studying"). The second most frequently cited motive was the desire to satisfy affiliative needs (e.g., hoping to "find someone who could really relate and understand").

These findings are consistent with other research in the social support literature regarding preferences for contact with experientially similar others. Taylor and Lobel (1989) and Molleman, Pruyn, and van Knippenberg (1986), as well as Kulik and Mahler (1989), also found that respondents' preferences for contact with experientially similar others were based on expectations that they could provide useful information. A plausible explanation for these findings, as well as the findings in this study, is that people attribute special credibility and expertise to experientially similar peers who are coping at a higher level. That is, they expect that upward-comparison experientially similar others will be able to impart their special knowledge in helping interactions. Such an explanation is consistent with Tinsley, Brown, de St. Aubin, and Lucek's (1984) findings that students' preferences for contact with different helpers were related to their expectations regarding interactions with these helpers. For example, students with strong expectations of a positive outcome from contacts with psychiatrists were significantly more likely to seek help from psychiatrists.

It is possible that the description in this study of the upward-comparison experientially similar helpers maximized expectations about their expertise. This type of helper was described as "another UCLA student who has learned some ways of coping that enabled him/her to significantly lessen discomfort and improve." Such language might maximize the appeal of these helpers, and one practical implication here is that the appeal of self-help groups may be maximized when more experienced members are described in such terms.

The possible impact of language on students' preferences also points to the close intertwining of the processes of coping and social comparison. However, in a survey study it is not possible to unconfound these two processes. It is possible that the language used here to describe the upward-comparison experientially similar helper influenced respondents to focus more on coping and problem-solving concerns than on social comparison concerns. However, the consistency of the findings here with previously reported findings suggests an alternative explanation—namely, that when information about how to cope with or master a problem is lacking, needs for information will be the most salient motivation for seeking help from experientially similar others. Kulik and Mahler's (1989) findings that cardiac patients preferred postoperative to preoperative roommates illustrate the influence of needs for information on affiliative preferences.

With reference to self-help groups, this suggests that needs for information for social comparison purposes become more important after basic needs for problem-focused information are satisfied. Over time, self-evaluative social comparison processes may come to be an important aspect of process and outcome in self-help groups. For example, over time, participants may come to make more in-group social comparisons—including upward, lateral, and downward ones— and compare themselves less to friends or to family members who are not group members.

That social comparison processes occur at the group level, as well as at the individual level, has been taken into account in other areas of social comparison research (e.g., research on relative deprivation) but not yet in relation to stress and coping. For example, it is well established that workers compare themselves more frequently with others who are members of their reference groups or in-groups (e.g., females compare their wages with the pay of other females; Major, 1990). In organizations, employees compare their wages with other employees with comparable levels of education and experience (Lansberg, 1989).

In a recent review of the literature on stigma and self-esteem, Crocker and Major (1989) have extended the analysis of social evaluation processes to the case of socially stigmatized groups (e.g., blacks, the physically disabled, the mentally retarded, and the mentally ill). After reviewing the anomalous findings that levels of self-esteem among members of these groups are not lower, as might be expected, they offer some relevant hypotheses to account for the findings. They suggest that

> members of stigmatized groups may (a) attribute negative feedback to prejudice against their group, (b) compare their outcomes with those of the ingroup, rather than with the relatively advantaged outgroup, and (c) selectively devalue those dimensions on which their group fares poorly and value those dimensions on which their group excels. (p. 608)

It can be speculated that, analogously, participation in self-help groups promotes in-group social comparisons, which protect the self-esteem of people with socially stigmatized problems. Clearly, there are self-help groups for all of the stigmatized groups mentioned in Crocker and Major's review. One question for future research is whether, over time, self-help group members increasingly compare themselves to fellow group members, and whether such comparisons are associated with gains in self-esteem. Future research might also examine the extent to which group members view themselves as oppressed, and the extent to which they devalue dimensions on which fellow group members do poorly and value those dimensions on which group members do well.

Other research suggests that social comparison processes are related to the behavioral outcomes of participation in self-help groups. Gibbons, Gerrard, Lando, and McGovern (in press), in a recent study of smoking cessation groups, report that adults who stopped smoking and remained abstinent perceived themselves as more dissimilar to and distant from "typical" smokers. The authors speculate that social comparisons with typical smokers can motivate changes in members' self-concepts—namely, changing from smokers to nonsmokers.

> In terms used by Markus and Nurius (1986), these people may have been employing a negative "possible self," i.e., future smoker, as a motivator to help them quit smoking. That particular possible self takes the form of the typical smoker, and as smokers attempt to avoid this negative self, they derogate the prototype. (p. 21)

Similar processes may be associated with behavioral changes in other self-help groups. For example, abstinence in AA may be associated with the downward comparisons members make between their current selves and their selves before they joined AA.

Low Frequency of Expectations
for Self-Enhancement

Given the emphasis in the literature on the motive of self-enhancement (Wills, 1983), the virtual absence of downward social comparisons in this study was surprising. Several factors may explain this. First, the literature may reflect people's tendencies to seek information about but not contact with worse-off others, as Taylor and Lobel (1989) argue. Although people are interested in knowing about or imagining worse-off others (Wood et al., 1985), their desire for contact with them may be minimal. Second, social desirability concerns may have made respondents reluctant to say that it would make them feel better to know someone else who was having a worse time than themselves. Additionally, as the above discussion suggests, downward comparison, along with social comparison processes generally, may simply be less salient during the initial phases of help-seeking.

Contextualizing the Findings

The findings here need to be considered in the context of the nature of the respondents' problems and their stages of coping with these problems. The students responded to the questionnaire primarily with reference to serious academic and relationship problems. For young adults in college, it might be expected that both types of problems would be perceived as amenable to improvement through increased efforts and/or new learning. However, in contrast to the problems on which these students focused, other types of problems may be intractable—for example, medical problems like AIDS or metastasized cancer. In such cases, the goal of self-improvement may be futile, and lateral comparisons may be most appealing. These speculations suggest that attributions regarding the controllability of the course of illness or of the solution to the problem are related to motives for help-seeking and preferences for helpers (see Brickman et al., 1982).

Brickman et al.'s (1982) distinction between attributions of responsibility for causing problems versus attributions of responsibility for solving problems is important here. At least one study suggests that help-seeking is discouraged when people blame themselves for causing the problem (e.g., with reference to alcoholism; Hingson, Mangione, Myers, & Scotch, 1982). Several studies show that help-seeking is increased when people believe they can control or influence the course of recovery or the solution to the problem. Findings in achievement contexts are that students will seek help if they attribute their failures to controllable factors, such as lack of effort (Ames & Lau, 1982; Testa & Major, in press). In studies of victimization—for example, rape—behavioral self-blame (as contrasted with characterological self-blame) has been linked to effective coping, presumably because such an attribution affords the possibility of control over future events.

What happens in situations where behavioral control is not possible? There appears to be little information about the extent to which desires for other types of control (e.g., decisional, cognitive, or informational) motivate help-seeking behavior. A recent study of a local chapter of the Alliance for the Mentally Ill (AMI)—a self-help group composed primarily of parents whose offspring have severe psychiatric disabilities—suggests that members do experience these other types of control as benefits of participation (Medvene & Krauss, 1989). The authors suggest that parents benefited from learning a schema about the illness of schizophrenia that included information about causes, symptoms, treatment, and probable outcomes. Learning this schema helped parents to develop coping techniques that increased their ability to influence (although not control) their adult sons' and daughters' symptomatic behaviors, anticipate future difficulties, and have more realistic expectations regarding outcomes. Questions for future research are the extent to which these findings are related to parents' motivations for joining AMI groups, as well as the extent to which these findings generalize to other self-help groups for caregivers.

The finding that locus of control was unrelated to preferences for potential helpers in this study may have been attributable to the insensitivity of the questionnaire items. Only five locus of control items were used, and these items concerned behavioral control only. Future research should include a larger number of items with more varied content.

Limitations of the Study and Future Research

Because the findings here only refer to students' stated preferences and not to their actual help-seeking behavior, the findings' generalizability may be limited. This is especially true given that the relationship between attitudes and behavior is often problematic (Ajzen & Fishbein, 1977). Additionally, students were responding to the questionnaire with reference to a variety of problems. Although the analysis was simplified by focusing on only academic and relationship problems, the results might have been clearer if there had been more respondents with each type of problem.

Future research should focus on a population with a single type of problem, and it should include measures of actual help-seeking behavior, as well as preferences for helpers. Additionally, future research ought to include populations with highly stigmatized problems, as many self-help groups are organized for people with socially undesirable conditions (e.g., mental illness, physical and sensory disabilities, and counternormative life-styles). Such stigmatized populations ought to be included in future studies because it is possible that stigma constitutes a limiting condition of the findings reported here. Stigma, or the fear that one's social identity or self-esteem will be "soiled" by contact with others, may inhibit the tendency to seek help from experientially similar others in various ways: (a) Negative stereotypes may discourage contact—for example, "Most divorced women are losers, and as a divorced woman I don't want to be associated with losers;" or (b) negative stereotypes may lead to rejection of self-inclusion in the social category—for example, "Welfare recipients are people who are on welfare for most of their adult lives, and since I'm just receiving welfare temporarily I'm not a welfare recipient."

Practical Implications

One implication of the findings is that self-help group heterogeneity with respect to coping skills and information is desirable. A likely way to attract new members would be to advertise that groups include members who are veterans of the problem area with high levels of coping skills. Success in attracting new members would also be a likely way to maintain the participation of skilled "old-timers." As suggested by the earlier discussion of AA, the old-timers can help the newer members and, at the same time, benefit from downward comparisons with them. From the point of view of social comparison theory, the ideal self-help group would be one that is homogeneous with respect to problem type and heterogeneous with respect to coping skills or level of mastery.

Second, recruiting peer helpers who have had problems themselves in the areas in which they are counseling others—for example, academic, health, or social—would be a relatively novel approach (Giddan, 1988) and ought to be tried. Given the literature on "wounded healers" (Farber, 1983), it may be that peer helpers are experientially similar to help-seekers more often than is explicitly acknowledged. In such cases, the issue of self-disclosure becomes important. There is a body of literature that indicates that friendship and intimacy are characterized by a pattern of reciprocal self-disclosures (Altman & Taylor, 1973). Within the psychotherapy literature, self-disclosures are recognized as tools for communicating empathy and understanding

(Goodman & Esterly, 1988; Truax & Carkhuff, 1965). However, where experiential similarities have not been explicitly stated initially, later disclosures may need to be made strategically so that the helper's role in the relationship is not undermined. An examination of the consequences of self-disclosure in peer counseling relationships would be a useful topic for future research.

A third implication of the findings is that self-disclosure is a crucial aspect of process in self-help groups. Self-disclosure creates opportunities for "me-too" self-disclosures (Goodman & Esterly, 1988), which may reduce threats to self-esteem, and it may also function as a request for help. This suggests that group facilitators will be most effective when they create conditions that are safe for self-disclosure. Established techniques for creating safety include (a) developing rules for confidentiality, (b) modeling comfortable self-disclosure behavior, and (c) not pressuring people to self-disclose (Medvene, in press). Mental health professionals could be helpful by training facilitators in these techniques using a variety of media, including consultation agreements, instructional manuals (Medvene, Pannor, & Strachan, 1989), audiotapes (e.g., *The Common Concern Program*; Goodman & Jacobs, 1987), and videotapes.

In summary, the findings here suggest a number of ways in which social comparison theory, as well as theories of stress and coping, promise to be useful in exploring the motivations for participation in self-help groups. Lewin's dictum that "there is nothing so practical as a good theory" is pertinent to these theories, and the theories and research findings suggest a number of questions that should guide future research.

References

Ajzen, I., & Fishbein, M. (1977). Attitude-behavior relations: A theoretical analysis and review of empirical research. *Psychological Bulletin, 84*, 888-918.

Altman, I., & Taylor, D. (1973). *Social penetration: The development of interpersonal relations*. New York: Holt, Rinhart, & Winston.

Ames, R., & Lau, S. (1982). An attributional analysis of help-seeking in academic settings. *Journal of Educational Psychology, 74*, 414-432.

Atkinson, D. R., & Schein, S. (1986). Similarity in counseling. *The Counseling Psychologist, 14*, 319-354.

Borkman, T. (1976). Experiential knowledge: A new concept for the analysis of self-help groups. *Social Service Review*, *50*, 445-456.

Brickman, P., Rabinowitz, V. C., Karuza, J., Jr., Coates, D., Cohn, E., & Kidder, L. (1982). Models of helping and coping. *American Psychologist*, *37*, 368-384.

Burke, R. J., & Weir, T. (1976). Personality characteristics associated with giving and receiving help. *Psychological Reports*, *38*, 343-353.

Byrne, D. (1971). *The attraction paradigm*. New York: Academic Press.

Coates, D., & Winston, T. (1983). Counteracting the deviance of depression: Peer support groups for victims. *Journal of Social Issues*, *39*(2), 169-194.

Collins, R. E., Dakof, G. A., & Taylor, S. E. (1988). *Social comparison and adjustment to a threatening event*. Manuscript submitted for publication.

Cottrell, N. B., & Epley, S. W. (1977). Affiliation, social comparison, and socially mediated stress reduction. In J. M. Suls & R. L. Miller (Eds.), *Social comparison processes: Theoretical and empirical perspectives* (pp. 43-68). Washington, DC: Hemisphere.

Crocker, J., & Major, B. (1989). Social stigma and self-esteem: The self-protective properties of stigma. *Psychological Review*, *96*, 608-630.

Dabbs, J. M., & Helmreich, R. L. (1972). Fear, anxiety, and affiliation following a role-played accident. *Journal of Social Psychology*, *86*, 269-278.

DePaulo, B. M., Tang, J., Webb, W., Hoover, C., Marsh, K., & Litowitz, C. (1989). Age differences in reactions to help in a peer tutoring context. *Child Development*, *60*, 423-439.

Farber, B. A. (1983). *Stress and burnout in the human service professions*. New York: Pergamon.

Festinger, L. (1954). A theory of social comparison processes. *Human Relations*, *7*, 117-140.

Fischer, E. H., & Turner, J. L. (1970). Orientations to seeking professional help: Development and research utility of an attitude scale. *Journal of Consulting and Clinical Psychology*, *35*, 79-90.

Fisher, J. D., & Nadler, A. (1982). Determinants of recipient reactions to aid: Donor-recipient similarity and perceived dimensions of problems. In T. A. Wells (Ed.), *Basic processes in helping relationships* (pp. 131-153). New York: Academic Press.

Gibbons, F. X., Gerrard, M., Lando, H. A., & McGovern, P. G. (in press). Social comparison and smoking cessation: The role of the "typical smoker." *Journal of Experimental Social Psychology*.

Giddan, N. S. (1988). *Community and social support for college students*. Springfield, IL: Charles C Thomas.

Goodman, G., & Esterly, G. (1988). *The talk book: The intimate science of communicating in close relationships*. Emmaus, PA: Rodale.

Goodman, G., & Jacobs, M. K. (1987). *The Common Concern Program—A self-led audiotaped and print materials program to start and train self-help groups* [Cassette recording]. Oakland, CA: New Harbinger.

Hakmiller, K. L. (1966). Threat as a determinant of downward comparison. *Journal of Experimental Social Psychology*, *2*(Suppl. 1), 32-39.

Harris, A., Tessler, R., & Potter, J. (1977). The induction of self-reliance: An experimental study of independence in the face of failure. *Journal of Applied Social Psychology*, *7*, 313-331.

Hingson, R., Mangione, T., Myers, A., & Scotch, N. (1982). Seeking help for drinking problems: A study in the Boston metropolitan area. *Journal of Studies on Alcohol, 43,* 273-288.

Hough, R. L., Landsverk, J. A., Karno, M., Burnam, A., Timbers, D. M., Escobar, I. J., & Regier, D. A. (1987). Utilization of health and mental health sources by Los Angeles Mexican Americans and non-Hispanic Whites. *Archives of General Psychiatry, 44,* 702-709.

Jacobs, M. K., & Goodman, G. (1989). Psychology and self-help groups: Predictions on a partnership. *American Psychologist, 44,* 536-545.

Katz, A. H., & Bender, E. T. (1976). *The strength in us: Self-help groups in the modern world.* New York: New Viewpoint.

Kulik, J. A., & Mahler, H. I. M. (1987). Effects of preoperative roommate assignment on preoperative anxiety and recovery from coronary-bypass surgery. *Health Psychology, 6,* 525-543.

Kulik, J. A., & Mahler, H. I. M. (1989). Stress and affiliation in a hospital setting: Preoperative roommate preferences. *Personality and Social Psychology Bulletin, 15,* 183-193.

Lansberg, I. (1989). Social categorization, entitlement, and justice in organizations: Contextual determinants and cognitive underpinnings. *Human Relations, 41,* 871-899.

Leerhsen, C., Lewis, S., Pomper, S., Davenport, L., & Nelson, M. (1990, February 5). Unite and conquer. *Newsweek,* pp. 50-55.

Lefcourt, H. M., Martin, R. A., & Saleh, W. E. (1984). Locus of control and social support: Interactive moderators of stress. *Journal of Personality and Social Psychology, 47,* 378-389.

Lieberman, M. A., & Videka-Sherman, L. (1986). The impact of self-help groups on the mental health of widows and widowers. *American Journal of Orthopsychiatry, 56,* 435-447.

Lin, K. M., Inui, T. S., Kleinman, A. M., & Womack, W. M. (1982). Sociocultural determinants of the help-seeking behavior of patients with mental illness. *Journal of Nervous and Mental Disease, 170,* 78-85.

Major, B. (1990). Gender differences in comparisons and entitlement: Implications for comparable worth. *Journal of Social Issues, 45*(4), 99-115.

Markus, H., & Nurius, P. (1986). Possible selves. *American Psychologist, 41,* 954-969.

Medvene, L. (1990). *Selected highlights of research on effectiveness of self-help groups.* Unpublished manuscript, University of California, California Self-Help Center, Los Angeles.

Medvene, L. (in press). Family support organizations: The functions of similarity. In T. Powell (Ed.), *Working with self-help.* Silver Spring, MD: National Association of Social Workers.

Medvene, L., & Krauss, D. (1989). Causal attributions and parent-child relationships in a self-help group for families of the mentally ill. *Journal of Applied Social Psychology, 19,* 1413-1430.

Medvene, L., Pannor, F., & Strachan, A. (1989). *A "how to" manual for facilitating AMI "Caring And Sharing" support groups.* Unpublished manuscript, Claremont Graduate School, Claremont, CA.

Mirels, H. L. (1970). Dimensions of internal vs. external control. *Journal of Consulting and Clinical Psychology, 34,* 226-228.

Molleman, E., Pruyn, J., & van Knippenberg, A. (1986). Social comparison processes among cancer patients. *British Journal of Social Psychology, 25,* 1-13.

Nadler, A. (1987). Determinants of help-seeking behavior: The effect of helper's similarity, task centrality, and recipient's self-esteem. *European Journal of Social Psychology, 17,* 57-67.

Nadler, A., & Fisher, J. D. (1986). The role of threat to self-esteem and perceived control in recipient reaction to help. In L. Berkowitz (Ed.), *Advances in experimental social psychology* (Vol. 19, pp. 81-122). New York: Academic Press.

Norcross, J. C., & Prochaska, J. O. (1986). The psychological distress and self-change of psychologists, counselors, and lay persons. *Psychotherapy, 23,* 102-114.

Powell, T. (1987). *Self-help organization and professional practice.* Silver Spring, MD: National Association of Social Workers.

President's Commission on Mental Health (1978). [Report]. Washington, DC: Government Printing Office.

Riessman, F. (1965). The "helper" therapy principle. *Social Work, 10,* 27-32.

Rosenberg, M. (1965). The Rosenberg Self-Esteem Scale: Short version. In M. Rosenberg (Ed.), *Society and the adolescent self image* (pp. 305-307). Princeton, NJ: Princeton University Press.

Russell, D. W., Peplau, L. A., & Cutrona, C. E. (1980). The revised UCLA Loneliness Scale: Concurrent and discriminant validity. *Journal of Personality and Social Psychology, 39,* 472-480.

Sarason, I. G., Sarason, B. R., Shearin, E. N., & Pierce, G. R. (1987). A brief measure of social support: Practical and theoretical implications. *Journal of Social and Personal Relationships, 4,* 497-510.

Sarnoff, I., & Zimbardo, P. G. (1961). Anxiety, fear, and social affiliation. *Journal of Abnormal and Social Psychology, 67,* 643-648.

Schachter, S. (1959). *The psychology of affiliation.* Stanford, CA: Stanford University Press.

Spiegel, D., Bloom, J. R., Kraemer, H. C., & Gottheil, E. (1989, October 14). Effect of psychosocial treatment on survival of patients with metastatic breast cancer. *The Lancet, 2,* 888-891.

Surgeon General's Workshop on Self-Help and Public Health. (1988). Public Health Service, Human Resources, and Service Administration, Bureau of Maternal and Child Health and Resource Administration (DHHS Publication No. 224-250-88-1). Washington, DC: Government Printing Office.

Taylor, S. E., Aspinwall, L. G., Dakof, G. A., & Reardon, K. (1988). *Stress, storytelling, social comparison, and social support: Victims' reactions to stories of similar victims.* Unpublished manuscript.

Taylor, S. E., Falke, R. L., Shoptaw, S. J., & Lichtman, R. R. (1986). Social support, support groups, and the cancer patient. *Journal of Consulting and Clinical Psychology, 54,* 608-615.

Taylor, S. E., & Lobel, M. (1989). Social comparison activity under threat: Downward evaluation and upward contacts. *Psychological Review, 96,* 569-575.

Taylor, S. E., & Mettee, D. (1971). When similarity breeds contempt. *Journal of Personality and Social Psychology, 20,* 75-81.

Testa, M., & Major, B. (in press). The impact of social comparisons after failure: The moderating effects of perceived control. *Basic and Applied Social Psychology.*

Tinsley, H. E. A., Brown, M. T., de St. Aubin, T. M., & Lucek, J. (1984). Relation between expectancies for a helping relationship and tendency to seek help from a campus help provider. *Journal of Counseling Psychology, 31*, 149-160.

Truax, C. B., & Carkhuff, R. R. (1965). Client and therapist transparency in the psychotherapeutic encounter. *Journal of Counseling Psychology, 12*, 3-9.

Veroff, J. B., Kulka, R. A., & Douvan, E. (1981). *Mental health in America: Patterns of help-seeking, 1957-1976.* New York: Basic Books.

Weiner, B. (1986). *An attributional theory of motivation and emotion.* New York: Springer-Verlag.

Wills, T. A. (1981). Downward comparison principles in social psychology. *Psychological Bulletin, 90*, 245-271.

Wills, T. A. (1983). Social comparison in coping and help-seeking. In B. M. DePaulo, A. Nadler, & J. D. Fisher (Eds.), *New directions in help-seeking* (Vol. 2, pp. 109-142). New York: Academic Press.

Wills, T. A., & DePaulo, B. M. (1991). Interpersonal analysis of the help-seeking process. In C. R. Snyder & D. R. Forsyth (Eds.), *Handbook of social and clinical psychology* (pp. 350-375). Elmsford, NY: Pergamon.

Wood, J. V., Taylor, S. E., & Lichtman, R. R. (1985). Social comparison in adjustment to breast cancer. *Journal of Personality and Social Psychology, 49*, 1169-1183.

4

Elements of Supportive Interactions: When Are Attempts to Help Effective?

CHRISTINE DUNKEL-SCHETTER
DAVID E. BLASBAND
LAWRENCE G. FEINSTEIN
TRACY BENNETT HERBERT

A central focus in our research has been to understand the factors that determine when actions are supportive or not for someone who is suffering. This issue is actually two intertwined questions: First, what factors increase or decrease the likelihood of a support attempt or a negative reaction taking place? Second, what factors mediate the effects of a support attempt? The former question concerns the quantity of support, with the possibilities ranging from no support to large amounts of support received. The second question concerns the quality of support received, which varies from poor to excellent. This chapter attempts to shed light on the latter issue—that is, why some support attempts succeed and others fail.

For the past 10 years, the senior author has been interested in how people cope with stress and the role of others' reactions, both positive and negative, in their adjustment. Her work has focused on social support processes in general such as the definition and measurement of social support (Dunkel-Schetter & Bennett, 1990; Wortman & Dunkel-Schetter, 1987), and on specific issues such as the determinants of support receipt (Dunkel-Schetter, Folkman, & Lazarus, 1987; Dunkel-Schetter & Skokan, 1990).

This program of research has been concerned with the social support that occurs when someone is suffering in some way. Usually, the person is experiencing a specific stressful life event, but we have also been interested in social responses to emotional distress stemming from chronic stress and from psychopathologic origins. Some social support researchers have indicated that exposure to stressful circumstances often leads a person to mobilize supportive resources (e.g., Barrera, 1981; Eckenrode & Wethington, 1990; Gore, 1981; Gottlieb, 1983). Furthermore, social psychological research reviewed by Staub (1974) and Schwarz (1977) has shown that emotional distress elicits attempts to help, in part because it is an indicator of an individual's need. Still other studies on victims suggest that social responses to distress change over time and may be negative as well as positive (see reviews by Herbert & Dunkel-Schetter, in press; Dunkel-Schetter & Bennett, 1990; Wortman & Lehman, 1985). In summary, our interest has been in suffering or distress attributable to a variety of causes, where the negative effect and the events precipitating it act as the stimuli for a range of social responses—in particular, support attempts and negative reactions.

In addressing the issue of why some support attempts succeed and others fail, this chapter draws from our own research as well as research conducted by others. Work by our research group has involved people experiencing a variety of life stresses, including cancer, AIDS, diabetes, and stress in medical school and college. In this chapter, however, we base our discussion on two dissertation projects—that of Blasband (1990), who conducted interviews with 40 men with AIDS regarding their social experiences, and that of Feinstein (1988), who conducted interviews with 20 male and 20 female diabetics and their spouses regarding their support interactions. Other past research that has addressed the question of interest here includes investigations by Lehman, Ellard, and Wortman (1986) of the support experiences of bereaved adults, and by Dakof and Taylor (1990; Taylor & Dakof, 1988) of the support experiences of cancer patients. These studies and ours utilize a similar methodology and, as a set, they inform us about naturally occurring social responses to suffering and distress. Before turning to the observations that can be made based on this body of work, our framework for the conceptualization and study of social support is described.

A Framework for the Study of Social Support

Social support has been defined in many different ways. The definition of social support used here follows in the tradition of a number of researchers (e.g., House, 1981; Kahn & Antonucci, 1980; Shumaker & Brownell, 1984), all of whom focus on social support as interpersonal interactions, transactions, or exchanges. House (1981), for example, defines support as interpersonal transactions involving one or more of the following: emotional concern, instrumental aid, information about the environment, and information relevant to appraisal of self. Our support concept involves the actual exchange of support, sometimes referred to as *received support*.

It should be noted that this conceptualization is quite different from the concept of *available support*, which has been dominant in the literature in the past. Available support is the perception that others are there to depend upon if one needs them, whether or not they are active in providing resources of any kind (see Dunkel-Schetter & Bennett, 1990, for a discussion of this distinction). Conceptions of available support are dispositional and cognitive, whereas conceptions of received support are situational and behavioral, involving interaction among individuals. Both approaches are valuable, and they are not generally inconsistent (Sarason, Pierce, & Sarason, 1990).

Our specific focus has been on dyadic support interactions—ones having the two roles of support provider and support recipient. Figure 4.1 provides a working framework for conceptualizing the perspectives of these two roles within supportive interactions, and it adds the perspective of an observer or third party to the picture. A particular interaction can be seen from each of these three perspectives—that of the *provider* (Circle A), that of the *recipient* (Circle B), and that of the *third party* (Circle C). The third- party perspective might be operationalized as the perspective of a single observer or the average of several judges' assessments (a normative standard). This third perspective

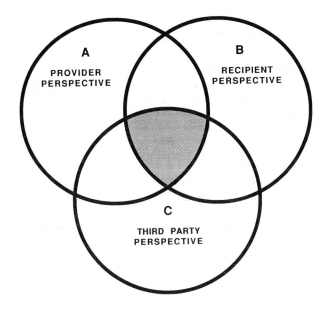

Figure 4.1. Three Perspectives of Supportive Interactions

accounts for the cultural and social relativity of social support interactions; what is viewed as support in one social class or culture may
not be seen as support in another. Overlap between two perspectives in
Figure 4.1 indicates agreement in the judgment of an interaction on a
particular dimension, whereas the absence of overlap suggests diver-
gence in two views of the interaction.

Two key dimensions of support interactions can be considered from
each of the three perspectives in this framework: (a) the *intentions*
behind a particular interaction or support attempt, and (b) the immediate *effects* of an interaction on the recipient. Each of these dimensions
is discussed below.

Intentions and Support Interactions

The importance of intentions in social support interactions was
highlighted by Shumaker and Brownell (1984) when they defined social

support as social exchanges in which either the provider or the recipient perceives that the provider had positive intent. The significance of intentions to social support research can also be justified in light of Ajzen and Fishbein's (1980) theory of planned action and of planned behavior (Ajzen, 1985). This theory states that the best predictor of a specific and volitional behavior is whether or not one intends to perform that behavior; the stronger the person's intentions, the greater the likelihood a specific behavior will be performed. Evidence for this theory's relevance to helping and social support is accumulating (Borgida, Simmons, Conner, & Lombard, 1990; Dalbert, Montada, & Schmitt, 1988; Montada, Dalbert, & Schmitt, 1982). Given that our goal is to predict the occurrence and quality of social support, the provider's intention seems to be a necessary component of models of support. Another reason for including it is that a long tradition of research in social psychology, and recent emphasis in social cognition research specifically, indicates that most complex social behaviors are goal based (for reviews and cogent discussion, see Bargh, 1990; Gollwitzer, 1990).

Support interactions could be altruistically motivated (which many are) or might involve other motives, chiefly egoistic ones. This distinction between altruistic and egoistic intentions is derived from the work of Batson in social psychological research on helping (Batson & Coke, 1981; Batson, O'Quin, Fultz, Vanderplas, & Isen, 1983). Examples of support attempts motivated by self-interest would include advice given with the expectation of some social reward, or to alter an aspect of the target person's behavior that is annoying. Altruistically motivated support attempts are those made without expectation of reward or personal gain.

This chapter is concerned with recipient, provider, and observer views of whether an act was intended altruistically or not—that is, whether the provider is viewed as intending to help the recipient primarily for the recipient's benefit. The provider is in the best position to know his or her intent, and providers' intentions can be assessed best prior to interaction. However, the perspective of the recipient about the provider's intentions is also important because the effects of support interactions are determined partly by the recipient's judgment of the intent underlying provider behaviors. Recipients who think an action was altruistically intended often view it as helpful, even though it would have had no effect without this imputed intent. Alternatively, recipients can misconstrue intentions, such as inferring ill intent when actions are well-meant. Hence, third-party or observer perspectives offer another source of information about imputed intentions that may be useful for comparison to recipient and provider views.

Effects of Support Interactions

In social support research, we are accustomed to thinking of the effects of support on physical and mental health outcomes, such as rates of depression, illness, or death. Considerable research has documented that support has many beneficial long-term effects for health, but researchers have been unsuccessful as yet in determining exactly why or how these effects occur (see Cohen, 1988; House, Umberson, & Landis, 1988; Thoits, 1985). Clues to the process by which support is health protective might be found in research on supportive interactions.

When an interactional approach to support is applied, the more immediate or proximal effects of support become evident. Specific immediate effects (for a recipient) of a particular interaction, or a series of consecutive interactions between two individuals, might include one or more of the following: a change in mood, attitude, optimism, or esteem; an enhanced motivation or sense of self-efficacy in coping; new knowledge or information of use in addressing the sources or effects of distress; or the accomplishment of a necessary or intended task. On each of these dimensions, a social support attempt can have *beneficial effects*, *no effect*, or *harmful effects*.

Table 4.1 provides a preliminary sketch of possible ways in which the different effects of support attempts might be conceptualized. Patterns of interaction over time within an individual's entire social network may influence the person's physical and mental health directly or indirectly. For example, social support interactions may enhance the perception that support is available, or may buffer the individual from the detrimental effects of stress on health.

Specific support interactions usually have several co-occurring immediate effects, some of which are helpful and some harmful. For example, aid in tasks can be provided in a manner that is instrumentally effective but that reduces self-esteem or sense of self-efficacy at the same time (Fisher, Nadler, & Whitcher-Alagna, 1982). In addition to considering the multiple effects of any particular interaction, the over-

Table 4.1
Possible Dimensions and Effects of Support Attempts

Dimension	Effects		
	Benefits	*No effect*	*Harm*
Mood/affect	improved	no change	made worse
Attitude	increased optimism	no change	increased pessimism
Self-esteem	enhanced	no change	diminished
Coping	greater motivation/ enhanced efficacy	no change	demotivated/ decreased efficacy
Knowledge	gained	not gained	incorrect information
Task	accomplished	not accomplished	performed incorrectly or ineptly

all effect can be viewed globally (from each of the three perspectives shown in Figure 4.1) as primarily beneficial, having no effect, or harmful (Shumaker & Brownell, 1984). Global effects of support interactions have been studied in the past almost exclusively from the recipient's perspective. Sometimes social support has even been defined as the recipient's perception that others have been helpful (e.g., Cobb, 1976). One problem with such a definition is that whether an interaction is defined as social support can only be known post hoc.

Another problem is that recipients may be less than veridical reporters of the effects of interactions. For instance, recipients may think that something was helpful when it does not seem so from the perspective of either the provider or a third party. Alternatively, a recipient of a support attempt may fail to observe beneficial effects of the interaction that would be reported by support providers or third persons, or that are objectively verifiable. Yet long-term benefits of social support interactions may be less likely to occur if the recipient is not aware of any immediate positive effects of social support interactions. Thus it is essential to obtain recipient perspectives of the effects of support interactions, but, because they may be biased by the immediacy of the person's support needs, the perspective of third parties also needs to be considered. It may be useful to consider provider perspectives of the effects of interactions as well, but provider reports are also likely to be biased, usually in the direction of perceiving one's support attempts as helpful.

In summary, our framework for the study of support views social support as a subgroup of all forms of social interaction, and takes three perspectives on these interactions (recipient, provider, and observer/ third party) along two key dimensions of interactions (intentions and immediate effects). The three perspectives of an interaction on each of these two dimensions may converge or diverge within this general framework.

Definitions for Different Forms of Support-Related Interactions

Using this framework, definitions of several further constructs are possible. First, *social support attempts* are any behaviors with altruistic intent directed toward another individual. Second, one way in which beneficial or *effective support interactions* may be defined is as interactions with perceived benefit in the eyes of the recipient. This phenomenological view of support effects emphasizes the cognitions of the recipient, who is pivotal in determining long-term effects.

This framework can also be used to operationalize various different forms of support interactions. The circles in Figure 4.2 represent that the provider has positive or altruistic intentions to benefit the recipient (Circle A), that the recipient perceives that personal benefit has occurred (Circle B), and that an outside observer or third party (or the consensus of several outsiders) would define the interaction as supportive (Circle C). The shaded area in Figure 4.2 represents social interactions in which the provider acts with altruistic intention, the recipient perceives benefit, and a third party perspective views the interaction as social support.

Although this shaded area represents classic or prototypical support interactions, interactions represented in other areas of the figure are also worth considering in attempts to understand a broad range of social

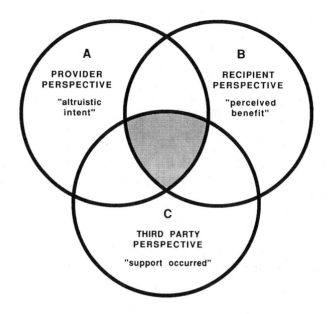

Figure 4.2. A Definitional Framework for Studying Social Support

support phenomena. For example, many support interactions involve positive intentions but no immediate beneficial effects for recipients (i.e., the area of Circle A that does not overlap Circle B); these could be labeled *ineffective support attempts.* Conceivably, an interaction that is not altruistically intended could be perceived as beneficial by a recipient (i.e., *unintended effective support,* or the area of Circle B that does not overlap Circle A). For example, a close relation who rarely gets angry may capture the attention of the distressed person by doing so. Although unintentional and not altruistically motivated, such rare temper outbursts may nonetheless reduce the recipient's maladaptive behavior and elicit his or her constructive action.

Finally, a provider and recipient may interact in ways they view as positively intended and beneficial but that are unrecognizable to an outsider as support acts (i.e., the overlap of Circles A and B that is not shaded). For example, in distressed marriages, criticizing, nagging, or other behaviors that are generally regarded as maladaptive may be viewed by participants as supportive. Another example involves the codependency occurring in families with substance abuse problems. Although these interactions do not fit the usual notions of what constitutes social support, they can be included in a broad conceptualization of support interactions. Also, given this framework, nonaltruistically intended interactions that are unhelpful or harmful are outside the domain of social support and constitute *negative social reactions* to distress or suffering.

The research covered in the next section of this chapter concentrates on just one aspect of this model—the recipient's global perceptions of benefit. We describe a naturalistic research paradigm for studying support interactions, and discuss the patterns of helpful and unhelpful interactions reported by recipients across studies using this paradigm. In the subsequent section, some of the factors and processes that appear to mediate the effects of a support attempt are explored.

A Naturalistic Paradigm for Studying Support

Pioneering work on social support by Gottlieb (1978) queried 40 single mothers regarding the things done by others that were seen as especially helpful in dealing with their problems. Later research by Dunkel-Schetter (1984), Wortman and Lehman (1985), and Dakof and Taylor (1990) has continued in this general tradition of asking respondents to answer in their own words regarding the most helpful and most unhelpful responses of others to their situation. These studies have focused on new mothers, cancer patients, bereaved parents, and bereaved spouses. Although other investigations have been conducted on various aspects of social support interactions, most do not utilize this methodology. The studies described in this chapter are the most systematic and extensive. The general paradigm used in these studies involves semistructured interviews with individuals who are going through some form of life stress, content analyses of their answers to open-ended questions regarding the most helpful and unhelpful responses of others, and, in some cases, ratings of satisfaction with different kinds of social support.

Background on Our Studies

Recently, we have employed this paradigm to study samples of Type II noninsulin-dependent diabetics (Feinstein, 1988), and gay and bisexual men with AIDS (Blasband, 1990). In our AIDS investigation, 40 gay or bisexual men with AIDS were sampled from an AIDS-assistance organization. They were interviewed in depth regarding their social experiences with family, friends, and lovers, as well as about stress and coping. Open-end and closed-end questions addressed effective and ineffective support received and negative reactions, particularly rejection, experienced by these men. The sample was similar to the population with AIDS in the United States in the mid 1980s in most ways, except that the men were all White and were somewhat better educated.

In the diabetes study, 20 male and 20 female diabetic patients and their spouses, recruited from southern California hospital outpatient programs, were interviewed and completed questionnaires regarding spouse support behaviors and other factors unrelated to this chapter. Open-end and closed-end questions addressed to both partners covered frequency and helpfulness of spouse support of several kinds, patient solicitation of it, and patient responses to support attempts. Standard scales of support and marital functioning were also completed by patients and spouses.

This sample of adult diabetics was characteristically obese, and respondents were experiencing the chronic stress of attempting to control their levels of blood glucose through strict dietary regimens. Continual and lifelong adherence to diet is necessary to prevent or minimize the adverse effects of this chronic disease. The inclusion of spouses in this study enabled us to obtain both recipient and provider perspectives on support interactions within a marital relationship. The spouse is especially important to consider because the diabetic's dietary requirements affect the daily life-style within the family.

The stresses faced by persons with AIDS (PWAs), cancer patients, and the bereaved have certain commonalities. In particular, they all experience a loss (e.g., the bereaved) or a combination of losses and threats of further loss (i.e., cancer and AIDS patients). In contrast, diabetes is somewhat different from many other stressful conditions in its disease characteristics. Diabetics who are noninsulin dependent do not experience a loss, but rather the stressful challenge of daily adherence to a difficult treatment regimen that involves monitoring virtually every bite consumed.

This distinction between challenge and threat/loss situations develops from work by Lazarus and Folkman (1984) in which they distinguish stress appraisals as benign or stressful, and in stressful situations they distinguish between appraisals of threat, loss, or challenge. An individual can appraise a situation as involving various degrees of each; however, we contend that most situations can be characterized as predominantly one or the other at any point in time. Bereavement is a loss event in general. Cancer and AIDS are typically described in the literature as threat/loss situations: During diagnosis, there is a threat; by early treatment, most people seem to experience a sense of loss; and after diagnosis, there is the continual threat of whether the cancer will recur. Type II diabetes mellitus is predominantly a challenge situation. Like other life-style and behavior change situations, it carries the constant challenge of monitoring and controlling one's behavior. This distinction between situations that can be characterized as predominantly challenge versus threat/loss appears to be important with respect to the effectiveness of support attempts, as elaborated below.

The next section of this chapter discusses general patterns of helpful and unhelpful interactions observed across studies that use the paradigm described. To illustrate these patterns, quotations from both diabetics and PWAs are included.

Recipient Perceptions of Helpful and Unhelpful Interactions

What Are the Most Helpful Types of Support Interactions?

The many discernible types of social support have been classified into a number of typologies, which overlap considerably (Wortman & Dunkel-Schetter, 1987). For the present purposes, we use a simple three-category classification of emotional support, informational support, and instrumental assistance (Dunkel-Schetter et al., 1987; Schaefer, Coyne, & Lazarus, 1976). Emotional support refers to a broad category involving emotional concern for the individual, acceptance, understanding, and encouragement. Informational support includes advice and information of any kind, including information about the environment and about one's self. Instrumental assistance or aid includes task assistance, such as help with chores, and material assistance, such as gifts or loans. Of these three, the last is most similar to the concept of helping typically studied in social psychology.

Of the three types of support, emotionally supportive behaviors seem uniformly extremely helpful. Respondents in all studies reiterate the same themes regarding the helpfulness of expressions of love, caring, concern, understanding, and affection (Blasband, 1990; Chesler & Barbarin, 1984; Dakof & Taylor, 1990; Dunkel-Schetter, 1984; Feinstein, 1988; Lehman et al., 1986). Prototypical illustrations from men with AIDS are "You are still Mike and we love you," and "Mother told me she loved me, and that's all that mattered." Others mentioned listening as a helpful form of support: "When I needed to talk to someone, he listened. Just having someone to listen told me that I was loved and that my friends cared." Emotional support includes not only expressions of love and concern, and listening, but also confirmation of one's physical presence or "just being there." For example, one PWA reported that friends who said, "We're here, we care, call if you need us," were extremely helpful. Another said, "My roommate says, 'Don't worry, I'll always be here for you,' and he really means it." The emotional support provided by knowing that others are available raises again the distinction between, and interconnectedness of, perceptions of available support and support received. When a support interaction involves communication of the availability of others, as in the quote above, it heightens one's sense of available support, which has been related to health benefits in past research (see Dunkel-Schetter & Bennett, 1990 for a review).

Instrumental aid or assistance was also reported by respondents as helpful in most or all of the studies. Grouped together in this category are both material aid and task assistance. The most helpful things done by friends for one PWA were described as follows:

> When I was in the hospital, he cleaned house, did banking, shopping, took care of my family when they came to visit. A friend from New York sent $200 for Christmas. One sent $100 out of the blue. A friend gave me $20 and took me out to lunch. My landlord let me slide on the rent for a month and a half.

Other PWAs vividly described forms of instrumental assistance or aid as among the most helpful things that others had done. For example, financial help, providing a place to stay, transportation to the hospital, and gifts of cars, furniture, dishes, and airline tickets were all seen as extremely helpful.

In contrast to emotional support and instrumental aid, information and advice were *not* seen as uniformly helpful across studies. In fact, this category of support attempt varies across studies from helpful to unhelpful. For example, when family or friends sent the PWAs in our study information about health, nutrition, alternative treatments, or research findings in books and newspapers, it was perceived as helpful. In contrast, there were instances such as this: "My sister-in-law is a born-again Christian. When I told her about AIDS, I got a lecture about drugs, what I'm doing to myself . . . [and] that I should turn to the Lord."

Advice was reported as especially unhelpful. The following is a characteristic comment by diabetic subjects about advice: "I think it is better when people are not telling me what is good for me. I do better when I reach that on my own." In addition, Lehman et al. (1986), in a study of bereaved individuals found advice was one of the two most frequently mentioned unhelpful behaviors. Interestingly, spouses of diabetics consistently reported in interviews in our study that they *knew* advice was not helpful, but they gave it anyway.

Advice appears to be more effective if provided in an emotionally supportive manner. For example, reminding a diabetic partner that he or she cannot eat certain foods is not as problematic if done with concern or affection. Thus, the effects of advice may vary as a function of whether it is provided in combination with other types of support. If provided with emotional support, advice is more likely to be viewed as altruistically intended, and consequently it is more frequently perceived as helpful. In contrast, when advice is given together with task or material assistance, the intent may be unclear or the act may be seen as egoistically motivated. In this form, advice may be seen by the recipient as a social influence attempt rather than as support.

Past research reporting differences in ratings of satisfaction with or helpfulness of different types of support is consistent with our observations (e.g., Camarillo, 1990). Zich and Temoshok (1987), for example, compared ratings of emotionally sustaining help and problem-solving help by 103 persons with ARC or AIDS and found that emotionally sustaining help was viewed as more desirable, more available, more often used, and more useful. Similarly, Cramer (1990) found that acceptance—as measured by listening, empathy, and other behaviors—was a more helpful reaction to personal problems and distress experienced by students than were behaviors labeled as guidance.

What Are the Most Unhelpful Types of Support Attempts?

There are two general themes across many studies regarding unhelpful support attempts. First, any advice that conveys a negative attribution of the recipient, including attributions of blame, incompetence, or failure, tends to be perceived by support recipients as unhelpful. This example from a man with AIDS is about the behavior of a friend: "As long as I had a positive attitude, it was okay with her. There was a time when I got very depressed, suicidal. She said, 'Well, you just don't have a fighting spirit.'" The motive of this friend is not clear. She may not have been altruistically inclined, and thus this would be labeled a negative social reaction rather than a support attempt by our definition. Alternatively, her intention may have been to cheer up the PWA, in which case it was an ineffective support attempt because he perceived her comment as critical and unhelpful.

A second unhelpful cluster of behaviors includes overinvolvement, intrusiveness, oversolicitousness, and overconcern. These behaviors are reported frequently by diabetics, but are also reported by PWAs and cancer patients. This pattern of unhelpful interaction has been discussed by Coyne, Wortman, and Lehman (1988), and by Thompson (see Chapter 5) in her work with stroke patients. A PWA in our study stated, "In the beginning, friends wouldn't let me do anything, wouldn't let me exert myself at all, like grabbing the grocery bags out of my hands. It made me feel like an old person." A diabetic stated, "When I'm doing my blood sugar, she'd ask me, 'Well what is it?' before the test is done. When I go out, she says, 'Oh what did you have? How much did you drink?' And, you know, that kind of thing is very irritating." Again, the motives behind these behaviors are not clear. Yet, it is reasonable to assume that such interactions are often positively motivated despite their ineffectiveness from the recipient's standpoint.

Determinants of Effective Support

Effects of Source of Support on Perceived Helpfulness

The consistent results across studies regarding the helpful and unhelpful patterns of behavior give us some idea of what to do and what not to do if we want to be good support providers, at least in the eyes of support recipients. But clearly more is involved than selecting the correct behavior. The results from various studies suggest additional aspects of support interactions that promote their effectiveness. One finding is that people in particular roles often provide support better than others. These main effects of source (or provider) of support have emerged consistently in the support literature (e.g., House & Wells, 1978; LaRocco, House, & French, 1980; Lieberman, 1982). However, past studies often have concerned effects of social support from different providers on health outcomes, rather than recipient-perceived differences in the helpfulness of social support from different providers (see Vachon & Stylianos, 1988).

One study that focused on the recipient's perceptions of support effectiveness found that rape victims reported that female friends were the most helpful supporters and that physicians were the least helpful (Popiel & Susskind, 1985). Dakof and Taylor (1990) found that spouses of cancer patients were most helpful by their mere physical presence and calm acceptance, and were most unhelpful by criticism of patient responses to cancer. In that study, friends were most helpful by practical assistance and were most unhelpful by avoiding social contact. Somewhat similarly, Camarillo (1990), in a study of ethnically diverse female college students, found students more satisfied with love and assistance from parents and romantic partners than from friends, but friends provided equally satisfactory advice and listening as parents and partners.

In our study of gay men with AIDS, we found that lovers were seen as more effective support providers compared to family and friends, both in the amount of support received and satisfaction with support of each of the three types (i.e., emotional, instrumental, and informational support). Interestingly, more than two thirds of the lovers of our respondents had AIDS, ARC, or were HIV positive themselves.

This similarity may have enabled lovers to be exceptionally supportive. The value of support from others going through similar circumstances has been discussed in the support and self-help literatures (Dakof & Taylor, 1990; Dunkel-Schetter & Wortman, 1982; Lieberman & Borman, 1979). Because they were in similar circumstances, and because of their close relationship to the respondent, lovers may have been capable of providing support of a quality no one else could match.

As mentioned earlier, advice is sometimes helpful but often unhelpful. In addition to the factor of whether it is provided in combination with emotional support, the particular person providing it seems to influence how helpful advice is perceived to be. Certain providers of support seem able to give advice effectively whereas others cannot. In a study of 79 cancer patients, Dunkel-Schetter (1984) found that information and advice from physicians were seen as helpful, but that the same behaviors were unhelpful when performed by family and friends (see also Dakof & Taylor, 1990). These results and those of others suggest that experts are viewed as more credible sources of advice than close personal relations (Zich & Temoshok, 1987). A PWA said that "qualified advice" from two friends, a nurse and a pharmacist, was especially helpful. In contrast, a diabetic respondent said, "I reject comments that come from lack of knowledge." It may be that general information can come from anyone, but that specific guidance, direction, and advice must come from someone perceived as experienced or knowledgeable. This may also explain why peer support, even from strangers, is valued and can be more effective than support from network members not experiencing the problem.

Overall, the results of all these studies indicate strongly that the *type* of support and the *provider* of support are important and interacting factors in determining the helpfulness of particular behaviors. It is also clear that the helpfulness of particular sources or providers varies depending on the stressful situation. In some situations, informal sources such as family members may be best able to provide effective support, whereas in others, particular formal sources of support who are experts may be in a better position to help. Even the effectiveness of different informal role relationships may be altered by the nature of the specific situation. Thus the joint effects of source of support and type of stressful situation warrant further investigation in research on social support effectiveness.

Effects of Type of Support and Type of Stressful Situation on Perceived Helpfulness

The type of stressful situation involved also seems to influence the *type* of support perceived by recipients as helpful or unhelpful. This is an interesting, yet largely unexplored, issue in support effectiveness. Gottlieb (1978), in his study of 40 low-income single mothers, found that the most helpful type of behaviors reported by women varied with the different problems they faced. Specifically, emotional support was perceived as most helpful for problems of an emotional nature, and instrumental support and active helping behaviors were most helpful for financial problems.

Similarly, we have observed differences in our work between the types of support that are perceived as effective in different situations. Although both emotional support and instrumental support were helpful in diverse circumstances, of the three types of support, emotional support seemed to be most helpful for cancer patients, PWAs, and the bereaved, whereas instrumental assistance seemed most helpful for diabetics. For example, a specific behavior that has been found helpful to cancer and AIDS patients in past research is encouragement, a form of emotional support. One PWA indicated that he appreciated it when his father offered encouragement not to give up, to be optimistic, and to do as much as he could. There were few or no instances like this reported in our diabetes study, although such encouragement might have been expected.

Why shouldn't diabetics find encouragement to stay on their diets helpful? It could be difficult to provide encouragement to diabetics that does not seem intrusive and disabling. Thus supporters may refrain from doing this or do it in an unskilled manner. Instead, instances of instrumental assistance were often related as most helpful by diabetics. Assistance for diabetics generally took the form of buying appropriate foods or preparing meals consistent with their diets.

There also appear to be different *unhelpful* interactions reported for different types of stress situations. Specifically, two types of unhelpful interactions seemed common to cancer, AIDS, and bereavement, and two types seemed unique to our sample of diabetics. One of the most frequent unhelpful behaviors for cancer patients in two studies was minimizing and trivializing their circumstances (Dakof & Taylor, 1990; Dunkel-Schetter, 1984). This occurred in anecdotes related by PWAs as well. For example: "A friend was encouraging me to date. It upset me. I had not had sex with anyone for a year. Dating wasn't on my agenda. My energy was into healing. It was a flippant remark—it trivialized all that I was going through." Minimization was reported as unhelpful by bereaved people in Lehman et al.'s (1986) study also, but it did not feature prominently in the interviews with diabetics. The underlying reasons that others may be inclined to minimize the situation of individuals in threat/loss situations, and not of those facing challenges, deserve exploration.

The second sort of unhelpful interaction that occurred for PWAs, cancer patients, and the bereaved involved closing off communication or changing the topic of conversation. Forty-three percent of PWAs reported that ex-lovers avoided or discouraged discussion of AIDS. This may have been attributable to denial and fear of infection, but it occurred with family members of PWAs somewhat as well. For example: "When I spoke to my sister while in the hospital and tried to tell her about my fears and sorrows, she didn't want to discuss it at all. She changed the subject." These behaviors were not evident in reports of diabetics. In contrast, the troubling behavior was raising the topic of the disease too much. A diabetic, describing what was unhelpful on the spouse's part, said: "Just talking about it, I think that's the thing. I don't really feel like talking about it. I know the situation, I know what I have to do, and I don't really feel like talking about it." Thus whether closing off communication is an unhelpful pattern of interaction or not may depend on the type of stress involved. Although we believe it is generally problematic to discourage communication about the stressful condition in threat/loss situations, there may be circumstances—such as the challenge of diabetes—that call for little discussion of the problem.

In addition to these two sorts of unhelpful interactions common in the AIDS, cancer, and bereaved samples, there were two types of unhelpful interactions specific to diabetes. First, attempts to show love and concern through offering temptations were described as especially unhelpful to diabetics. Spouses were described as constantly bringing home restricted foods such as donuts, cake, cookies, and candy as treats, and frequently offering foods that were not allowed on the diet. One woman said, "He brings home two loaves of hot French bread, fresh and hot. It's unhelpful to me. I think he is trying to be helpful by being nice—but in my mind he knows that I am going to eat more bread than I am supposed to eat." Another diabetic man's answer to the question of what was most unhelpful was the following: "When you are trying to stay on a diet and you are trying to count your calories, she pushes more food in front of you or offers to give you another portion." These instances seemed to reflect the desires of spouses to communicate their love and affection by offering food, a gesture of emotional support that recipients could not accept if they were to cope well with their diabetes.

A second unhelpful behavior specific to diabetes involved reminders of things the diabetic already knew and reprimands when the person had deviated from the diet. Four quotes illustrate this:

> I know he's right if he says, "You aren't supposed to eat that ice cream." But it isn't helpful for him to tell me because I'm going to do it anyway just because I have already made up my mind to do it, I guess.

> I'm not wanting someone to tell me what to do. I want to do things because I want to do them, because *I'm* motivated.

> It doesn't motivate me, it just annoys me, because I know I should do it.

> Reminders are unhelpful because I know she is right.

Behaviors involving reminders and reprimands, which were seen as demotivating and guilt eliciting, occurred in great frequency only in the diabetes study. "Nudging," as this is sometimes called, is perceived by the diabetic as debilitating rather than enabling. It seems to shift the balance of control or responsibility away from the diabetic, reducing feelings of self-efficacy, and arousing guilt.

In summary, it seems that different kinds of support attempts are helpful for people experiencing cancer, AIDS, and bereavement as compared to diabetes. Furthermore, these differences seem to reflect the underlying psychological properties of the two types of situations. Specifically, the differences observed in what was found to be helpful and unhelpful may reflect differences in the demands of threat/loss situations and challenge situations. On the basis of a review of empirical research and on theoretical premises, Cutrona (1990; Cutrona & Russell, 1990) argues that the controllability and life domain of a stressful life event are good predictors of the types of support associated with positive mental health outcomes. Although the focus here is on recipient perceptions of benefit, rather than health outcomes, the observation that life stresses must be distinguished into conceptual categories with different social support effects is a common feature in Cutrona's work and ours.

Effects of Relationship Characteristics on Perceived Helpfulness

Besides the provider, the type of support, and the type of stress involved, characteristics of the relationship between the provider and recipient are clearly important in determining whether support attempts will be perceived as effective (Albrecht & Adelman, 1987; Leatham & Duck, 1990; Reis, 1990). In one study, for example, Hobfoll, Nadler, and Lieberman (1986) found that intimacy of the relationship predicted satisfaction with support over time in Israeli new mothers, controlling for self-esteem and network characteristics.

In our diabetes study (Feinstein, 1988), qualities of the marital relationships were assessed by both partners using the Dyadic Adjustment Scale (DAS; Spanier, 1976) and the Communications Patterns Questionnaire (CPQ; Christensen, 1988; Christensen & Sullaway, 1984). The DAS contains subscales of cohesion, affective expression, marital satisfaction, and consensus. The CPQ has two subscales, mutual constructive communication (MCC) and demand/withdrawal communication (DWC) patterns. Couple averages on these instruments were tested for their relationships to measures of support available, support received, and the helpfulness of support. It was expected that spouse support would be more optimal in all ways in better functioning marriages.

Results showed that marriages that were rated as well-adjusted, mutually and constructively communicative, and low in demand/withdrawal patterns, had greater diet-related spouse support available, as perceived by the diabetic patients ($r = .64$, $p < .001$, DAS total; $r = .46$, $p < .001$, MCC; $r = -.52$, $p < .001$, DWC), and also greater general support perceived as available ($r = .50$, $r = .51$, and $r = -.42$, respectively, all $p < .001$). Correlations between support received and marital functioning were not as consistently significant. Frequency of spouse support (the average of both partners' ratings) was associated significantly only with cohesion in the marriage ($r = .28$, $p < .05$), marginally with marital satisfaction ($r = .20$, $p = .11$) and with demand/withdrawal communication patterns ($r = -.21$, $p = .09$), but not with consensus, affective expression, or mutual constructive communication. In contrast, helpfulness of spouse support (again, the average of both partners' ratings) was associated with consensus ($r = .29$, $p < .05$), marital satisfaction ($r = .33$, $p < .05$), cohesion ($r = .33$, $p < .05$), and mutual constructive communication ($r = .26$, $p < .05$) in marriages. Helpfulness was also marginally negatively associated with demand/withdrawal communication patterns ($r = -.20$, $p = .11$), but was not related significantly to affective expression.

Thus for these diabetic patients, marital functioning as assessed along several dimensions was strongly associated with perceptions that the spouse was *available* as a supporter, both in general and with regard to the diet. Marital functioning was also related to the *helpfulness* of the spouse's diet-related support, although much less strongly. Finally, marital functioning was only slightly associated with the *frequency* of spouse diet-related support. The particular dimension of marital functioning that seemed most important was cohesion, whereas affective expression was not related to spouse support at all. Other dimensions of marital functioning, such as mutual constructive communication, consensus, and satisfaction, were related more strongly to the *helpfulness* of spouse support than to the *frequency* of it. Frequency of support may not be predicted by aspects of the marital relationship because the spouse role carries the responsibility to provide fairly steady support. However, quality of the marital relationship does seem to be linked to the quality of support provided (i.e., its helpfulness). From these results, it is clear that at least some aspects of the quality of the marital relationship are important in determining support. In general, relationship characteristics warrant follow-up in future research on determinants of effective support transactions (Fincham & Bradbury, 1990; Reis, 1990).

Effects of Receptivity to Support and Mood of Recipient on Perceived Helpfulness

Whether support is wanted, and whether it is requested or sought, may also influence perceptions of its helpfulness. Most of the unhelpful spouse support described by diabetics was perceived as such because it was unneeded or unwanted (Feinstein, 1988). Diabetic patients' ratings of the degree to which spouse support was wanted and solicited were significantly related to ratings of helpfulness ($r = .45$, $p < .001$; $r = .39$, $p < .01$). In challenge situations, such as adherence to diet among diabetics, leaving patients alone when they feel they do not need support may convey confidence and encouragement better than most routine support attempts can. Thus assumptions that a person under stress needs active support may be quite erroneous in some situations, a possibility that deserves further attention. Even in threat/loss situations such as cancer or AIDS, unwanted support attempts are likely to be unhelpful. Thus potential support providers need to attend closely to cues from stressed individuals regarding their willingness to accept social support at a given time.

Furthermore, there are indications in our results that the effectiveness of support attempts depends on the mood of the recipient at the time of the interaction. Social psychological research has established that mood of the *helper* is a variable influencing willingness to help (Carlson & Miller, 1987). With respect to the effectiveness of support, mood of the support *recipient* seems to be an overlooked mediator. Seemingly arbitrary conditions such as a stressful day at work, unusually hot weather, or a bothersome viral infection at the time a support attempt occurs may influence its effects. One diabetic indicated that whether something was helpful or not "depends on the mood I'm in too. If I'm kind of uptight, it bothers me more than if I am not."

One implication of these results is that the effects of support attempts can be managed by providers of support through sensitive consideration of the context required for support efforts to help. Support providers can take into account a person's mood and receptivity in deciding when to attempt to provide social support. Skillful social support providers are probably adept at assessing receptivity and mood and targeting their actions accordingly.

Toward a Model of Support Effectiveness

In this chapter we have endeavored to provide a framework for studying social support interactions and an empirically-based description of some of the factors that might be important in determining the effectiveness of support attempts. These factors include characteristics of recipients, providers, and the relationship, and situational contexts in which the interaction takes place. The specific aspects discussed include the type of support offered, the provider offering it, the type of stressful situation involved, the quality of the relationship between recipient and provider, whether the support was desired or sought, and the mood of the recipient.

A Need to Take into Account the Three Perspectives

This discussion has built on the strong base of studies now available on perceptions of the recipients of support attempts. Regarding the value of this method of studying social support, Gottlieb (1978) has stated, "A classification of informal helping behaviors which is grounded in the everyday experience of those taking part in such transactions can inform our understanding of how citizens define social support and how its forms may differ in natural, as opposed to professional, ecologies" (p. 106).

Although it is extremely valuable to study the recipient's view of effective support interactions, ineffective support attempts, and harmful interactions, this paradigm does not offer information about provider or third-party perspectives. Lehman et al. (1986) studied providers as well as recipients, but they were not parties to the same interactions. Feinstein (1988) studied both diabetic and spouse reports of support interactions in marital relationships, but the study focused retrospectively on general interactions rather than on specific recent interactions. Thus more investment of effort on this topic is still needed. Studies of provider perspectives are especially valuable in contributing yet another view of social support interactions. Research on caregivers, which is an example of a provider focus, may offer much insight into this perspective and how it differs from that of support recipients (Biegel, Sales, & Schulz, in press; Thompson and Pitts, Chapter 5 of this volume).

Past research on social support has focused predominantly on recipients of support, represented in Circle B of Figure 4.1 (House, 1981; Wortman & Dunkel-Schetter, 1987). In contrast, much of social psychological research on helping has focused on providers or helpers (Circle A in Figure 4.1). Integration of our knowledge in these two areas is desirable in understanding support effectiveness (Dunkel-Schetter &

Skokan, 1990). Little research whatsoever has been conducted on third-party perspectives of support interactions (Circle C in Figure 4.1), and this seems a very fruitful area for future investigation. By studying observer views, we may be able to untangle the extent to which effective support is determined by perceptions of participants in an interaction, and to explore whether there are standard elements in most or all effective social support attempts that can be objectively defined. Also, if studies on third-party perspectives systematically vary the demographics of observers, we can learn about cultural differences in support. Thus naturalistic studies that involve recipient, provider, and observer perspectives of the same specific support interactions all within one research design have much to offer in the next stage of research.

Additional Factors Needing Study for Models of Support Interaction Effectiveness

In attempting to move this area of research forward, it would be useful to specify the theoretical factors determining whether a given support attempt will be effective or not, and to model the interrelationships among such factors. Many additional variables beyond those discussed here may help to predict effective support transactions. This section highlights two provider factors that may be central to improving our understanding of when support attempts succeed or fail—*provider diagnostic accuracy* and *provider support skills* (Dunkel-Schetter & Bennett, 1990). These factors are included within the constructs of social and relational competence (Jones, 1985).

Past research indicates that there is a positive relationship between the distressed person's social competence and perceived availability of support (Cauce, 1986; Heller, 1979; Heller & Swindle, 1983; Procidano & Heller, 1983; Sarason et al., 1990; Sarason, Sarason, Hacker, & Basham, 1985; Sarason, Sarason, & Shearin, 1986). However, social competence and related constructs have not been studied or developed much within the context of work on supportive interactions or received support. We focus here on the social competence of the provider of support as it influences the effectiveness of support transactions (Vaux, 1988). Our discussion of these factors is consistent with a view of social support interactions as a communication process (Albrecht & Adelman,

1987). Burleson's (1984) review and analysis of comforting communications, for example, concludes that the ability to comfort others
derives in part from a combination of social perception skills and
rhetorical skills.

Provider Diagnostic Accuracy

The accuracy of provider perceptions of what is needed in a particular situation is critical in determining whether a support attempt will
be helpful. Many authors propose that the health benefits of support are
related to the fit between the demands of the stressor and the support
provided (Caplan, 1974; House, 1981; Shinn, Lehman, & Wong, 1984;
Thoits, 1985). For example, Cohen and McKay (1984) argue that
support will buffer the effects of stress if the support provided meets
the needs created by the stressor (see also Cohen & Wills, 1985).

Similarly, a person-environment framework of adaptation has been
applied to support research (Caplan, 1974; House, 1981). For example,
Shinn et al. (1984) proposed that the appropriateness of the amount,
timing, sources, structure, and functions (types) of support will determine whether it is effective (see also Vachon & Stylianos, 1988, on
bereavement). Thus converging accounts point to the need to focus on
the support provider's cognitive and perceptual skills in diagnosing
what is needed in a particular situation prior to enacting specific support
behaviors (Burleson, 1984). The earlier discussion of the receptivity
and mood of recipients as factors in determining support interaction
effects suggests that providers must attend not only to what is needed
and when, but also to whether anything at all should be done.

Provider Support Skills

In addition to the accuracy of provider perceptions of recipient needs
in a particular situation, the provider's behavioral support skills are an
overlooked and important factor to study. Support skills are learned
over one's life course and can be practiced and improved upon in
adulthood. Early experience in observing and modeling the behavior of
parents should be influential in the formation of adult support skills.
For example, nurturing parents are likely to have more nurturing offspring. The ability to be nurturing in turn is a valuable skill in providing
emotional support.

The concept of social skills may be useful in conceptualizing support
skills specifically (Riggio, 1986). Also, communication research on

comforting has delineated many of the particular skills involved in certain forms of emotional support (Burleson, 1984, 1985, 1990). The topic of support skills and their developmental antecedents is a critical one for future investigation of social support interactions. A person with a very socially skilled partner or social network should stand a better chance of receiving effective support in times of need than someone with a less competent partner or network.

Conclusion

This chapter has distinguished between the determinants of quantity and quality of support, and has defined social support as a specific subcategory of the universe of all social interactions. It also has discussed some of the elements in effective support interactions, and has highlighted directions for future research and application. In discussing factors involved in support interaction effectiveness, we tried to illuminate both basic issues facing social psychologists studying helping and the relevance of these matters to professional efforts to provide help to stressed people. Many interesting social psychological variables are involved in support interaction effectiveness, and little work has been done to examine how they exert their effects or whether they interact. Furthermore, there are many implications of this work for helpers in applied settings, some of which have been noted. Like many topics in social psychology, the study of helping encompasses a rich array of closely intertwined basic and applied issues. Many aspects of supportive interactions remain largely unexplored, and they offer both promise and challenge to interested researchers.

References

Ajzen, I. (1985). From intentions to actions: A theory of planned behavior. In J. Kuhl & J. Beckman (Eds.), *Action-control: From cognition to behavior* (pp. 11-39). Heidelberg, Germany: Springer.

Ajzen, I., & Fishbein, M. (1980). *Understanding attitudes and predicting social behavior.* Englewood Cliffs, NJ: Prentice-Hall.

Albrecht, T. L., & Adelman, M. B. (1987). Communicating social support: A theoretical perspective. In T. L. Albrecht & M. B. Adelman (Eds.), *Communicating social support* (pp. 18-39). Newbury Park, CA: Sage.

Bargh, J. (1990). Auto-motives: Preconscious determinants of social interaction. In E. T. Higgins & R. M. Sorrentino (Eds.), *Handbook of motivation and cognition* (Vol. 2, pp. 93-130). New York: Guilford.

Barrera, M., Jr. (1981). Social support in the adjustment of pregnant adolescents: Assessment issues. In B. H. Gottlieb (Ed.), *Social networks and social support* (pp. 69-96). Beverly Hills, CA: Sage.

Batson, C. D., & Coke, J. S. (1981). Empathy: A source of altruistic motivation for helping? In J. P. Rushton & R. M. Sorrentino (Eds.), *Altruism and helping behavior* (pp. 167-187). Hillsdale, NJ: Lawrence Erlbaum.

Batson, C. D., O'Quin, K., Fultz, J., Vanderplas, M., & Isen, A. M. (1983). Influences of self-reported distress and empathy on egoistic versus altruistic motivation to help. *Journal of Personality and Social Psychology, 45*, 706-718.

Biegel, D. E., Sales, E., & Schulz, R. (in press). *Caregiving: Theory, practice, and policy.* Newbury Park, CA: Sage.

Blasband, D. E. (1990). *Social support, rejection, stress, and coping among gay men with AIDS.* Unpublished doctoral dissertation, University of California, Los Angeles.

Borgida, E., Simmons, R. G., Conner, C., & Lombard, K. (1990). The Minnesota living donor studies: Implications for organ procurement. In J. Shanteau & R. J. Harris (Eds.), *Psychological research on organ donation* (pp. 108-121). Washington, DC: American Psychological Association.

Burleson, B. R. (1984). Comforting communication. In H. E. Sypher & J. L. Applegate (Eds.), *Communication by children and adults: Social cognitive and strategic processes* (pp. 63-104). Beverly Hills, CA: Sage.

Burleson, B. R. (1985). The production of comforting messages: Social-cognitive foundations. *Journal of Language and Social Psychology, 4*, 253-273.

Burleson, B. R. (1990). Comforting as social support: Relational consequences of supportive behaviors. In S. Duck (Ed.), *Personal relationships and social support* (pp. 66-82). London: Sage.

Camarillo, J. (1990). *The adequacy of social support provided to female undergraduates in three ethnic groups from four relationships.* Unpublished doctoral dissertation, University of California, Los Angeles.

Caplan, G. (1974). *Support systems and community mental health.* New York: Behavioral Publications.

Carlson, M., & Miller, N. (1987). Explanation of the relation between negative mood and helping. *Psychological Bulletin, 102*(1), 91-108.

Cauce, A. (1986). Social networks and social competence: Exploring the effects of early adolescent friendships. *American Journal of Community Psychology, 14*, 607-628.

Chesler, M. A., & Barbarin, O. A. (1984). Difficulties of providing help in a crisis: Relationship between parents of children with cancer and their friends. *Journal of Social Issues, 40*(4), 113-134.

Christensen, A. (1988). Dysfunctional interaction patterns in couples. In P. Noller & M. A. Fitzpatrick (Eds.), *Perspectives on marital interaction.* Philadelphia: Multilingual Matters.

Christensen, A., & Sullaway, M. (1984). *Communication Patterns Questionnaire.* Unpublished questionnaire, University of California, Los Angeles.

Cobb, S. (1976). Social support as a moderator of life stress. *Psychosomatic Medicine, 38*, 300-314.

Cohen, S. (1988). Psychosocial models of the role of social support in the etiology of physical disease. *Health Psychology, 7*(3), 269-297.

Cohen, S., & McKay, G. (1984). Social support, stress, and the buffering hypothesis: A theoretical analysis. In A. Baum, J. E. Singer, & S. E. Taylor (Eds.), *Handbook of psychology and health* (Vol. 4, pp. 253-263). Hillsdale, NJ: Lawrence Erlbaum.

Cohen, S., & Wills, T. A. (1985). Stress, social support, and the buffering hypothesis. *Psychological Bulletin, 98*, 310-357.

Coyne, J. C., Wortman, C. B., & Lehman, D. R. (1988). The other side of support: Emotional overinvolvement and miscarried helping. In B. H. Gottlieb (Ed.), *Marshalling social support* (pp. 305-330). Newbury Park, CA: Sage.

Cramer, D. (1990, September). Helpful actions of close friends to personal problems and distress. *British Journal of Guidance and Counseling, 18*, 280-292.

Cutrona, C. E. (1990). Stress and social support—In search of optimal matching. *Journal of Social and Clinical Psychology, 9*, 3-14.

Cutrona, C. E., & Russell, D. W. (1990). Type of social support and specific stress: Toward a theory of optimal matching. In I. G. Sarason, B. R. Sarason, & G. R. Pierce (Eds.), *Social support: An interactional view* (pp. 319-366). New York: John Wiley.

Dakof, G. A., & Taylor, S. E. (1990). Victims' perceptions of social support: What is helpful from whom? *Journal of Personality and Social Psychology, 58*, 80-89.

Dalbert, C., Montada, L., & Schmitt, M. (1988). Intention and ability as predictors of change in adult daughters' prosocial behavior toward their mothers. *Verantwortung, Gerechitigkeit, Moral, 46*, 1-17.

Dunkel-Schetter, C. (1984). Social support and cancer: Findings based on patient interviews and their implications. *Journal of Social Issues, 40*(4), 77-98.

Dunkel-Schetter, C., & Bennett, T. L. (1990). Differentiating the cognitive and behavioral aspects of social support. In B. R. Sarason, I. G. Sarason, & G. R. Pierce (Eds.), *Social support: An interactional view*. New York: John Wiley.

Dunkel-Schetter, C., Folkman, S., & Lazarus, R. S. (1987). Correlates of social support receipt. *Journal of Personality and Social Psychology, 53*, 71-80.

Dunkel-Schetter, C., & Skokan, L. A. (1990). Determinants of social support provision in personal relationships. *Journal of Social and Personal Relationships, 7*, 437-450.

Dunkel-Schetter, C., & Wortman, C. B. (1982). The interpersonal dynamics of cancer: Problems in social relationships and their impact on the patient. In H. S. Friedman & M. R. DiMatteo (Eds.), *Interpersonal issues in health care* (pp. 69-100). New York: Academic Press.

Eckenrode, J., & Wethington, E. (1990). The process and outcome of mobilizing social support. In S. Duck (Ed.), *Personal relationships and social support* (pp. 83-103). London: Sage.

Feinstein, L. G. (1988). *Social support, dietary adherence, and blood glucose control among patients with non-insulin-dependent diabetes mellitus.* Unpublished doctoral dissertation, University of California, Los Angeles.

Fincham, F. D., & Bradbury, T. N. (1990). Social support in marriage: The role of social cognition. *Journal of Social and Clinical Psychology, 9*, 31-42.

Fisher, J. D., Nadler, A., & Whitcher-Alagna, S. (1982). Recipient reactions to aid. *Psychological Bulletin, 91*, 27-54.

Gollwitzer, P. (1990). Action phases and mind-sets. In E. T. Higgins & R. M. Sorrentino (Eds.), *Handbook of motivation and cognition* (Vol. 2, pp. 53-92). New York: Guilford.

Gore, S. (1981). Stress-buffering functions of social support: An appraisal and clarification of research models. In B. S. Dohrenwend & B. P. Dohrenwend (Eds.), *Stressful life events and their contexts* (pp. 202-222). New York: Prodist.

Gottlieb, B. H. (1978). The development and application of a classification scheme of informal helping behaviors. *Canadian Journal of Behavioral Science, 10,* 105-115.

Gottlieb, B. H. (1983). *Social support strategies: Guidelines for mental health practice.* Beverly Hills, CA: Sage.

Heller, K. (1979). The effects of social support: Prevention and treatment implications. In A. P. Goldstein & F. H. Kanfer (Eds.), *Maximizing treatment gains* (pp. 353-382). New York: Academic Press.

Heller, K., & Swindle, R. (1983). Social networks, perceived support, and coping with stress. In R. D. Felner, L. A. Jason, J. N. Moritsugu, & S. S. Farber (Eds.), *Preventive psychology: Theory, research, and practice* (pp. 87-103). New York: Pergamon.

Herbert, T. L., & Dunkel-Schetter, C. (in press). Social reactions to distress and suffering. In S. H. Filipp, L. Montada, & M. Lerner (Eds.), *Adjustment to crises and loss in the adult years.* Hillsdale, NJ: Lawrence Erlbaum.

Hobfoll, S. E., Nadler, A., & Lieberman, J. (1986). Satisfaction with social support during crisis: Intimacy and self-esteem as critical determinants. *Journal of Personality and Social Psychology, 51,* 296-304.

House, J. S. (1981). *Work, stress, and social support.* Reading, MA: Addison-Wesley.

House, J. S., Umberson, D., & Landis, K. R. (1988). Structure and processes of social support. In W. R. Scott & J. Blake (Eds.), *Annual review of sociology* (Vol. 14, pp. 293-318). Palo Alto, CA: Annual Reviews.

House, J. S., & Wells, A. J. (1978). Occupational stress, social support, and health. In A. McLean, G. Black, & M. Colligan (Eds.), *Reducing occupational stress: Proceedings of a conference* (DHEW-NIOHS Publication No. 78-140, pp. 8-29). Washington, DC: Government Printing Office.

Jones, W. H. (1985). The psychology of loneliness: Some personality issues in the study of social support. In I. G. Sarason & B. R. Sarason (Eds.), *Social support: Theory, research, and application* (pp. 225-242). The Hague, The Netherlands: Martinus Nijhoff.

Kahn, T. L., & Antonucci, T. C. (1980). Convoys over the life course: Attachment, roles, and social support. *Life Span Development and Behavior, 3,* 269-276.

LaRocco, J. M., House, J. S., & French, J. R. P. (1980). Social support, occupational stress, and health. *Journal of Health and Social Behavior, 21,* 202-218.

Lazarus, R. S., & Folkman, S. (1984). *Stress, appraisal, and coping.* New York: Springer.

Leatham, G., & Duck, S. (1990). Conversations with friends and the dynamics of social support. In S. Duck (Ed.), *Personal relationships and social support* (pp. 1-29). London: Sage.

Lehman, D. R., Ellard, J. H., & Wortman, C. B. (1986). Social support for the bereaved: Recipients' and providers' perspectives on what is helpful. *Journal of Consulting and Clinical Psychology, 54,* 438-446.

Lieberman, M. A. (1982). The effects of social supports on responses to stress. In L. Goldberg & S. Breznitz (Eds.), *Handbook of stress* (pp. 764-783). New York: Free Press.

Lieberman, M. A., & Borman, L. D. (Eds.). (1979). *Self-help groups for coping with crisis*. San Francisco: Jossey-Bass.

Montada, L., Dalbert, C., & Schmitt, M. (1982). Interpersonale verantwortlichkeit erwachsener Tochter ihren Muttern gegenüber: Hypothesen über zusammenhänge innerhalb der Kernvariablen und zwischen Kernvariablen und Kovariaten [Interpersonal responsibility of adult daughters toward their mothers: Hypotheses about relationships among core variables as well as between core variables and covariates]. *Verantwortung, Gerechtigkeit, Moral, 15*.

Popiel, D. A., & Susskind, E. C. (1985). The impact of rape: Social support as a moderator of stress. *American Journal of Community Psychology, 13*, 645-676.

Procidano, M. E., & Heller, K. (1983). Measures of perceived social support from friends and family: Three validation studies. *American Journal of Community Psychology, 11*, 1-24.

Reis, H. T. (1990). The role of intimacy in interpersonal relations. *Journal of Social and Clinical Psychology, 9*, 15-30.

Riggio, R. E. (1986). Assessment of basic social skills. *Journal of Personality and Social Psychology, 51*, 649-660.

Sarason, B. R., Pierce, G. R., & Sarason, I. G. (1990). Social support: The sense of acceptance and the role of relationships. In B. R. Sarason, I. G. Sarason, & G. R. Pierce (Eds.), *Social support: An interactional view* (pp. 97-128). New York: John Wiley.

Sarason, B. R., Sarason, I. G., Hacker, T. A., & Basham, R. B. (1985). Concomitants of social support: Social skills, physical attractiveness, and gender. *Journal of Personality and Social Psychology, 49*, 469-480.

Sarason, I. G., Sarason, B. R., & Shearin, E. N. (1986). Social support as an individual difference variable: Its stability, origins, and relational aspects. *Journal of Personality and Social Psychology, 50*, 845-855.

Schaefer, C., Coyne, J. C., & Lazarus, R. S. (1976). The health-related functions of social support. *Journal of Behavioral Medicine, 4*, 381-406.

Schwarz, S. H. (1977). Normative influences on altruism. In L. Berkowitz (Ed.), *Advances in experimental social psychology* (Vol. 10, pp. 221-279). New York: Academic Press.

Shinn, M., Lehman, S., & Wong, N. W. (1984). Social interaction and social support. *Journal of Social Issues, 40*(4), 55-75.

Shumaker, S. A., & Brownell, A. (1984). Toward a theory of social support: Closing conceptual gaps. *Journal of Social Issues, 40*(1), 11-36.

Spanier, G. B. (1976). Measuring dyadic adjustment: New scales for assessing the quality of marriage and similar dyads. *Journal of Marriage and Family, 38*, 15-28.

Staub, E. (1974). Helping a distressed person: Social personality, and stimulus determinants. In L. Berkowitz (Ed.), *Advances in experimental social psychology* (Vol. 7, pp. 293-341). New York: Academic Press.

Taylor, S. E., & Dakof, G. A. (1988). Social support and the cancer patient. In S. Spacapan & S. Oskamp (Eds.), *The social psychology of health* (pp. 95-116). Newbury Park, CA: Sage.

Thoits, P. A. (1985). Social support and psychological well-being: Theoretical possibilities. In I. G. Sarason & B. R. Sarason (Eds.), *Social support: Theory, research, and application* (pp. 51-72). The Hague, The Netherlands: Martinus Nijhoff.

Vachon, M. L. S., & Stylianos, S. K. (1988). The role of social support in bereavement. *Journal of Social Issues, 44*(3), 175-190.

Vaux, A. (1988). *Social support: Theory, research, and intervention.* New York: Praeger.

Wortman, C. B., & Dunkel-Schetter, C. (1987). Conceptual and methodological issues in the study of social support. In A. Baum & J. Singer (Eds.), *Handbook of psychology and health* (Vol. 5, pp. 63-108). Hillsdale, NJ: Lawrence Erlbaum.

Wortman, C. B., & Lehman, D. R. (1985). Reactions to victims of life crises: Support attempts that fail. In I. G. Sarason & B. R. Sarason (Eds.), *Social support: Theory, research, and application* (pp. 463-489). The Hague, The Netherlands: Martinus Nijhoff.

Zich, J., & Temoshok, L. (1987). Perceptions of social support in men with AIDS and ARC: Relationships with distress and hardiness. *Journal of Applied Social Psychology, 17*, 193-215.

5

In Sickness and in Health: Chronic Illness, Marriage, and Spousal Caregiving

JENNIFER S. PITTS

The leading causes of death in the United States today are three chronic diseases: coronary heart disease, cancer, and stroke. Most individuals who live to early old age are likely to develop one of these diseases or another common disabling illness, such as arthritis, emphysema, or Alzheimer's disease. Thus, when newlyweds promise to be committed to their partners "in sickness and in health, for better and for worse," the chances are good that eventually this vow will be tested by the care of a chronically ill spouse.

Despite the prevalence of chronic illness and the profound changes it can bring to individual lives, there has not been a great deal of research examining the effects of a long-term illness on the marital relationship, nor on ways in which well spouses help or hinder the adjustment of their ill partners. Our program of research on stroke patients' adaptation to their changed circumstances indicates that relationships can play a major role in psychological recovery from a chronic disorder. Thus this is a particularly interesting topic both at the practical level, because of its relevance to the daily life of many individuals, and at the theoretical level, because consideration of these issues ties together work in many disparate areas: social support, marriage and the family, helping, social exchange, coping with stress, and health psychology. To begin to address these issues, the present chapter reviews the research that has been done in this area.

The review focuses on the effects of chronic illness on the marital relationship, and ways in which well partners affect their spouses' adjustment to the illness. However, first we describe theoretical perspectives on the family and on relationships, which can provide a framework for understanding and interpreting the research in this area and can suggest avenues for further exploration.

Theoretical Perspectives

The structure and function of relationships in general, and in families and marriages in particular, have been studied in many different disciplines. Social psychologists interested in close relationships have studied the exchange process in casual and intimate relationships, the role and maintenance of power in relationships, and the structure of relationships in terms of the interdependence of outcomes of the participants. Health psychologists have been interested in the effects of supportive social relations on health and coping outcomes. Clinical psychologists have proposed that problems arise in relationships because of family dynamics, the overinvolvement of family members, and the reinforcement of maladaptive behavior by the family. Sociologists have been concerned with the enactment of roles within relationships, have studied the effects of social networks on health and quality of life outcomes, and have viewed the family from a systems theory perspective. Clearly, there is no lack of relevant theories to apply to questions about the effects of illness on a marriage. The next three sections present brief summaries of three major categories of approaches that seem to have the most applicability to the issues at hand.

Social Exchange Theories

Social exchange theory, equity theory, and interdependence theory are similar in that they propose that people enter relationships because they expect to gain rewards, and remain in them because of the rewards that the relationships provide (Shaw & Costanzo, 1982). Social support ideas also fit with these approaches because support provision involves a type of exchange that is governed by the same rules (Shumaker & Brownell, 1984). The rewards that are exchanged in relationships need not be immediately available. In their model of incremental social exchange, Huesmann and Levinger (1979) include the idea that people will defer present rewards for future ones if they anticipate the value of the eventual reward to be greater than possible immediate payoffs.

According to these approaches, an individual will seek maximum rewards at minimum costs; however, there are group sanctions that keep the pursuit of rewards in check (Walster, Berscheid, & Walster, 1973). Societal norms and sanctions make it profitable to behave equitably, and they provide punishment for inequitable behavior. Because of the internalization of these standards, inequitable relationships can lead to distress for both the beneficiaries and the victims of the inequity. Those who feel they are getting more than they deserve are likely to feel guilt, and the underbenefited may experience anger and a desire to leave the relationship (Walster et al., 1973). These distressing emotions can lead both individuals in an inequitable situation to work to restore real equity by changing the balance of costs and rewards, to restore psychological equity by changing perceptions so the balance seems fair, or to end the relationship.

Kelley's (1979; Kelley & Thibaut, 1978) theory of interdependence adds the idea that the outcomes received or exchanged in the relationship occur at two levels, the *given* level (the direct, concrete outcomes each receives from the other partner's behavior) and the *dispositional* level (the implications of the behavior for the partners' dispositional qualities). For example, each partner receives concrete outcomes, such as a clean house or an unmowed yard, as well as dispositional outcomes, such as the chance to be a loving person or the perception that the other is not trustworthy.

Social exchange theories have obvious implications for the case of chronic illness, where the spouse of the ill partner takes on more burdens because of the illness and, at the same time, receives fewer rewards from the partner. The theories suggest that both spouses would be distressed as the result of inequities in the benefits and costs that each incur in the relationship. The well spouse may be vulnerable to feelings of anger, resentment, and lessened commitment to the relationship. The ill partner may experience guilt, fears of being a burden, and worries about being deserted. These changes at the given level will be accompanied by changes at the dispositional level (Kelley, 1981). The greater dependence of the ill spouse allows his or her partner to express love and caring and to demonstrate general altruistic dispositions, but this dispositional benefit is accompanied by poor given outcomes that can lead to expressions of resentment and anger. Thus chronic illness is likely to have a serious, negative impact on the relationship.

Social support ideas deal with the provision of resources to a needy member of a relationship. Social support "theory" is not a theory per se, so much as a loosely connected set of ideas deriving from the central notion that social relationships provide benefits that can affect physical and psychological well-being. So, in applying this approach to the effects of chronic illness on marriage, some questions are (a) How would the chronic illness of one spouse affect the need for, the provision of, and the effects of support for one or both partners? and (b) How would it enhance or hinder coping efforts?

Wortman and Conway (1985) make the reasonable suggestion that physical illness will increase needs for support from others because of the fears, problems, and threats to self-esteem associated with physical disease. It also seems likely that the spouse providing care will experience an increase in the need for emotional and tangible support. The provision of support in a chronic illness condition may differ from the support provided for everyday situations or one-time traumatic stressors. One possibility is that the diversity of potential support providers for the chronic patient is restricted and, in time, becomes limited mainly to the spouse or other close family members because of the patient's physical or cognitive limitations. A second possibility is that well spouses may become overwhelmed with the support needs of the ill partner when they themselves are experiencing decreased availability of potential support.

The social support perspective leads to further questions about the source of the support. Do marital partners provide unique benefits that cannot be adequately obtained in other types of relationships (Brown & Harris, 1978; Weiss, 1974)? Finally, in what ways does the support provided by spouses help or hinder the coping efforts of the ill partner? Wives and husbands seem to be in a unique position to provide important benefits to their spouses, but they may also be uniquely able to interact in unhelpful, harmful ways.

Family Dynamics Theories

The second category of theories, including family systems theory (Minuchin, 1974), behavioral approaches (Block, Kremer, & Gaylor, 1980), and role theory (Parsons & Fox, 1958), focuses on the family as a social environment that generates and maintains the behaviors of its individual members.

According to family systems theory, there are several features of families that play an important part in their functioning. First, the family operates as a system, and, as in all systems, there are pressures toward maintaining the status quo. One implication is that the family will try to avoid change even if the present state is maladaptive (Turk & Kerns, 1985). Second, families vary in the degree of rigidity or openness of the boundaries between members. At one extreme are enmeshed families in which boundaries between members are very diffuse, leading to members being overly involved in each other's lives at the expense of individual autonomy (Minuchin, 1974). At the other end of the continuum are disengaged families that foster extreme independence in family members, accompanied by low feelings of belongingness and commitment to the group. Third, the family has well-defined beliefs or myths about family members, their characteristics, and their roles in the group, and it will resist threats to these beliefs. For example, if one member typically plays the role of "incompetent," the family will act to support this myth if disconfirming evidence is encountered. Fourth, the interpersonal behavior of individual family members can be understood as attempts by the individual to influence others in the family (Christensen, 1983). Thus each member's actions can be understood only within the context of the role that person plays in the family dynamics.

The second theory in this group, a behavioral approach to relationships, is concerned with the ways in which family members reinforce and, therefore, contribute to the maintenance of the behavior of other family members (Block et al., 1980). Attention, approval, and other social rewards are seen as powerful reinforcers that shape and maintain behavior. Because spouses are in a position to provide or withhold these reinforcers, they can have important effects on their partners' behaviors (Fordyce, 1976).

Much of the work applying a behavioral approach to the area of chronic illness and marriage has examined spousal influences on chronic pain patients. It has been proposed that marital partners reinforce the pain behaviors of chronic pain patients and, thereby, contribute to the increase and maintenance of the pain (Flor & Turk, 1985). For example, a patient's grimacing in response to pain may elicit sympathy and attention from his or her spouse. The sympathy is reinforcing and increases the probability of grimacing and other expressive pain behaviors. Spouses may also reinforce the patient for pain expression by taking over chores and activities that are the patient's responsibility (Block, 1981; Block et al., 1980).

The third family dynamic theory, role theory, analyzes individual behavior within the family context. Each family member is seen as playing a role in the family setting that is an integral part of the family system and its functioning (Turk & Kerns, 1985). Of particular interest here is the "patient" or "sick" role. Parsons and Fox (1958) suggest that adoption of the sick role is socially determined because one is allowed to take on this role only with the agreement of significant others. Family members influence both whether or not someone can adopt the sick role and how long someone can claim this status with its associated rights and responsibilities. At one end of this continuum, some families may be overly supportive of the patient, which may encourage perpetuation of the illness. At the other end, the family may be overly intolerant of sickness and unwilling to make allowances for the illness, which would greatly reduce illness-related behaviors. Thus a spouse is seen as in a position to modify the expression of behaviors associated with illness.

Although these three family dynamic approaches are very different in some respects, they are similar in that they propose that the family generates and maintains even the maladaptive, undesired behavior of its members. There are at least two implications for chronic illness in the family. First, it seems likely that the chronic illness of one spouse could change the role of that partner in the system and the system dynamics. Although families resist change and challenges to their beliefs, some of the changes in physical or cognitive functioning associated with chronic disease may overwhelm the desire to maintain the system in its previous form. For example, it would be difficult for a husband to maintain a role as the dominant family member and principal decision maker if a stroke had reduced his ability to communicate and to care for himself physically. Thus the marriage may suffer a crisis because of the resulting challenge to the established roles and myths that maintained the system.

In some cases, however, illness of one member may be welcomed by the family because it gives stability to a threatened system (Flor & Turk, 1985). For example, the diagnosis of chronic illness in one spouse may take pressure off a troubled marriage and allow the couple to avoid facing problems in the relationship, or it may provide the well spouse with an excuse to avoid his or her problems (MacVicar & Archbold, 1976). If this situation arises, then the well spouse and the patient may "collude" to maintain the definition of the patient as ill so they can continue to realize the benefits (Delvey & Hopkins, 1982; MacVicar & Archbold, 1976). Collusion may take the form of both members refusing to recognize the remission of illness and continuing in their use of language and behaviors toward each other to treat one spouse as ill.

The second implication is that two types of maladaptive relationships can occur. In the language of family systems theory, the openness of the boundaries in the family will define the types of problems that the couple faces with chronic illness. The well spouse in an enmeshed, overinvolved couple may tend to be overprotective of the ill partner; overly rigid boundaries, on the other hand, may make it difficult for the patient to accept dependence and help from the partner. From a behavioral perspective, well spouses may respond with social reinforcers when the patient expresses depression, thereby inadvertently increasing depressed behaviors. For a variety of reasons, such as a desire to be helpful or a need to express their own power in the relationship, well spouses may support and maintain their partners' dependency by reinforcing dependent actions and either not reinforcing or punishing attempts to be independent. A number of areas of research have shown that, especially for older adults, the social environment often does not provide reinforcement for independence (Baltes & Reisenzein, 1986) and that overly protective behaviors can reduce the recipient's motivation and competence (Avorn & Langer, 1982).

Family Resource and Coping Theories

The two theories in this section focus on the resources that families have to cope with stresses such as illness, and how they adapt to changed circumstances.

Family stress theory proposes that life stressors for individuals should be studied as family-level phenomena (McCubbin & Patterson, 1983). This approach is based on Hill's (1949, 1958) ABCX crisis model, which identifies three factors that influence the extent to which a crisis will lead to disorganization or disruption in the family system: the nature of the stressor; the family resources (e.g., common interests, affection, and agreed-upon goals); and the family's interpretation of the crisis (e.g., a challenge or an uncontrollable threat). The interaction of the type of stressor encountered, the resources the family can call upon, and how the situation is interpreted determine whether or not the crisis will be successfully weathered. More recently, McCubbin and Patterson (1983) have incorporated three additional factors into the model: the pileup of family demands, the modification of meaning within the family, and family coping strategies. In addition, they broadened consideration of the effects of the crisis to include not just the disruption it causes in the family, but also the extent to which the family achieves successful adaptation.

This model has a number of implications for marriage and chronic illness. As illustrations, three applications will be mentioned. First, the "nature of the stressor" factor has usually referred to whether the stressor is normative or nonnormative (Lavee, McCubbin, & Olson, 1987). Normative events are less exceptional and occur at a predictable time in life. Nonnormative events are sudden, unexpected, or at the wrong stage in life, and as such have a greater potential to be disruptive to the family. Applying this idea to chronic illness, which is nonnormative in early and middle adulthood but normative during later adulthood, we would expect that the life stage in which an illness occurs would influence how disruptive it is for the marriage and the individuals. Second, couples who are more satisfied with their relationship are more likely to have the family resources of closeness and caring that the model identifies as important. Thus marital adjustment before the illness and in the face of the illness should be one indicator of ability to cope with the crisis. Third, the notion of "pileup of demands" suggests that families will handle the illness better if they are not facing other crises that drain family resources.

The second theory that focuses on family resources is a model of how couples deal with chronic illness, developed by Corbin and Strauss (1984) using grounded theory techniques. Their approach examines ways in which couples collaborate and coordinate their activities in order to manage the illness successfully. The concepts of biography, trajectory, and work help clarify what couples must go through in order to interact collaboratively.

Biography refers to the events, both expected and unexpected, that make up the substance of one's life. Biographical projections are the goals people have for their future, or the way they expect their lives to proceed. Their biographical scheme is the plan they have for carrying out their hopes and dreams. In the case of a couple, they will likely have separate biographical projections and schemes, as well as ambitions and desires for their life together.

The *trajectory* of the illness refers to how it will proceed, the effects it will have on the couple, and the plan of action each has for dealing with the illness. *Work* refers to the tasks and chores that are necessary to manage the various aspects of the biography, the couple's life together, and the illness. Chronic illness can be very disruptive to the couple's biographies, both shared and individual. The realities of the situation may dictate that the couple postpone, rearrange, or even cancel important plans. If the illness strikes relatively early in life when the partners are still in pursuit of career goals, it may be particularly difficult. The biographical projection of either partner may be changed or delayed in ways that take a heavy toll. At any age, though, the couple will have central issues of biography that could be affected by the illness, such as where and how to spend their retirement years.

Problems can also develop around the illness trajectories and the work of the couple. For example, partners may have different conceptions of the trajectory of the illness. If the well partner feels that the patient should be recovering faster than is evidently the case, it may lead to disappointment and resentment, especially if the slower recovery interferes with plans of the well spouse. The illness has probably introduced additional work for the well spouse, some of which may require the cooperation of the ill partner, so the work associated with daily life and with the illness may require a high level of coordination between the spouses. Couples who are unable or unwilling to coordinate their work and schedules will have difficulties.

The way in which the illness affects the relationship will depend on a number of factors. If both partners are highly committed to the marriage, there will be less resentment attributable to broken plans and unfulfilled goals. A second important factor is each partner's reaction to the effects of the illness. Couples who work best together seem to be those who have accepted the terms of the illness (Kaplan, Smith, Grobstein, & Fischman, 1973). They may not be happy about it, but they have accepted it as a fact with which they have to deal. Communication is another important influence, as it enables the coordination and organization that are necessary for successful management of a chronic illness.

Common Themes and Unique Perspectives

There are two common views on the issue of marriage and chronic illness that emerge from the theories covered above. The first is that the inequities in outcomes and in dependence that chronic illness can create have serious implications for the marital relationship. A lack of equity has the potential to change each partner's perception of and satisfaction with the relationship. It is not unreasonable to expect at least some resentment and anger on the part of the well spouse, and guilt and worry by the patient. Except for the idea in equity theory that this situation can be resolved through either actual or perceived changes in outcomes, none of the approaches give much attention to how couples handle this important issue.

A second common theme is that spouses may act in overprotective and oversolicitous ways, which increase or support sick-role behavior on the part of the patient. It is assumed that this leads to negative consequences for the patient, such as increased dependency, lowered competence, and greater depression. The theories that suggest this possibility differ in whether or not they also propose that there are positive payoffs to the spouse for being overinvolved.

Although some themes common to two or more of the theories can be found, these approaches also represent a remarkable diversity of views on relationships. Some of the approaches view the partners as engaging in a rational and, to some extent, conscious analysis of the costs and benefits they stand to incur, and acting on that basis. At the other extreme are theories that focus on largely unconscious motives that lead people to act in ways that are against their own best interests. In the framework of some of these theories, relationships are seen as providing positive, adaptive resources of self-esteem maintenance and help in times of trouble. Contrasted with that view are approaches that identify family systems as fostering maladaptive behavior because the stability of the system, not individual adaptation, is the primary driving force. A third way in which the theories differ is the extent to which they focus entirely on factors occurring within the family to explain family responses and adaptation, versus also including in their analysis extrafamilial factors, such as the timing of the event, family financial and educational resources, and additional stressors.

The following review of the literature on marriage and chronic illness incorporates many of the concepts that these three general approaches have identified as important. It addresses two issues: the effects of chronic illness on the marriage, and ways in which the spouse affects the patient's ability to cope with the illness. We have tried to include all the research relevant to this topic; however, because the work that has been done is scattered among a variety of disciplines (e.g., public health, relationships, health psychology, clinical psychology, nursing, sociology, medicine), this may not always be an exhaustive review.

Effects of Chronic Illness on the Marital Relationship

In order to understand how the chronic illness of one spouse might affect the marriage, it is important to consider indirect effects that may occur because of consequences for the well spouse as well as direct influences on the relationship. Thus we will first look at how the well spouse is affected by his or her partner's illness, then at how the illness affects the outcomes received by both spouses in the relationship, and finally at effects on satisfaction with the marriage. First, however, we present an overview of the numerous methodological problems that arise repeatedly in this area.

Methodological Issues

Most of the research in this area has used questionnaire or interview methods with correlational designs, so it is usually not possible to determine if relationship factors are a consequence or a cause of health status. For example, an ill person may be depressed or psychologically distressed because of problems in his or her primary relationship, or the person may have a troubled relationship because of the depression or distress (Pagel, Erdly, & Becker, 1987). Coyne and DeLongis (1986) point out the additional possibility of selection factors in that a person who is physically healthy and interpersonally skilled may be more likely to have a satisfying marriage. These kinds of interpretational problems can be avoided through the use of longitudinal research that studies relationship and outcome measures at various points through the illness (Pagel et al., 1987; Schulz, Tompkins, & Rau, 1988). However, most studies rely on single, retrospective measures of relationship variables, usually taken long after the change in health status. Although prospective designs are difficult to carry out, they would increase the capacity for drawing causal interpretations, as well as help uncover any sequential processes that may be present (Jung, 1984).

An additional complaint that has been leveled at this area is that there is no clear, universally accepted definition of concepts such as "social support" (Coyne & DeLongis, 1986; Jung, 1984; Suls, 1982). For example, several researchers have attempted typologies that break down support into its constituent parts (Fiore, Becker, & Coppel, 1983; Jung, 1984; Kahn & Antonucci, 1982; Wills, 1985). The components are generally very similar, and overlap quite a bit. For instance, the typology used by Jung (1984) was originally proposed by House (1981), who suggested that there were four basic kinds of support: emotional (e.g., esteem, concern, listening), instrumental (e.g., money, labor, time), informational (e.g., advice, suggestions, information), and appraisal (e.g., affirmation, feedback, social comparison). Both the Fiore et al. (1983) and Wills (1985) classification systems have very similar elements but use different names for them. Because of this lack of clarity and because of the tremendous variety in events that respondents are undergoing in different studies (e.g., various diseases, aging, accidents, death in the family), it is difficult to generalize about collective findings.

Another common problem is that the reliability and validity of indices used to assess concepts may not be measured at all, or may be quite low (Dean & Lin, 1977; Jung, 1984; Suls, 1982). For example, what a researcher classifies as support may actually be a troublesome relationship in the judgment of the ill person. The general lack of checks on construct validity leaves studies open to alternative interpretations. As a related point, Jung (1984) suggests that there is a need for multiple outcome measures of coping. If research focuses completely on depression or any other single indicator as an outcome, some other important effects such as changes in health status, or in levels of compliance with treatment regimens, may be missed. These limits to interpretation should be kept in mind in the following review.

Effects on the Well Spouse

Numerous studies have found that caregivers providing care for elderly or ill family members suffer anxiety (Wade, Legh-Smith, & Hewer, 1986; Wellisch, Fawzy, Landsvere, Pasnau, & Wolcott, 1983); depression (Kiecolt-Glaser et al., 1987; Skelton & Dominian, 1973); low ratings of life satisfaction and self-esteem (Kiecolt-Glaser et al., 1987); complaints of restricted social and recreational activities (Deimling & Bass, 1986); self-reports of worry, frustration, and sadness (Fengler & Goodrich, 1979); poor health outcomes (Haley, Levine, Brown, Berry, & Hughes, 1987); and compromised immune system functioning (Kiecolt-Glaser et al., 1987).

Not all the effects are negative; providing care for another person can increase the giver's sense of efficacy, and can contribute to a positive self-image as a nurturant person, for example (Shumaker & Brownell, 1984). However, many more costs than benefits have been identified, and in balance there is little doubt that taking on the duties of a caregiver can be a major life stressor.

Even if the illness does not necessitate long-term physical care or dependency of the patient, well partners may experience considerable stress. Pederson and Valanis (1988), for example, identified seven coping problems facing the husband of a woman with breast cancer: responding to the patient's emotional needs, dealing with his own emotional reactions, getting medical information, reorganizing home responsibilities, communicating with his wife and children, handling additional stressors, and maintaining the marital relationship. These problems represent a number of sources of stress for spouses, including fears about the patient's mortality or declining health, the spouse's own feelings of vulnerability and loss of control, worries about effects of the illness on other family members, concerns about the financial burden of the illness, and dealing with medical care providers.

In addition to fear associated with the partner's future health and increased depression, two frequently mentioned emotional reactions of well spouses are guilt and some combination of anger and/or resentment. The guilt seems to have a number of potential sources, including blaming oneself for the illness (Doehrman, 1977; Skelton & Dominian, 1973), feeling that one is not now doing enough to help the spouse (Bilodeau & Hackett, 1971) or is focusing too much on one's own needs (Vess, Moreland, Schwebel, & Kraut, 1988), and a reaction to one's hostility or firmness shown toward the ill partner (Shambaugh & Kantor, 1969; Skelton & Dominian, 1973). The source of the anger and resentment has not been directly studied, but it seems likely that it is attributable to increased restrictions in the caregiver's life as a result of the spouse's illness (Burish & Lyles, 1983; Fengler & Goodrich, 1979; Thompson & Sobolew-Shubin, 1990) or is in response to the perception that the ill partner is not sufficiently motivated (Thompson & Sobolew-Shubin, 1990), or is overly demanding or irritable (Bilodeau & Hackett, 1971; Skelton & Dominian, 1973).

It is significant that well spouses face these stressors and negative emotional reactions at a time when they may have lessened social support themselves. This is particularly true when the spouse's primary or only source of emotional support is within the marriage. According to Dunkel-Schetter and Wortman (1982), family members and friends may be reluctant to discuss issues relating to a victimization for fear of upsetting the victim. Thus in many families there is not an open discussion of the fears, worries, and emotional reactions engendered by the traumatic event. It may also seem terribly inappropriate to burden an ill partner with one's own concerns (Vess et al., 1988), especially if they are caused by the partner's illness. It is probably even more difficult to express anger and resentment toward someone who already has to deal with major life changes and losses and who has not intentionally brought about the situation. The reluctance to communicate about negative affect may leave many well spouses without the emotional support of the person who is usually their closest confidant.

Effects on the Marriage

Outcomes

Marital partners affect each other's outcomes in numerous ways: some rewarding or reinforcing, others aversive or punishing. One important way in which chronic illness can affect a marriage is through changes in the extent to which each partner provides reinforcing or aversive outcomes for the other. First, let us consider how outcomes might change for the patient.

It is likely that the chronically ill spouse will be faced with restricted opportunities for satisfying outcomes outside of the relationship. Kerns and Turk (1984) discuss how pain patients come to experience fewer and fewer positive sources of reinforcement because of the loss of social, vocational, and recreational opportunities for instrumental behavior. Depending on the nature and severity of the disease, other individuals with a chronic disorder have similar limitations in outside sources of reinforcement. At the same time, the ill spouse is likely to experience increased reliance on the partner. Many conditions associated with chronic illness—such as fatigue, pain, physical disability, cognitive impairments, a complicated treatment regimen, or emotional distress—necessitate obtaining help from others (Burish & Bradley, 1983). Because the well spouse is likely to be the help provider, his or her opportunities to supply positive outcomes increase both in absolute and in relative terms.

However, as ill partners become more dependent on the relationship, just the opposite process may be working for the caregiving spouse. Many of the changes brought about by the illness can have the effect of decreasing the benefits and increasing the costs that the well partner receives from the marriage.

Changes in positive outcomes received from the ill partner can occur in a number of areas. The well spouse may assume the daily duties of the partner if the chronic illness makes it difficult or impossible for that person to continue those tasks. For example, there is a change in the family roles of postmyocardial-infarction men. The men become less active than they were before the infarction, and their wives take on more responsibility for family maintenance (Croog & Levine, 1977). The changes in roles may be particularly dramatic if the illness involves cognitive impairment (Rosenbaum & Najenson, 1976). Thus benefits that the patient formerly contributed to the marriage, such as performance of household chores, organization of the family finances, or coordination of social activities, will no longer be provided for the well spouse, leading to a decreased dependence on the patient (Leventhal, Leventhal, & Nguyen, 1985).

Sexual benefits may also be less available. Across a variety of chronic illnesses, such as coronary heart disease, stroke, cancer, and chronic pain, there is evidence that frequency and satisfaction with sexual functioning decreases in marriages following the onset of the illness (Burish & Lyles, 1983; Doehrman, 1977; Krantz & Deckel, 1983; Maruta & Osborne, 1978; Vess et al., 1988). Maruta, Osborne, Swanson, and Halling (1981), for example, found that 84% of the well partners of chronic pain patients reported reductions in sexual activity attributable to their partner's pain problems. Finally, as discussed earlier, well spouses may experience less emotional support from their partners as a result of their own worries about bringing up issues that might upset the patient. Thus, for the caregiver, several important benefits from the marriage may be curtailed or no longer available.

One of the effects of increased benefits and dependence for the ill partner and decreased benefits and dependence for the well partner is that the marital relationship increases in importance for the patient and may decrease for the well spouse. Chronic pain patients, for example, are more depressed if the quality of their marital relationship is poor, indicating that their emotional outcomes are dependent on the quality of the relationship with the spouse (Kerns & Turk, 1984). However, the same is not true for their spouses; depression levels of well partners are not related to how well they perceive the marriage to be functioning. Thus inequalities in the centrality of the relationship and dependence on it are likely to develop.

Satisfaction

Given the importance of the topic, it is surprising that so little empirical research has examined the effects of chronic illness on marital adjustment. The few studies that have been done show mixed results.

Some studies suggest that marriage is not negatively affected by a chronic illness and that, within a reasonable period of time following the onset of the illness, most families adjust and return to normal functioning. This is true for a myocardial infarction (Croog & Levine, 1977), physical disability (Shellhase & Shellhase, 1972), colostomy

(Burnam, Lennard-Jones, & Brooke, 1976), or cancer (Morris, Greer, & White, 1977; Spiegel, Bloom, & Gottheil, 1983). However, a number of studies find some decreased satisfaction. Meyerowitz, Sparks, and Spears (1979) reported that 23% of women receiving chemotherapy for breast cancer had disruptions in their marital or family relationships. This was offset somewhat by their additional finding that 17% of the women reported improved family relationships. There are frequently problems in marital maladjustment reported by chronic pain patients (Flor & Turk, 1985). Maruta and Osborne (1978), for example, found that over 30% of pain patients perceived decreases in marital satisfaction. Another study reported that 25% of pain patients experienced deterioration in their marriages following the onset of the pain (Maruta et al., 1981). However, well spouses in this study perceived considerably more deterioration in the relationship than their ill partners did; 65% of the spouses of the pain patients felt less satisfied with their marriage than before the onset of the pain.

One explanation for these conflicting findings could be that the chronic pain population is different in some critical way from other chronic illness groups. However, overall conclusions are not easy to reach, even when research has examined the same chronic illness. In one study, women who had had a mastectomy did not rate their marital relationships lower than a control group of women who were diagnosed with benign breast disease (Morris et al., 1977). In contrast, Burish and Lyles (1983) cited three studies to support their conclusion that marital dissatisfaction is a frequently reported consequence of mastectomy.

In view of the mixed findings, it might be more fruitful to focus on the factors that affect whether or not chronic illness leads to deterioration, enhancement, or no change in satisfaction with one's marriage. One possible factor, suggested by folk wisdom, is the premorbid functioning of the couple—a good marriage may get better as the couple pulls together to face a common crisis, and a bad marriage may be further weakened by the stresses of a crisis. Consistent with this idea, the impact of husbands' myocardial infarction on their marriages was found to be related to the quality of their premorbid relationships (Skelton & Dominian, 1973). However, the data in this study consisted of impressions from unstructured interviews with the wives, so it is possible that these retrospective reports were colored by the wives' current satisfaction with their husbands or by beliefs in the folk wisdom stated above. Unfortunately, other research has not examined this important issue.

A second factor that may affect changes in marital satisfaction of chronically ill individuals is how the partners handle their emotional reactions to the situation. Several studies have found that couples who are able to express to each other their feelings and emotions about the illness have higher levels of marital satisfaction (Taylor, Lichtman, & Wood, 1984; Wills, 1985). Also, spouses of ill partners have better emotional outcomes if they consider their partners as confidants (Fengler & Goodrich, 1979) and if the family environment encourages the expression of feelings (Spiegel et al., 1983). Presumably, more positive emotional outcomes for the well spouse would increase the likelihood that the marriage would not deteriorate.

A third influence on whether or not the marriage is affected may be the age of the spouses. Women with breast cancer who report marital problems as a result of their cancer tend to be younger than those who do not report problems (Smith, Redman, Burns, & Sagert, 1985). Consistent with this, the relationships of younger cancer patients were more impaired by the illness than were those of older patients, although in general the older well spouses were more depressed and overwhelmed (Wellisch et al., 1983). It could be that the issues of unfairness and of impairment of sexuality raised by some diseases will be felt more strongly in younger couples. Another possibility is that these findings reflect a cohort difference. The older cohort may have stronger marriages, for example, and that may be responsible for their better coping. Studies in other areas have not reported age differences, but it is not known whether this is because the researchers have not examined these effects or because no relationships were found.

Conclusions Regarding Effects on the Marriage

Based on the evidence presented above that the spouses of chronically ill individuals are experiencing major stress themselves, and that the illness creates or exacerbates inequalities in dependence and outcomes between the spouses, one might expect to find dramatic (or at least consistent) negative effects of chronic illness on marital relationships. In contrast, the work done so far suggests far more modest effects. Although one should be cautious because so few studies have been done in this area, especially relative to the tremendous diversity among types of chronic disease, the most reasonable conclusion at this point seems to be that some—but certainly not all—marriages will experience some problems because of the illness. The chances that the quality of the marriage will suffer may be affected by the openness of the couple's communication and other factors such as the strength of the marriage and the age of the couple.

Why have stronger effects of chronic illness on the marital relationship not been found? One interesting possible answer to this question is suggested by the study mentioned earlier that reported that the well spouses of pain patients were far more likely to report low satisfaction with the marriage than were the patients themselves (Maruta et al., 1981). Along the same lines, stroke patients were more likely than their partners to report that the stroke brought the couple closer together, although they did not differ in judgments of whether or not the stroke had caused conflict (Thompson, Bundek, & Sobolew-Shubin, 1990). In the latter study, the participants were asked to rate themselves and their partners on interpersonal attributes (e.g., appreciative, demanding, understanding) and stroke patients had significantly more positive impressions of their partners than the partners had of the patients (Thompson, 1986). Ill partners' views of how the marriage has been affected may be more positive than those of their partners because of the benefits that the ill spouses receive and their dependence on the relationship. Thus studies that obtain ratings from only the ill spouse may get an incomplete picture of how the marriage has been affected.

A second possible reason why stronger effects have not been found may be that all the studies have been retrospective. As Nisbett and Wilson (1977) argue, people's assessments of whether or not attitudes have changed are heavily influenced by current attitudes. There may be a tendency for both partners to see the earlier relationship as consistent with present feelings and to be unaware of changes in their satisfaction with the marriage.

The above two explanations for weak effects assume that the problem is methodological: The marriage has been affected, but the research is not uncovering these effects. A final possible reason why chronic illness has not been found to have strong consistent effects on marital satisfaction is that couples may adjust their expectations or their behaviors to preserve satisfaction with the relationship. The well spouse may see care of the partner during illness as part of the commitment of long-term marriage and may focus on earlier benefits he or she has received. A related possibility is that the ill partner may work to provide increased benefits for the well spouse that compensate for the costs incurred. Clearly, more research is needed in this area before a reliable picture of the effects of chronic illness on marriage can be drawn.

The Influence of Spouses on Patients' Adjustment

For married individuals, it is highly likely that the spouse will be the primary person to provide physical care and emotional support in a long-term illness (Ervin, 1973). This section examines ways in which spousal caregivers have an impact on the patients' coping efforts and their psychological and social adjustment, including differences that can be attributed to marital status, and to how help is provided by the spouse.

Marriage is associated with many benefits, including better psychological well-being (Campbell, 1981) and lower mortality rates (House, Robins, & Metzner, 1982). It seems obvious that, if faced with a major life stressor, married persons would fare better than those who are single. Consistent with this, many studies do find that spouses are an especially important source of support (Brown & Harris, 1978; Ervin, 1973; Lieberman, 1982). However, some studies find that single status is associated with better adjustment. Parmelee (1983) compared the aged who received care from a spouse to those who received care from a younger relative. Contrary to predictions, those who were cared for by a spouse had more worries, expressed more negative affect toward their caregiver, and felt that the caregiver was more negative toward them than those who relied on another relative.

In a similar vein, cancer patients given home care were significantly more anxious, depressed, and irritable than those not cared for by their spouse at home (Hinton, 1979). Other studies find that stroke patients being cared for by the spouse show less physical improvement than do single patients (Rogoff, Cooney, & Kutner, 1964), particularly if the potential for overprotection by the family is great (Hyman, 1972). Stroke patients who live alone are also less likely than those who live with their families to decrease outside socializing following the stroke

(Labi, Phillips, & Greshman, 1980). Some of these effects could be attributable to younger or professional caregivers giving better care, but at any rate, it cannot be automatically assumed that the chronically ill who are married will fare better than those who are not.

Considerable research finds that supportive relationships are associated with positive physical and psychological outcomes (Kessler & McLeod, 1985; Thoits, 1984; Wills, 1985; Wortman & Dunkel-Schetter, 1987), and therefore it seems surprising that the availability of an intimate marital relationship can sometimes lead to worse physical and psychological status. Granted, not all spouses are supportive, but still, on the average, married individuals would be expected to have a better chance of getting the emotional and tangible benefits of close social relationships than would single individuals, some of whom may not have even one close network member. This section explores the possibility that, in addition to the benefits of social support, there are costs associated with relationships as well. Intimate others may at times exacerbate problems, reduce motivation, and contribute to emotional distress.

The Dilemma of Caregiving

Some of these problems stem from the nature of providing help to and receiving help from another adult with whom one has a long-term relationship. Any provision of help is inherently ambiguous; the aid can be seen as an expression of concern, an attempt to manipulate, a laudable sacrifice on the part of the giver, an indication of the friendship between the two participants, the recipient's due, or a reflection of the receiver's dependence and incompetence (Gergen & Gergen, 1983; Jung, 1987). In the case of chronic illness, both the caregiver and the patient face the "dilemma of caregiving"—in other words, providing assistance indicates love and caring but also reflects the dependence and neediness of the recipient. Thus, providing care for someone can be seen as supportive and caring, but also as controlling and overprotective. The ambiguity in help-giving may not be important in short-term, acute situations where the recipient will have ample opportunities at a later date to take the role of giver, but with a chronic illness the roles of who helps and who is dependent on that help are likely to be less flexible. This analysis suggests that two specific ways of giving help may cause problems: overprotective styles and complaining styles. We will discuss each of these styles and then describe our own research that has examined their effects in a population of chronically ill individuals.

Overprotection

For the chronically ill, who may be experiencing limitations in their ability to care for themselves and to function as autonomous adults, increased dependency on others is an important issue. Overprotection by family members emphasizes the dependency in the relationship and thereby reduces patients' feelings of control and motivation to work on their own. There is considerable evidence to support the idea that overprotective care is dysfunctional. Chronically ill individuals who have overprotective caregivers come to exhibit more disability than those who are not overprotected even when the initial level of impairment is controlled for (Hyman, 1971). Overprotected congestive heart failure patients are less likely to return to work following convalescence (Lewis, 1966). Stroke patients who are overprotected by family members are more depressed and less motivated to work in physical therapy programs (Evans & Miller, 1984; Newman, 1984). Thus overprotection by intimates is associated with a variety of negative consequences.

One reason why overprotective care has these negative effects is that it may make it difficult for the recipients to maintain feelings of control over their own lives. Cancer patients complain that family members perform tasks that the patients are capable of, thereby frustrating the patients' attempts to regulate their own lives (Nerentz & Leventhal, 1983). In addition, a curvilinear relationship has been found between the amount of social support received by older adults and their locus of control scores (Krause, 1987). Increases in emotional support are associated with a more internal locus of control up to a point. Beyond that, more emotional support is related to less internality in control.

Criticism

The second pattern of providing help that may also have negative effects is that of criticizing the patient and complaining about the demands of the caregiving role. Assistance accompanied by criticism and complaints gives the message that the help is not being given out of concern for the patient. In an indirect way it emphasizes inequalities in the relationship through the implication that the caregiver is unfairly burdened by the illness. Some research has examined this topic. Manne and Zautra (1989) found that women with rheumatoid arthritis whose husbands were highly critical had poorer adjustment and engaged in less adaptive coping behaviors than those whose husbands were not critical. This finding is consistent with studies on the effects of family members with recently hospitalized schizophrenia patients. Research in this area has measured "expressed emotion," which consists of hostility toward the patient and emotional overinvolvement with the patient (Brown, Monck, Carstairs, & Wing, 1982). High levels of expressed emotion of family members has been found to predict those schizophrenic patients who are likely to relapse and return to the hospital (Brown, Birley, & Wing, 1972; Karno et al., 1987; Vaughn & Leff, 1976). Similar effects on relapse rates were found in a non-psychiatric population of women who were trying to maintain their successful weight loss (Fischmann-Havstad & Marston, 1984). Thus across a number of areas it appears that critical, complaining caregivers are associated with poorer patient outcomes.

Stroke Patients and Caregiving Styles

In a series of studies, Thompson and her colleagues have investigated these two caregiving styles and their effects for stroke patients and their families. In the first study (Thompson, Sobolew-Shubin, Graham, & Janigian, 1989), we interviewed 40 pairs of stroke patients who were entering outpatient therapy and their primary caregivers, usually spouses. Three classes of predictors of poststroke depression were measured: objective factors that might affect depression (such as the severity of the stroke and site of the stroke), patients' interpretations of their situation, and the quality of the patient-caregiver relationship. As can be seen in Table 5.1, patients were more depressed when the stroke was more serious, when they had negative interpretations of their situation, and when the quality of the patient-caregiver relationship was poor. Most important for the current discussion is that the quality of the patient-caregiver relationship (RC) predicted patient depression even when the effects of the objective circumstances (OC) were controlled for by their prior entry in the regression equation (see the first row of Table 5.1; there is a significant increase of .22 in R^2 as a result of the

Table 5.1
Multiple Regression Results for Variables Predicting
Depression and the Increase in Variance Accounted for
When a Second Set Is Added to the Equation: First Study

Set of variables entered in equation	R	R^2	Increase in R^2 due to subsequent entry of		
			OC	PI	RC
Objective circumstances (OC)	.52**	.27	—	.23**	.22**
Patient interpretation (PI)	.61**	.36	.13*	—	.12*
Relationship with caregiver (RC)	.62***	.38	.10*	.11**	—

*p < .05; **p < .01; ***p < .001.

subsequent entry of RC). The relationship measure that was the strongest correlate of patient depression was feeling overprotected by the caregiver, $r(39) = .56$, $p < .01$. Patients who perceived themselves as being overprotected were significantly more depressed than those who did not feel overprotected, even when the effects of characteristics of the stroke and patient interpretation variables were controlled for in a multiple regression analysis.

In a second study, these results were replicated with a sample of 52 stroke patients who attended a resocialization program (Bundek & Thompson, 1989). Those who felt overprotected were more depressed, $r(51) = .44$, $p < .01$, and they also had lower perceptions of control over stroke-related outcomes, such as recovery and avoidance of a second stroke, $r(51) = -.46$, $p < .01$. In this second study, we developed and included a measure of criticism—the extent to which patients felt blamed and pushed by their family members to work harder, which we called "held to unrealistic expectations." Feeling that one's family members had unrealistic expectations was significantly correlated with patient depression, $r(51) = .47$, $p < .01$. Thus it appears that for stroke patients two types of relationships with the caregiver are problematic: feeling overprotected, and feeling pushed to do more and blamed for not trying harder.

These first two studies established that there is a strong, reliable relationship between feeling overprotected and worse psychological outcomes for stroke patients, but they did not examine the source of feelings of overprotection. Are they an accurate reflection of how family members treat the patient, or are they a misperception on the part of the patient? For example, patient perceptions may be a fairly accurate reflection of caregivers engaging in behaviors that lead to unnecessary dependency. Alternatively, patients may overestimate their own abilities and judge appropriate help from the family to be unnecessary and, therefore, overprotective. Our third study addressed four different possible explanations for stroke patients' feelings of overprotection (Thompson & Sobolew-Shubin, 1990): (a) low patient physical or mental functioning or a discrepancy between patient and caregiver estimates of patient functioning; (b) caregivers who restrict patient physical activities for benign reasons, such as fear for the patient's safety, expediency, and for the patient's own good; (c) caregivers who try to protect patients emotionally (e.g., shield them from stressful decisions); and (d) caregivers with resentful, negative attitudes toward the patient.

To examine these issues, 60 pairs of stroke patients and their caregivers were interviewed using closed-ended scales to measure patients' physical and mental functioning, discrepancies between patients and caregivers in judging patients' functioning, caregivers' self-ratings of helping or restricting the patient for three specific reasons (fear for the patient's safety, expediency, and for the patient's own good), emotional shielding of the patient, and negative attitudes of the caregiver toward the patient (e.g., resentment, infantilization). The results showed that stroke patients' feelings of being overprotected were not related to their degree of disability, nor to the number of helpful behaviors on the part of their spouses. Rather, patients who felt overprotected were those whose spouses were most resentful of the caregiving role and, independent of that, those whose spouses shielded the patient from upsetting news or difficult decisions. (See Table 5.2 for the zero-order correlations.)

A stepwise multiple regression, predicting overprotection from the four categories of variables described above, confirmed the pattern of results shown in the zero-order correlations—only two variables entered the equation: emotional shielding (standardized beta = .37, $t = 3.2$, $p < .01$) and negative attitudes (standardized beta = .28, $t = 2.4$, $p < .02$). The multiple R was .50, $p < .001$. Thus it appears that overprotective behaviors could arise from two independent sources—intentions on the part of the caregiver to shield the patient from stress and

Table 5.2
Correlations With Overprotection: Third Study

Variables	r	p
Physical functioning	−.04	ns
Disparity between caregiver and patient in judgments of patient physical functioning	−.01	ns
Mental status[a]	.02	ns
Caregiver protective behaviors	.01	ns
Emotional shielding	.42	.001
Caregiver negative attitudes	.36	.01

a. Higher scores indicate lower mental functioning.

expressions of, or possibly compensations for, negative resentful attitudes toward the patient.

Another issue is the relationship between the two caregiving styles that we have identified as maladaptive: overprotection and pushing/blaming. We had originally assumed that the two styles reflected the two ends of a continuum of helping: overhelping versus pushing the recipient to be independent. Contrary to our expectations, the two caregiving styles were positively, not negatively, correlated in the second study. Previously unpublished data from the third study replicated this finding: Judging that one's caregiver had unrealistic expectations was positively correlated with patient depression, $r(59) = .36$, $p < .01$, *and* with feeling overprotected, $r(59) = .33, p < .01$.

An examination of the other correlates of feeling held to unrealistic expectations sheds some light on these findings. Feeling held to unrealistic expectations was not associated with the severity of the stroke, but it was related to the extent to which caregivers rated themselves as having negative attitudes (e.g., resentment, infantilization) toward the patient, $r(59) = .32, p < .01$. Thus caregivers with negative attitudes toward the patient tended both to be overprotective and also to push the patient to do more. This finding fits with Watzlawick and Coyne's (1980) suggestion that family caregivers sometimes alternate between using coercive techniques, such as being critical and demanding and, when this is not successful, giving up and doing too much for patients. Thus the same caregivers may be both critical and overprotective.

Adaptive Interaction Styles

Not all well spouses are overprotective or critical of their chronically ill partners. It seems that there must be adaptive ways of giving help that circumvent the caregiving dilemma so that patients receive appropriate help in ways that do not increase dependency and reduce control.

One possibility is that successful caregiving allows for or encourages reciprocity so that patients have opportunities to repay their spouses for the help that has been provided. Reciprocity is an important issue in helping situations between strangers or acquaintances; it is an open question, however, whether or not more intimate relationships are similarly governed by issues of exchange and reciprocity (Clark, 1983). One important difference is that, in close relationships, there is more latitude in the types of benefits that could repay a particular helpful act, and perhaps a longer time frame in which the exchange could take place (Hatfield, Utne, & Traupmann, 1979). A problem with attempting to increase reciprocity is that chronically ill individuals may have limitations on the benefits they can give to their partners, so it is likely to be difficult for the ill spouse to return the same level of benefits that he or she has received. However, the patient's limited resources may be taken into account by the well spouse; even small gestures of reciprocation may be recognized and have an impact that is disproportionate to their size.

Perhaps what is important is not that the exchange be equal, but that there be flexibility in the helper and help-seeker roles. If neither partner is ill, caregiving and care-receiving roles are probably open to negotiation. There does not seem to be empirical research on this topic, but it seems likely that many couples work out on a daily basis who will be the support giver and who will receive support. If one partner has excessive stress, is depressed, or physically ill that day, he or she becomes the support receiver and gets the attention, emotional support, and maybe even the freedom from chores that goes with that role. On another day, the other partner may be seen as the one deserving of support, and the roles will be reversed. It may be problematic for both spouses if a situation like chronic illness reduces the flexibility in these roles so that the well spouse is always the support provider. Couples that manage their relationship more successfully during a chronic illness may be those that allow the ill spouse to be the care provider at times, giving emotional, informational, and perhaps also some physical assistance to the well spouse.

A second adaptive style of caregiving may be to make it clear that the help is given because of caring and love for the recipient. The recipient's perception of the caregiver's regard for him or her has a strong effect on the interpretation of aid (Gergen & Gergen, 1983). Help that is given without caring for the recipient can be seen as manipulative and controlling. This may be the reason why critical, nagging spouses are associated with poor patient outcomes. Their obvious low regard for the patient makes it seem that caring is not the primary motive for their help, and it may be particularly demeaning to have to accept help from someone who gives it unwillingly.

One way that couples may establish an adaptive interaction style during chronic illness is by the well spouse making it unambiguous that positive intentions and love for the patient are the motivating factors behind the help. Corbin and Strauss (1984) found that couples who worked collaboratively despite a chronic illness used "sentimental types of interactions, such as giving affection, saying please and thank you, giving compliments, telling the other how much what has been done is appreciated, and doing special little things for the other" (p. 112). Assistance in the context of an affectionate relationship may be less controlling and dependency inducing.

A third adaptive way for couples to function when one partner has a chronic illness may be to find ways to avoid or handle some of the resentment that can easily develop from the burdens of caregiving. Open communication and a chance to vent one's feelings may be one way to reduce resentment. For example, having opportunities to express some of their feelings and frustrations to others was associated with less caregiver burden and resentment for stroke caregivers (Thompson & Sobolew-Shubin, 1990). Couples dealing with chronic illness who have good communication have higher levels of marital satisfaction (Spiegel et al., 1983; Taylor et al., 1984). Unfortunately, many studies find that chronic illness can have deleterious effects on communication because the family may feel that dwelling on problems is not in the patient's best interest (Dunkel-Schetter & Wortman, 1982; Taylor & Dakof, 1988). There may be a tendency to engage in what Vess and his colleagues call "fair weather communication"—avoiding negative information and feelings (Vess et al., 1988). Thus communication may become difficult or restricted in some areas just when open expression of feelings may be most important. Caregivers who can maintain good communication with their spouses may be able to avoid some of the negative caregiving styles that seem to stem from unexpressed resentment.

Two qualifications on these adaptive caring styles should be noted. First, adaptive caregiving may be more difficult to carry out if the spouse's illness has resulted in cognitive impairments. Life satisfaction is especially low for wives whose ill husbands are aphasic (Fengler & Goodrich, 1979). Rosenbaum and Najenson (1976) found that wives of brain-injured men have more disruptions in their everyday lives and more negative affect than do wives of paraplegics. Similarly, caregivers of those stroke patients who are more cognitively impaired are more likely to think that the stroke has caused conflict in the relationship (Thompson et al., 1990). The communication difficulties of the cognitively impaired may make reciprocity, positive affect, and open communication particularly difficult.

Second, because so little is known about how the quality of the premorbid relationship affects the marriage, it is possible that adaptive caregiving styles are entirely a reflection of the quality of the marriage before the illness. It is reasonable that couples who had satisfying interactions prior to the onset of the disease are more likely to maintain harmonious relations. Alternatively, a satisfying marital relationship before the illness may make it especially difficult for some couples to face the contrast of a chronic caregiving situation. The general point is that it may be misleading to suggest that the style of care is adopted by the caregiver, independent of the couple's long history of interaction.

Linking Theory and Research

It is beyond the scope of this chapter to examine the implications of the research that has been reviewed here for each of the theoretical viewpoints presented in the first section. Instead, we will explore the research support for the two general issues that occur across a number of the approaches.

The first theme is that chronic illness leads to inequities in outcomes and dependencies that are likely to have negative effects on the marriage. There is definite support for the first part of this proposition. Well spouses experience increased stress and declining benefits as a result of their spouses' illness, and some resentment of these additional burdens appears to be fairly common. At the same time, patients increase their reliance on their spouses and become more dependent on the relationship. However, these inequities do not seem to have the expected negative effects on the marital adjustment of most couples. Some marriages do seem to suffer, but a clear, consistent negative impact of the illness does not seem to be the rule. This lack of a strong effect has different implications within the frameworks of various theories. We will explore three of these implications.

From the perspective of equity theory, it is possible that most spouses are able to restore actual or psychological equity, despite the imbalance in costs and rewards associated with the illness. Ill partners might restore actual equity by providing new positive outcomes for their spouses. They may be able to take on chores that help the partner or to provide benefits, such as emotional social support or a positive re-flected image of the spouse, at a higher level than before the illness. A more likely possibility, given the restrictions in resources that many chronically ill individuals face, is that both partners restore equity through psychological means. This could be accomplished if the couple used an extended time frame to judge equity and felt that earlier rewards from the partner offset the current costs. Partners may also judge what is fair based on what the partner would be *willing* to do, not just what has been done to date. For instance, a well husband may feel that the circumstances are fair because, if the situation had been reversed and he had been the one to get ill, his wife would have provided the same care for him. Another possibility is that what ill spouses are *able* to do is taken into account in judging the adequacy of their contributions.

Kelley's theory of relationships might suggest that inequities in outcomes at the given level have not been found to have a strong impact because each partner makes adjustments at the dispositional level. The fact that, in addition to resentment, many well spouses often feel guilt about how well they are fulfilling their caregiving role indicates that carrying out those duties may have a symbolic value. For some care-givers, the satisfaction associated with being nurturant and a good care provider may compensate for the loss of benefits at the given level. Another possibility is that the increases in the patient's dependency may be welcomed by some well spouses, who prior to the illness felt ignored, unappreciated, or in need of more attention and interaction with their partners. Thus increases in one partner's dependency may change the structure of the relationship, but not necessarily have negative effects.

A third theoretical perspective on the finding that many marriages are not adversely affected by chronic illness comes from family stress theory. Because this theory specifically examines the factors that lead to good and poor functioning when faced with a family crisis, it has clearly spelled out ideas about the ability of many relationships to survive without major problems. Relationships with a strong premorbid commitment, for example, should weather the crisis well, as should those in which the partners have good coping strategies and outside resources on which to draw. From this point of view, it is not surprising that the marital adjustment of many couples is not seriously affected by an illness.

The second theme that is common to a number of theories in this area is that an overprotective, overinvolving relationship style will be associated with poor outcomes for the patient. There is a fair amount of support for this idea: Overprotected patients tend to be depressed and to have low perceptions of control.

Three theories have perspectives that explain why overprotective styles are not unusual. First, according to family systems theory, the overinvolvement reflects a stable pattern of openness in the boundaries between family members. Presumably, the overprotective style would probably not develop just in response to the illness, but would be evident in the premorbid relationship. Alternatively, role theories suggest that the spouse's conception of the sick role could lead to overprotective behavior. Some well partners may believe that those identified as sick deserve solicitous and protective care; thus they may engage in overly helpful behaviors that inadvertently reduce patients' independence. A third theoretical possibility, from equity theory, is that the anger and resentment that many caregivers feel can lead to overly protective care that, in part, reflects a desire to control the patient. Our own research has found that overprotection is associated both with resentment and with a presumably more benign motivation of trying to protect the patient from emotional stress, indicating that both benign and less benign motives may be responsible for overprotective behaviors toward the chronically ill.

It is clear that considerably more research is needed in this area to develop a more complete picture of the effects of chronic illness on marriage. Further investigation into ways in which spouses can affect the adjustment of the patient is also indicated. We hope that the application of these theoretical perspectives will help researchers to understand more fully the problems that can occur in relationships where one of the partners is chronically ill. This understanding is a necessary step toward developing and implementing useful interventions that can help couples deal with the effects of long-term illness. At this time there is no single coherent theory that can describe and explain all of the complexities involved in successful coping with chronic illness. However, from the viewpoint of the family relationship and dyadic interactions, an approach that integrates some combination of theories such as those described in this chapter may be especially useful for gaining fresh insight.

References

Avorn, J., & Langer, E. (1982). Induced disability in nursing home patients: A controlled clinical trial. *Journal of the American Geriatrics Society, 30*, 397-400.

Baltes, M. M., & Reisenzein, R. (1986). The social world in long-term care institutions: Psychosocial control toward dependency? In M. M. Baltes & P. B. Baltes (Eds.), *The psychology of control and aging* (pp. 315-344). Hillsdale, NJ: Lawrence Erlbaum.

Bilodeau, C. B., & Hackett, T. P. (1971). Issues raised in a group setting by patients of myocardial infarction. *American Journal of Psychiatry, 128*, 105-110.

Block, A. R. (1981). An investigation of the response of the spouse to chronic pain behavior. *Psychosomatic Medicine, 43*, 415-422.

Block, A. R., Kremer, E. F., & Gaylor, M. (1980). Behavioral treatment of chronic pain: The spouse as a discriminative cue for pain behavior. *Pain, 9*, 243-252.

Brown, G. W., Birley, J. L. T., & Wing, J. K. (1972). Influence of family life on the course of schizophrenic disorders: A replication. *British Journal of Psychiatry, 121*, 241-258.

Brown, G. W., & Harris, G. (1978). *Social origins of depression: A study of psychiatric disorder in women.* New York: Free Press.

Brown, G. W., Monck, E. M., Carstairs, G. M., & Wing, J. K. (1982). The measurement of family activities and relationships. *Human Relations, 19*, 241-263.

Bundek, N. I., & Thompson, S. C. (1989). *Stroke patient depression: An investigation of patient and caregiver relationships.* Manuscript under review.

Burish, T. G., & Bradley, L. A. (1983). Coping with chronic disease: Definitions and issues. In T. G. Burish & L. A. Bradley (Eds.), *Coping with chronic disease* (pp. 3-12). New York: Academic Press.

Burish, T. G., & Lyles, J. N. (1983). Coping with the adverse effects of cancer treatments. In T. G. Burish & L. A. Bradley (Eds.), *Coping with chronic disease* (pp. 159-189). New York: Academic Press.

Burnam, W. R., Lennard-Jones, J. E., & Brooke, B. N. (1976). The incidence and nature of sexual problems among married ileostomists. *Gut, 17,* 391-392.

Campbell, A. (1981). *The sense of well-being in America.* New York: McGraw-Hill.

Christensen, A. (1983). Intervention. In H. H. Kelley, E. Berscheid, A. Christensen, J. H. Harvey, T. L. Huston, G. Levinger, E. McClintock, L. A. Peplau, & D. R. Peterson (Eds.), *Close relationships* (pp. 397-448). San Francisco: Freeman.

Clark, M. S. (1983). Some implications of close social bonds for help-seeking. In B. M. DePaulo, A. Nadler, & J. D. Fisher (Eds.), *New directions in helping: Help-seeking* (Vol. 2, pp. 205-228). New York: Academic Press.

Corbin, J. M., & Strauss, A. L. (1984). Collaboration: Couples working together to manage chronic illness. *Image: The Journal of Nursing Scholarship, 16,* 109-115.

Coyne, J. C., & DeLongis, A. (1986). Going beyond social support: The role of social relationships in adaptation. *Journal of Consulting and Clinical Psychology, 54,* 454-460.

Croog, S. H., & Levine, S. (1977). *The heart patient recovers: Social and psychological factors.* New York: Human Sciences Press.

Dean, A., & Lin, N. (1977). The stress buffering role of social support: Problems and prospects for systematic investigation. *Journal of Nervous and Mental Disorders, 165,* 403-417.

Deimling, G. T., & Bass, D. M. (1986). Symptoms of mental impairment among elderly adults and their effects on family caregivers. *Journal of Gerontology, 41,* 778-784.

Delvey, J., & Hopkins, L. (1982). Pain patients and their partners: The role of collusion in chronic pain. *Journal of Marital and Family Therapy, 8,* 135-142.

Doehrman, S. R. (1977). Psycho-social aspects of recovery from coronary heart disease: A review. *Social Science and Medicine, 11,* 199-218.

Dunkel-Schetter, C., & Wortman, C. B. (1982). The interpersonal dynamics of cancer: Problems in social relationships and their impact on the patient. In H. D. Friedman & M. R. DiMatteo (Eds.), *Interpersonal issues in health care* (pp. 69-100). New York: Academic Press.

Ervin, C. V. (1973). Psychologic adjustment to mastectomy. *Medical Aspects of Human Sexuality, 1,* 42-65.

Evans, R. L., & Miller, R. M. (1984). Psychosocial implications of treatment of stroke. *Social Casework: The Journal of Contemporary Social Work, 65,* 242-247.

Fengler, A. P., & Goodrich, N. (1979). Wives of elderly disabled men: The hidden patients. *Gerontologist, 19,* 175-183.

Fiore, J., Becker, J., & Coppel, D. B. (1983). Social interactions: A buffer or a stress. *American Journal of Community Psychology, 11,* 423-439.

Fischmann-Havstad, L., & Marston, A. R. (1984). Weight loss maintenance as an aspect of family emotion and process. *British Journal of Clinical Psychology, 23,* 265-271.

Flor, H., & Turk, D. C. (1985). Chronic illness in an adult family member: Pain as a prototype. In D. C. Turk & R. D. Kerns (Eds.), *Health, illness, and families: A life span perspective* (pp. 255-278). New York: John Wiley.

Fordyce, W. E. (1976). *Behavioral methods in chronic pain and illness.* St. Louis, MO: C. V. Mosby.

Gergen, M. M., & Gergen, K. J. (1983). Interpretive dimensions of international aid. In A. Nadler, J. D. Fisher, & B. M. DePaulo (Eds.), *New directions in helping* (Vol. 3, pp. 329-348). New York: Academic Press.

Haley, W. E., Levine, E. G., Brown, S. L., Berry, J. W., & Hughes, G. H. (1987). Psychological, social and health consequences of caring for a relative with senile dementia. *Journal of the American Geriatrics Society, 35*, 405-411.

Hatfield, E., Utne, M. K., & Traupmann, J. (1979). Equity theory and intimate relationships. In R. L. Burgess & T. L. Huston (Eds.), *Social exchange in developing relationships* (pp. 99-133). New York: Academic Press.

Hill, R. (1949). *Families under stress.* New York: Harper & Row.

Hill, R. (1958). Generic features of families under stress. *Social Casework, 39*, 139-150.

Hinton, J. (1979). Comparison of places and policies for terminal care. *Lancet, 1*, 29-32.

House, J. S. (1981). *Work stress and social support.* Reading, MA: Addison-Wesley.

House, J. S., Robins, C., & Metzner, H. L. (1982). The association of social relationships and activities with mortality: Prospective evidence from the Tecumseh Community Health Study. *American Journal of Epidemiology, 116*, 123-140.

Huesmann, L. R., & Levinger, G. (1979). Incremental exchange theory: A formal model for progression in dyadic social interaction. In L. Berkowitz & E. Walster (Eds.), *Advances in experimental social psychology* (Vol. 9, pp. 191-229). New York: Academic Press.

Hyman, M. D. (1971). Social isolation and performance in rehabilitation. *Journal of Chronic Disease, 25*, 85-97.

Hyman, M. D. (1972). Social psychological determinants of patients' performance in stroke rehabilitation. *Archives of Physical Medicine and Rehabilitation, 53*, 217-226.

Jung, J. (1984). Social support and its relation to health: A critical evaluation. *Basic and Applied Social Psychology, 5*, 143-169.

Jung, J. (1987). Toward a social psychology of social support. *Basic and Applied Social Psychology, 8*, 57-83.

Kahn, R. L., & Antonucci, T. C. (1982). Convoys over the life course: Attachment, roles, and social support. In P. B. Baltes & O. Brim (Eds.), *Life-span development and behavior* (Vol. 3, pp. 253-286). Lexington, MA: Lexington Press.

Kaplan, B. H., Smith, A., Grobstein, R., & Fischman, S. E. (1973). Family mediation of stress. *Social Work, 17*, 60-69.

Karno, M., Jenkins, J. H., de la Selva, A., Santana, F., Telles, C., Lopez, S., & Mintz, J. (1987). Expressed emotional and schizophrenic outcome among Mexican-American families. *Journal of Nervous and Mental Disease, 175*, 143-151.

Kelley, H. H. (1979). *Personal relationships: Their structure and processes.* Hillsdale, NJ: Lawrence Erlbaum.

Kelley, H. H. (1981). Love and commitment. In H. H. Kelley, E. Berscheid, A. Christensen, J. H. Harvey, T. L. Huston, G. Levinger, E. McClintock, L. A. Peplau, & D. R. Peterson (Eds.), *Close relationships* (pp. 265-314). San Francisco: Freeman.

Kelley, H. H., & Thibaut, J. W. (1978). *Interpersonal relationships: A theory of interdependence.* New York: Wiley-Interscience.

Kerns, R. D., & Turk, D. C. (1984). Depression and chronic pain: The mediating role of the spouse. *Journal of Marriage and the Family, 46*, 845-852.

Kessler, R. C., & McLeod, J. D. (1985). Social support and mental health in community samples. In S. Cohen & S. L. Syme (Eds.), *Social support and health* (pp. 219-240). New York: Academic Press.

Kiecolt-Glaser, J. K., Glaser, R., Shuttleworth, E. C., Dyer, C. S., Ogrocki, P., & Speicher, C. E. (1987). Chronic stress and immunity in family caregivers of Alzheimer's disease victims. *Psychosomatic Medicine, 49*, 523-535.

Krantz, D. S., & Deckel, A. W. (1983). Coping with coronary heart disease and stroke. In T. G. Burish & L. A. Bradley (Eds.), *Coping with chronic disease: Research and applications* (pp. 85-112). New York: Academic Press.

Krause, N. (1987). Understanding the stress process: Linking social support with locus of control beliefs. *Journal of Gerontology, 42*, 589-593.

Labi, M. L., Phillips, T. F., & Greshman, G. E. (1980). Psychosocial disability in physically restored long-term stroke survivors. *Archives of Physical Medicine and Rehabilitation, 61*, 561-565.

Lavee, Y., McCubbin, H. I., & Olson, D. H. (1987). The effect of stressful life events and transitions on family functioning and well being. *Journal of Marriage and the Family, 49*, 857-873.

Leventhal, H., Leventhal, E. A., & Nguyen, T. V. (1985). Reactions of families to illness: Theoretical models and perspectives. In D. C. Turk & R. D. Kerns (Eds.), *Health, illness, and families: A life-span perspective* (pp. 108-145). New York: John Wiley.

Lewis, C. E. (1966). Factors influencing the return to work of men with congestive heart failure. *Journal of Chronic Disease, 19*, 1193-1209.

Lieberman, M. A. (1982). The effects of social supports on responses to stress. In L. Goldberger & S. Berenznitz (Eds.), *Handbook of stress* (pp. 764-781). New York: Free Press.

MacVicar, M. G., & Archbold, P. (1976). A framework for assessment in chronic illness. *Nursing Forum, 15*, 180-194.

Manne, S. L., & Zautra, A. J. (1989). Spouse criticism and support: Their association with coping and psychological adjustment among women with rheumatoid arthritis. *Journal of Personality and Social Psychology, 56*, 608-617.

Maruta, T., & Osborne, D. (1978). Sexual activity in chronic pain patients. *Psychosomatics, 19*, 531-537.

Maruta, T., Osborne, D., Swanson, D. W., & Halling, J. M. (1981). Chronic pain patients and spouses: Marital and sexual adjustment. *Mayo Clinic Proceedings, 56*, 307-310.

McCubbin, H. I., & Patterson, J. M. (1983). The family stress process. In H. I. McCubbin, M. B. Sussman, & J. M. Patterson (Eds.), *Social stress and the family: Advances in family stress theory and research* (pp. 7-37). New York: Hawthorne.

Meyerowitz, B. E., Sparks, F. C., & Spears, I. K. (1979). Adjuvant chemotherapy for breast carcinoma: Psychological implications. *Cancer, 43*, 1613-1618.

Minuchin, S. (1974). *Families and family therapy.* Cambridge, MA: Harvard University Press.

Morris, T., Greer, H. S., & White, P. W. (1977). Psychological and social adjustment to mastectomy: A two-year follow-up. *Cancer, 40*, 2381-2387.

Nerentz, D. R., & Leventhal, H. (1983). Self-regulation theory in chronic illness. In T. Burish & L. Bradley (Eds.), *Coping with chronic disease: Research and applications* (pp. 13-37). New York: Academic Press.

Newman, S. (1984). The social and emotional consequences of head injury and stroke. *International Review of Applied Psychology, 33*, 427-455.

Nisbett, R. E., & Wilson, T. D. (1977). Telling more than we can know: Verbal reports on mental processes. *Psychological Review, 84*, 231-256 .

Pagel, M. D., Erdly, W. W., & Becker, J. (1987). Social networks: We get by with (and in spite of) a little help from our friends. *Journal of Personality and Social Psychology, 53*, 793-804.

Parmelee, P. A. (1983). Spouse versus other family caregivers: Psychological impact on impaired aged. *American Journal of Community Psychology, 11*, 337-349.

Parsons, T., & Fox, R. (1958). Illness, therapy, and the American family. *Journal of Social Issues, 8*, 31-44.

Pederson, L. M., & Valanis, B. G. (1988). The effects of breast cancer on the family: A review of the literature. *Journal of Psychosocial Oncology, 6*, 95-117.

Rogoff, J. B., Cooney, D. V., & Kutner, B. (1964). Hemiplegia: A study of home rehabilitation. *Journal of Chronic Disability, 17*, 539-550.

Rosenbaum, M., & Najenson, R. (1976). Changes in life patterns and symptoms of low mood as reported by wives of severely brain-injured soldiers. *Journal of Consulting and Clinical Psychology, 44*, 881-888.

Schulz, R., Tompkins, C. A., & Rau, M. T. (1988). A longitudinal study of the psychosocial impact of stroke on primary support persons. *Psychology and Aging, 3*, 131-141.

Shambaugh, P. W., & Kantor, S. S. (1969). Spouses under stress: Group meetings with spouses of patients on hemodialysis. *American Journal of Psychiatry, 125*, 100-108.

Shaw, M. E., & Costanzo, P. R. (1982). *Theories of social psychology* (2nd ed.). New York: McGraw-Hill.

Shellhase, L. J., & Shellhase, F. E. (1972). Role of the family rehabilitation. *Social Casework, 53*, 544-550.

Shumaker, S. A., & Brownell, A. (1984). Toward a theory of social support: Closing conceptual gaps. *Journal of Social Issues, 40*(1), 11-36.

Skelton, M., & Dominian, J. (1973). Psychological stress in wives of patients with myocardial infarction. *British Medical Journal, 14*, 101-103.

Smith, E. M., Redman, P., Burns, T. L., & Sagert, K. M. (1985). Perceptions of social support among patients with recently diagnosed breast, endometrial, and ovarian cancer. *Journal of Psychosocial Oncology, 3*, 65-81.

Spiegel, D., Bloom, J. R., & Gottheil, E. (1983). Family environment as a predictor of adjustment to metastatic breast carcinoma. *Journal of Psychosocial Oncology, 1*, 33-44.

Suls, J. (1982). Social support, interpersonal relations, and health: Benefits and liabilities. In G. S. Sanders & J. Suls (Eds.), *Social psychology of health and illness* (pp. 255-277). Hillsdale, NJ: Lawrence Erlbaum.

Taylor, S. E., & Dakof, G. A. (1988). Social support and the cancer patient. In S. Spacapan & S. Oskamp (Eds.), *The social psychology of health* (pp. 95-116). Newbury Park, CA: Sage.

Taylor, S. E., Lichtman, R. R., & Wood, J. V. (1984). Attributions, beliefs about control, and adjustment to breast cancer. *Journal of Personality and Social Psychology, 46*, 489-502.

Thoits, P. A. (1984). Coping, social support, and psychological outcomes. In P. Shaver (Ed.), *Review of personality and social psychology* (Vol. 5, pp. 219-238). Beverly Hills, CA: Sage.

Thompson, S. C. (1986). [Psychosocial adjustment to stroke: Patient and spousal perceptions]. Unpublished data.

Thompson, S. C., Bundek, N. I., & Sobolew-Shubin, A. (1990). The caregivers of stroke patients: An investigation of factors associated with depression. *Journal of Applied Social Psychology, 20*, 115-129.

Thompson, S. C., & Sobolew-Shubin, A. (1990). *Overprotective relationships: A non-supportive side of social networks.* Manuscript under review.

Thompson, S. C., Sobolew-Shubin, A., Graham, M. A., & Janigian, A. S. (1989). Psychosocial adjustment following a stroke. *Social Science and Medicine, 28*, 239-247.

Turk, D. C., & Kerns, R. D. (1985). The family in health and illness. In D. C. Turk & R. D. Kerns (Eds.), *Health, illness, and families: A life-span perspective* (pp. 1-22). New York: John Wiley.

Vaughn, C. E., & Leff, J. P. (1976). The influence of family and social factors on the course of psychiatric illness. *British Journal of Psychiatry, 129*, 125-137.

Vess, J. D., Moreland, J. R., Schwebel, A. I., & Kraut, E. (1988). Psychosocial needs of cancer patients: Learning from patients and their spouses. *Journal of Psychosocial Oncology, 6*, 31-51.

Wade, D. T., Legh-Smith, J., & Hewer, R. L. (1986). Effects of living with and looking after survivors of a stroke. *British Medical Journal, 293*, 418-420.

Walster, E., Berscheid, E., & Walster, G. W. (1973). New directions in equity research. *Journal of Personality and Social Psychology, 25*, 151-176.

Watzlawick, P., & Coyne, J. C. (1980). Depression following stroke: Brief, problem focused family treatment. *Family Process, 19*, 13-18.

Weiss, R. S. (1974). The provisions of social relationships. In Z. Rubin (Ed.), *Doing unto others* (pp. 17-26). Englewood Cliffs, NJ: Prentice-Hall.

Wellisch, D. K., Fawzy, F. I., Landsvere, J., Pasnau, R. O., & Wolcott, D. L. (1983). Evaluation of psychosocial problems of the home bound cancer patient: The relationship of disease and the sociodemographic variables of patients to family problems. *Journal of Psychosocial Oncology, 1*, 1-15.

Wills, T. A. (1985). Supportive functions of interpersonal relationships. In S. Cohen & S. L. Syme (Eds.), *Social support and health* (pp. 61-108). New York: Academic Press.

Wortman, C. B., & Conway, T. L. (1985). The role of social support in adaptation and recovery from physical illness. In S. Cohen & S. L. Syme (Eds.), *Social support and health* (pp. 281-302). New York: Academic Press.

Wortman, C. B., & Dunkel-Schetter, C. (1987). Conceptual and methodological issues in the study of support. In A. Baum & J. E. Singer (Eds.), *Handbook of psychology and health: Vol. V. Stress* (pp. 63-108). Hillsdale, NJ: Lawrence Erlbaum.

6

Costs and Benefits of Providing Care to Alzheimer's Patients

RICHARD SCHULZ
GAIL M. WILLIAMSON
RICHARD K. MORYCZ
DAVID E. BIEGEL

T he population of the United States is aging, and the prevalence of age-related disorders is increasing. One of these disorders, Alzheimer's disease (AD), has become a major focus of investigation for a large segment of the scientific community. For social psychologists, issues concerning the care of AD patients present opportunities to answer important questions about the human capacity to endure long-term chronic stress—specifically, stress in the form of providing large amounts of help for extended periods of time.

In this chapter, we first describe Alzheimer's disease, including its prevalence and clinical course. Next, we review existing research on the impact of this illness on informal caregivers, followed by a social psychological analysis of caregiving. In the remainder of the chapter,

AUTHORS' NOTE: This research was supported by a grant from the National Institute on Aging (AG 05444).

we present data from a longitudinal study of caregivers of AD patients and offer interpretations of these data.

Alzheimer's Disease

More than 70 different conditions can cause dementia. In elderly persons, the two most common causes are Alzheimer's disease and stroke. A clinical diagnosis of AD is based on presence of dementia symptoms, insidious onset followed by progressive deterioration, and exclusion of all other testable causes of dementia and dementia-like symptoms by history, physical examination, laboratory tests, and psychometric and other studies. AD is also associated with various physiological changes in the brain, including loss of neurons, widened fissures, narrower and flatter ridges, senile plaques scattered throughout the cortex, and replacement of normal nerve cells in the basal ganglia with tangled threadlike structures.

Prevalence and Disease Course

Results of a recent community population study reveal that current prevalence of AD may be higher than previously estimated. Earlier figures (e.g., Gurland et al., 1983) placed prevalence among individuals over 65 at approximately 5% in the United States. However, using stringent criteria for diagnosing AD in a community population, Evans et al. (1989) determined that 10.3% of the noninstitutionalized residents over 65 years of age of East Boston, Massachusetts were probable victims of Alzheimer's disease. They also found dramatic increases with age. Among those between 65 and 74 years of age, prevalence was 3.0%. Among those 75 to 84 years of age, the rate of probable AD was 18.7%. Of those individuals 85 and older, an astonishing 47.2% were probable Alzheimer's cases. Currently, there are approximately 1 million cases of severe AD and 3 million cases of mild to moderate AD in the United States. Severe cases are expected to increase to approximately 4.5 million by the year 2040. AD is estimated to account for 100,000 to 120,000 deaths annually, making it the fourth leading cause of death in the United States.

The onset of AD is deceptively mild, and its course is one of steady deterioration. In Stage One, patients may exhibit minor symptoms and mood changes. They may have less energy and drive, be less spontaneous and slower to learn or react, and forget some words. They may lose their temper more easily than they did before. Frequently, these symptoms go undetected or are attributed to temporary changes in the environment or the individual.

In Stage Two, patients may still be able to perform familiar activities but need help with complicated tasks. Ability to speak and understand are noticeably impaired. They may be insensitive to others' feelings. Stage Three is characterized by profound memory deficits, particularly for recent events. Patients may forget where they are, as well as the date, time, and season. They may fail to recognize familiar people. Behavioral problems may become prominent with manifestation of psychotic symptoms (e.g., delusions, hallucinations, paranoid ideation, severe agitation).

Memory continues to deteriorate in Stage Four, and patients are likely to need help with all activities. They are frequently disoriented, unable to recognize close friends and family members, and often lose bowel and bladder control. Finally, patients become completely mute, inattentive, and totally incapable of caring for themselves. The process of deterioration ultimately leads to death. The total illness course is 1 to 10 years.

At this time, dementia of the Alzheimer's type cannot be prevented, nor can its course be slowed or reversed. However, in many cases, its severity of impact on the individual and/or family may be reduced through early detection and appropriate treatment of associated problems.

Impact on the Patient

In some ways, dealing with AD is the reverse of dealing with cancer. It leaves bone and flesh intact while erasing judgment, memory, and the sense of self. In contrast, most types of cancer destroy physical being while leaving cognitive abilities intact. However, in the respect that both present profound, life-shattering challenges to individuals, they have much in common.

An AD diagnosis has been likened to receiving a death sentence. Patients respond with a variety of strong emotions, including shock, anger, disbelief, fear, and despair. A few refuse to acknowledge their condition altogether.

Themes of death and loss are prominent in patients' responses to a diagnosis of AD, in large part because the illness conveys an image of profound loss and is perceived as incurable and life shortening. In the early stages, many patients are desperate to talk about what AD means for the future and their family (Cohen & Eisdorfer, 1988). Patients want to remain as active as possible for as long as possible and to be included in family decisions and plans for the future. Fear and sadness are characteristic in this stage. Patients know that as the disease progresses, they will be unable to relate to others with dignity and respect.

Perhaps most distressing for AD patients is existing in that transitional limbo where they are aware of having profound cognitive deficits that will only worsen. Observing the unraveling of a self-identity created over a lifetime is a burden virtually no one can bear with equanimity.

These observations are derived primarily from case studies (Cohen & Eisdorfer, 1988). Systematic studies of representative samples of Alzheimer's patients and their responses to diagnosis and subsequent decline are nonexistent. This lack can be attributed to several factors. First, an AD diagnosis typically evolves gradually over an extended period of time. As a result, it is usually difficult to pinpoint exactly when patients become aware of the diagnosis and the extent to which their responses are influenced by events and experiences that occurred before diagnosis. The ideal situation would be to begin studying patients when they first suspect dementia problems and follow them through the diagnostic process.

A second factor hampering systematic study is that data on patient responses to illness are usually based on self-reports. In this case, the disease itself may interfere with patients' ability to provide useful self-report data. Data could, however, be collected from patients in early to middle stages. Finally, it can be argued that collecting such data may be stressful for patients by causing them to dwell on feelings related to their own impending decline and death. Although this argument applies to some patients, others would benefit from opportunities to discuss their feelings. On the whole, researchers generally have been concerned with assessing patients' cognitive and functional status and with differentiating AD from other illnesses such as depression. Little attention has been paid to how patients feel about what is happening to them.

Impact on Family Members

In contrast, the literature on the impact of AD on caregivers is extensive and continues to grow rapidly. Early research focused primarily on documenting the burdens of caregiving. As a result, it is now well established that providing care to an Alzheimer's patient creates emotional, physical, and financial strain. Specific problems that have been identified include undesirable changes in one's social life, feeling overwhelmed, developing depression and anxiety, strained relations with other family members, and general feelings that life is uncontrollable (e.g., Barnes, Raskind, Scott, & Murphy, 1981; Morycz, 1985; Rabins, Mace, & Lucas, 1982; Zarit, Reever, & Bach-Peterson, 1980).

Although distress is characteristic in all caregiving situations, regardless of patient disability, it is generally believed that caring for a demented individual presents the greatest challenge of all. The cognitive impairment and unusual behavioral disorders associated with dementia create burdens that are uniquely and severely stressful to caregivers (George & Gwyther, 1986; Mace & Rabins, 1981). Frequently, families must assist demented patients with dressing, feeding, bathing, and management of incontinence. Physical demands are aggravated by witnessing the deterioration of a loved one's personality, a process described by caregivers as a "living death" (Haley, Levine, Brown, Berry, & Hughes, 1987). The constant, unremitting nature of caring for a relative with dementia has been called a "36-hour day" (Mace & Rabins, 1981).

In addition to documenting the burdens and distress associated with AD caregiving, researchers have investigated psychiatric and physical morbidity effects. Mental health impacts have been assessed in two types of studies: (a) those using standardized self-report inventories to measure psychiatric symptomatology (e.g., depressive affect), and (b) those using clinical assessment procedures to identify the prevalence of actual clinical cases. Overall, the literature on psychiatric morbidity is suggestive but not conclusive (see Biegel, Sales, & Schulz, 1991, for a review of this literature). There is strong evidence for increased symptom reports of depression and demoralization among *most* caregivers. There is also evidence of increased clinical psychiatric illness among *some* caregivers. In addition, one large survey revealed higher rates of psychotropic drug use among caregivers than among noncaregivers (George & Gwyther, 1986).

Although the findings are somewhat inconsistent, research suggests that caregiving may also adversely affect physical health. Three categories of outcomes have been examined as indicators of physical illness effects among caregivers. First, the most frequently used measures are self-reports of health status, illness, and illness-related symptoms. Second, a few studies have examined health care utilization as an indicator of physical morbidity (George & Gwyther, 1986; Haley et al., 1987; Pruchno & Potashnik, 1989). Finally, one study assessed immune function as an indicator of susceptibility to disease (Kiecolt-Glaser et al., 1987).

Self-report data consistently show lower levels of health among caregivers than age-matched peers (Stone, Cafferata, & Sangl, 1987), but it is difficult to infer causality from these data. Health care utilization studies yield mixed results. One study (Haley et al., 1987) reports more frequent physician visits and more prescription drug use among caregivers compared to a matched group of noncaregivers. However, two others (George & Gwyther, 1986; Kiecolt-Glaser et al., 1987) found that caregivers did not use more medical services compared to age-specific normative data or matched controls. One study (Kiecolt-Glaser et al., 1987) showed impaired immune function among caregivers compared to matched controls, although no relation was found between immune function and self-report health data (see Schulz, Visintainer, & Williamson, in press, for a detailed review of the morbidity literature).

Research on predictors of caregiver outcomes is more consistent. As one would expect, increased patient disability is consistently related to unfavorable caregiver outcomes, although the relation is only moderate. Being female, being married to the patient, and living with the patient are associated with higher rates of distress and depression, and availability of social support from others seems to attenuate the negative impact of caregiving.

Social Psychological Approaches
to Caregiving

Much of the literature on caregiving represents an attempt to link some antecedent variables to the well-being of individuals who provide support to disabled relatives. A typical antecedent (independent) variable is patient functional or behavior status. Representative measures of caregiver well-being (dependent variables) include a variety of assessments of psychosocial status, physical health, and mental health (e.g., morale, life satisfaction, depression, perceived strain or burden). Sandwiched between independent and dependent variables are many individual and situational conditioning variables characteristic of all stress-coping models (e.g., caregiver age, gender, and socioeconomic status; type and quality of the relationship between caregiver and patient; social support available to caregivers; individual characteristics of caregivers, such as self-esteem, locus of control, and religiosity). The inclusion of conditioning or intervening variables is justified by findings of relations between independent variables (e.g., patient impairment) and caregiver outcomes (e.g., depression) that are only moderate. This basic model has been elaborated by a number of researchers (e.g., Cohler, Groves, Borden, & Lazarus, 1989; Haley, Levine, Brown, & Bartolucci, 1987; Montgomery, Stull, & Borgatta, 1985; Schulz, Tompkins, & Rau, 1988; Schulz, Tompkins, Wood, & Decker, 1987).

In an effort to develop a framework for understanding physical and psychological costs and benefits of providing support to disabled individuals, Schulz et al. (1987) adapted a stress-coping model from House (1974) and George (1980) that identifies relevant variables and their interrelations. As illustrated in Figure 6.1, four categories of variables are incorporated in the model: (a) objective conditions conducive to stress, (b) individual perceptions of stress or perceived burden, (c) enduring outcomes of perceived stress, and (d) individual and situational conditioning variables that affect relations among the other three sets of factors. In this chapter, we focus on objective stressors and conditioning variables as predictors of caregiver distress.

Among caregivers, objective stressors include the patient's functional disability, which can be characterized on such dimensions as

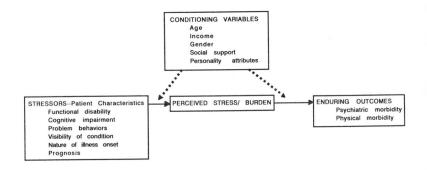

Figure 6.1. Caregiver Stress and Coping Model

inability to care for self, degree of cognitive impairment, and frequency of problem behaviors. Other illness-related factors are also likely to influence caregiver response to patient disability. For instance, how *visible* the condition is to others may significantly affect caregivers' social lives. Victims of AD often exhibit behaviors (e.g., aggressiveness, incontinence, inappropriate sexual behaviors) that may be embarrassing to caregivers. Examples of additional factors likely to influence caregiver response are the *nature of illness onset* (sudden or insidious) and *prognosis* (recuperative, stable, degenerative, or terminal). Equivalent levels of functional disability may have differential impacts depending on the perceived natural history and stage of illness.

As Figure 6.1 shows, it is hypothesized that a variety of conditioning variables mediate the direct relation between objective stressors and enduring caregiver outcomes. They may (a) attenuate or prevent perceptions of stress; or (b) influence enduring outcomes by reducing emotional reactions, lessening physiological reactions, or altering maladaptive behavior. Conditioning variables include demographics (e.g., caregiver age, income, gender), social support, caregiver personality factors, and coping strategies.

Major components of this model have been examined in two prior studies, one focusing on primary support persons of middle-aged and elderly spinal cord injured persons (Schulz et al., 1987) and the other dealing with caregivers of stroke patients (Schulz et al., 1988). The study of spinal cord support persons was cross-sectional and provided general support for the model. After controlling for health and income, the well-being of support persons was strongly related to the amount of social support received, adequacy of social contacts, and feelings of control over their lives. In addition, the amount of time spent each day assisting the disabled person was a strong independent correlate of the support person's depression.

The stroke study was longitudinal. Approximately 150 stroke victims and their caregivers were interviewed three times: (a) an average of 7 weeks after a first completed stroke, (b) 6 months later, and (c) a year after the initial interview. In the acute phase (7 weeks poststroke), caregiver adjustment was highly related to aspects of the stroke (e.g., severity). Conditioning variables such as age and income played relatively minor roles in attenuating these relations. However, 8 and 14 months after the stroke, well-established demographic factors (health, income, and age) were significant predictors of caregiver depression levels. Older individuals in good health with higher incomes were least depressed. In addition, change in depression was related to changes in the expected direction in two measures of social support—the amount of reciprocal confiding, and satisfaction with the quality of social contacts. Declines in these indices were associated with increases in depression.

Taken together, these studies make three important points. First, the stress-coping model appeared to do a good job of representing the large number of variables important in understanding caregiving outcomes. Second, results underscored the importance of longitudinal data by showing that the impact of an illness during the acute phase may differ from its long-term impact. Finally, both studies demonstrated that most individuals adjust fairly well to caring for family members with long-term disabling conditions.

However, we should be cautious about generalizing these findings to other disabling conditions—in particular, those with different prognoses. AD prognosis differs from that for stroke or spinal cord injury in important ways. Both spinal cord injury and stroke have stable prognoses; AD is characterized by an unpredictable downward course. Although caregivers can be certain that patients will get worse, they cannot know how quickly the decline will occur nor how the illness will manifest itself behaviorally. Another feature unique to AD is the implication that caregivers are also vulnerable to the illness through genetic similarity to the patient and/or shared environmental exposures. Thus daughters must not only cope with the stress of caring for a dementing parent but also the possibility that they, too, will be afflicted with the illness. Spouses of Alzheimer's patients often feel vulnerable because the disease may be linked to environmental toxin exposure.

In sum, Alzheimer's caregiving provides an applied context with a number of unique features. It affords researchers the opportunity to test hypotheses concerning individual caregivers' willingness and ability to provide diverse types of help at high levels for long periods of time, and it provides a context for exploring the limits of human exposure to chronic stress. Using the stress-coping model described above as a general heuristic device, our goal in this chapter is to describe the impact of Alzheimer's disease on caregiver symptoms of depression, identify major correlates of depression in caregivers, and determine how patient decline affects caregivers over time.

Method

Sample and Procedure

Participants were identified through Alzheimer's disease (AD) and related diseases diagnostic centers in the Pittsburgh and Cleveland metropolitan areas. Individuals were eligible if they were primary caregivers of family members diagnosed with possible or probable Alzheimer's dementia. Diagnoses were based on clinical symptoms, psychological testing, and laboratory studies as outlined in the NINCDS/ADRDA criteria (McKahn et al., 1984). Only caregivers of noninstitutionalized patients scoring between 12 and 27 on the Folstein Mini-Mental State Exam (MMS; Folstein, Folstein, & McHugh, 1975) were eligible for inclusion in the study. The MMS assesses orientation, memory, and attention with questions requiring verbal responses (e.g., "What is the date?" and "Where are we?") as well as the ability to name objects, follow commands, write a sentence, and copy a figure. The highest possible score on the MMS is 30, with lower scores reflecting greater cognitive impairment.

Caregiving individuals who met these criteria ($N = 244$) received a letter describing the project and inviting them to participate. Of these, 174 (71%) agreed. Those who agreed did not differ from those who refused in gender, familial relationship to the patient, age of the patient, or patient MMS scores. Participants were usually interviewed in their own homes. Initial interviews were conducted in 1986 and 1987, and on average, 27 months had elapsed since the patient's AD was first diagnosed. Each interview took approximately 90 minutes to complete and included questions eliciting information about demographic characteristics, problem behaviors exhibited by patients, the amount and type of help provided by caregivers, support received by caregivers from others, and caregiver symptoms of depression. These interviews were repeated at Time 2 (6 months after the initial interview) and Time 3 (12 months after Time 2). Interviewers requested that patients not be present during interviews. Two participants did not give enough data at Time 1 to be included in the analyses, leaving $N = 172$ at intake.

Measures

Analyses focused on three categories of quantitative data: (a) indicators of patient functional status (objective stressors); (b) demographic characteristics of patients and caregivers, quality of relationship between caregiver and patient prior to AD onset, social support, and caregiver health (conditioning variables); and (c) caregiver depression (enduring outcome). In addition, an open-ended question was asked to ascertain positive aspects of caregiving. Specific topics covered within each category are briefly described below.

Objective Stressors (Patient Status)

Patient cognitive function was assessed using the Folstein Mini-Mental State Exam (Folstein et al., 1975) described previously. The amount of help that patients received from their caregivers was assessed with 18 items from the Older Americans Resource and Services scales (OARS; Center for the Study of Aging and Human Development, 1978) measuring activities of daily living (ADL) such as bathing, dressing, and eating, and instrumental activities of daily living (IADL) such as managing money, laundry, and shopping for personal items. Each item was rated on a 5-point scale, with 0 indicating no help given and 4 indicating complete help given. Scores could range from 0 to 72.

Caregivers were also asked to indicate to what extent patients exhibited 40 different behavioral problems associated with Alzheimer's disease (e.g., wandering, asking repetitive questions, losing things, trouble dressing, failing to recognize familiar people). Frequency of problem behavior occurrence was rated on a 5-point scale of 0 (*never*) to 4 (*almost always*). Scores could range from 0 to 160.

Demographic Characteristics

Traditional demographic data collected included age, gender, household income, and number of people living in the caregiver's household. Caregivers were also asked how they were related to the patient (e.g., husband, wife, daughter-in-law, friend) and whether the patient lived in their household. Additional questions included the perceived adequacy of caregiver's household income (scored 1 = *much more than adequate*, 5 = *not at all adequate*) and the number of people who helped care for the patient.

Social Support

Perceived social support was measured using a 6-item version of the Interpersonal Support Evaluation List (ISEL; Cohen, Mermelstein, Kamarck, & Hoberman, 1985). On a scale of 0 (*definitely true*) to 3 (*definitely false*), respondents rated these statements: (a) "When I feel lonely, there are several people I can talk to;" (b) "I often meet or talk with family or friends;" (c) "If I were sick, I could easily find someone to help me with my daily chores;" (d) "When I need suggestions on how to deal with a personal problem, I know someone I can turn to;" (e) "If I had to go out of town for a few weeks, it would be difficult to find someone who would look after my house or apartment" (reverse scored); and (f) "There is at least one person I know whose advice I really trust." Higher scores indicated lower levels of perceived support.

Responses to three items were summed to yield an index of satisfaction with social contact: (a) "How satisfied would you say you have been with the amount of social contacts you've had in the past 6 months?"; (b) "What about the quality or closeness of the contacts you have had?"; and (c) "Compared to 6 months ago, has the number of people you feel close to increased, stayed about the same, or decreased?" Responses to items a and b were scored on a scale of 1 (*very dissatisfied*) to 5 (*very satisfied*); scores on item c were reversed. Higher scores indicated greater satisfaction with social contact.

Negative support was assessed by summing responses to five questions asking caregivers the number of network members who "criticize your handling of things," "don't [help] as much as [you] thought they would," "try to help but wind up making things worse," "seem to be out to make problems for you," and have "withdrawn from you or [patient]." Higher scores represented more negative social support.

Caregiver Health Status

A measure of caregiver objective health was obtained by summing (a) the number of disabilities that limited activities in the last 6 months, (b) the number of other chronic health problems, and (c) the number of prescription drugs taken. Subjective health was assessed by asking caregivers to rate their current overall health (1 = *excellent,* 5 = *poor*).

Prior Relationship

To measure quality of caregiver/patient relationship before AD, 14 items were selected from the Communication, Affective Expression, and Involvement subscales of the Dyadic Relationship component of the Family Assessment Measure (Skinner, Steinhauer, & Santa-Barbara, 1983). Items selected measured the quality of the prior relationship in terms of communication (e.g., "I knew what this person meant when he/she said something"), affect expression (e.g., "When I was upset, this person usually knew why"), and involvement (e.g., "This person and I weren't close to each other;" reverse scored). Prior relationship quality was assessed only at Time 1.

Depressive Symptomatology

The primary outcome measure was the Center for Epidemiologic Studies Depression Scale (CES-D; Radloff, 1977). The CES-D is a 20-item self-report scale designed to identify individuals at risk for depression. This instrument measures current levels of symptoms by asking respondents to indicate on a 4-point scale (0 to 3) how often they experienced each symptom during the previous week. Scores could range from 0 to 60, with higher scores reflecting more depressive symptoms. Individuals scoring 16 or above on the CES-D are generally considered to be "at risk" for developing clinical depression.

Positive Aspects of Caregiving

At the end of each interview, respondents were asked, "Has there been any purpose or positive meaning that [patient's]) illness has had in your life?" Those replying "yes" were then asked to describe the purpose(s) and/or positive meaning(s).

Results

Few changes occurred between Time 1 and Time 2 in outcome and predictor variables, reflecting the relatively brief period of time (6 months) between data collection intervals. As a result, the focus of our analyses is on Times 1 and 3, an 18-month period during which most patients experienced substantial declines in functioning.

Results are presented in progressive stages. First, we describe attrition from Time 1 to Time 3. Next, we present descriptive data for major outcome and predictor variables. This is followed by correlational analyses examining predictors of depression at Time 1 and Time 3. Changes in predictor and outcome variables from Time 1 to Time 3 are described next, followed by a series of analyses contrasting three distinct subgroups of caregivers: (a) those that became considerably more depressed over time, (b) those that changed little, and (c) those that became considerably less depressed. A final set of qualitative analyses identifies some possible benefits of caregiving and their correlates.

Attrition from Time 1 to Time 3

Twenty-four caregivers (14%) were lost to attrition, leaving $N = 148$. The attrition group included 16 caregivers who could not be located or who refused to participate at Time 3 without giving a reason. Six others refused to continue in the study because their patient had died ($n = 4$) or had been placed in an institution ($n = 2$). One caregiver had died and another had become terminally ill. Of the 24, 15 (62.5%) were female— 9 daughters, 4 wives, 1 niece, and 1 granddaughter. Of the 9 men lost to attrition, 3 were sons, 5 were husbands, and 1 was a grandson. An additional 26 participants (21 females and 5 males) continued in the study even though they were no longer acting as caregivers at Time 3, either because their patient was deceased ($n = 19$) or institutionalized ($n = 7$). The majority (76.9%) of these were children of the patient (11 daughters, 4 sons) or other relatives (4 daughters-in-law, 1 sister) rather than spouses (5 wives, 1 husband).

One-way ANOVAs (Ss lost to attrition versus Ss no longer acting as caregivers versus continuing caregivers) revealed no significant differences between groups in patient status at Time 1 (on MMS, ADL, IADL, and frequency of disturbing behaviors), all $Fs < 2.90$, ns. Caregivers in the three groups did not differ from each other in age, income, indicators of social support, prior relationship quality, number of people in the household, or number of people who helped care for the patient; all $Fs < 1.85$, ns. Not surprisingly, given this overall lack of differences in predictor variables, the groups also did not differ in symptoms of depression at Time 1. Moreover, caregivers whose patients had either died or been placed in an institution were neither more nor less depressed at Time 3 than those who continued in the caregiving role. Thus we concluded that the 122 individuals who continued to provide care at Time 3 were representative of the original sample and did not differ systematically from those lost to attrition or those whose patients had died or been placed in a nursing home. Unless otherwise noted, the 26 individuals who were no longer caregivers at Time 3 are not included in the analyses reported below.

Descriptive Analysis of Patients and Caregivers

Patients

Patients were predominantly female (70%). Their average age was 76 years (range = 56 to 98). The mean MMS score for this sample was 19.9 (out of 30), indicating moderate levels of cognitive impairment at intake. A typical patient required some assistance with 9 of 18 ADL and IADL items.

Caregivers

Means describing the total caregiver sample at intake ($N = 172$) are presented in Table 6.1. The mean caregiver age was 58 years, and most were female. About one third of the women were spouses of the patients, and slightly more than half were daughters. Male caregivers were somewhat older than females and were more likely to be spouses than adult children of the patients. This sample is similar in age, gender, and type of relationship to national estimates of caregivers of demented

Table 6.1
Caregiver Characteristics by Gender at Time 1

Characteristic	Male (n = 51) (29.0%)	Female (n = 121) (71.0%)	Total sample (N = 172)
Age	62.7	55.7	57.8
Modal income	$20-25K	$20-25K	$20-25K
Kinship: spouse	58.8%	33.1%	40.7%
child	37.2%	56.2%	50.6%
other	4.0%	10.7%	8.7%
Number in household	1.4	2.1	1.9
CES-D	8.7	14.6	12.8
Objective health[a]	2.5	2.5	2.5
Subjective health[a]	2.2	2.6	2.5
ADL assistance frequency	4.3	4.9	4.7
IADL assistance frequency	24.3	23.3	23.6
Problem behavior frequency	59.1	62.0	61.1
Number of people who help with patient care	0.9	0.9	0.9
Satisfaction with social contacts	10.4	9.6	9.8
Perceived social support	4.9	4.8	4.8
Negative social support	3.6	3.4	3.5
Prior relationship quality[b]	21.8	25.6	24.5

a. Higher scores = poorer health.
b. Higher scores = less close.

elderly. The modal yearly household income for both males and females was between $20,000 and $25,000.

Mean levels of depression for both male and female caregivers were substantially higher than population means for similarly aged individuals (Berkman et al., 1986). Women reported significantly more depressive symptoms than men, $F(1,167) = 13.89, p < .0001$. In fact, the mean level of depression for women (14.6) was very close to the cutoff score (16) for being at risk for clinical depression. Overall, at Time 1, 39% of the women and 16% of the men qualified as being at risk for clinical depression.

Men and women caregivers reported providing equal amounts of ADL and IADL assistance and identified about equal numbers of problem behaviors in their patients. There were no gender differences at Time 1 in self-reported measures of caregiver health status (either objective or subjective). Nor did males and females differ in

Table 6.2
Correlates of Depression at Time 1 and Time 3
(Total Sample)

Variable	Time 1	Time 3
Gender (1 = female; 2 = male)	−.27**	−.17*
Age	−.10	.01
Income	−.09	−.16*
Income adequacy (higher values = less adequate)	.21**	.18**
Number of people in household	−.03	−.03
Objective health (higher scores = poorer health)	.13	.08
Subjective health (higher scores = poorer health)	.33**	.30**
ADL assistance provided	.12	.13
IADL assistance provided	.09	.17*
Problem behaviors	.21**	.27**
Number of people helping with care	.01	−.17*
Satisfaction with social contacts	−.36**	−.45**
Perceived social support (higher scores = less support)	.11	.31**
Negative social support (higher scores = more negative support)	.05	.26**
Prior relationship quality	.01	.07

*$p < .05$; ** $p < .01$.

the number of people who helped care for the patient, their satisfaction with social contacts, perceptions of social support available, or reports of negative social support. However, women rated their relationship with the patient prior to the illness onset less favorably than did men, $F(1, 168) = 7.25, p < .007$. Women also reported having more people living in their household than did men, $F(1, 170) = 6.27$, $p < .01$.

Correlates of Depression at Time 1 and Time 3

First, zero-order correlations were calculated between predictor variables and depression for the total sample at Time 1 and for those continuing as caregivers at Time 3. The results are shown in Table 6.2. At both measurement points gender, income adequacy, caregiver subjective health, patient problem behaviors, and satisfaction with social contacts were significantly related to the caregiver's level of depression. In addition, at Time 3, income, IADL assistance provided, number of people helping with patient care, perceived social support, and negative social support were significantly related to depression. The direction of all of these relationships was as expected.

Hierarchical multiple linear regression analyses were carried out to examine the combined effects of these variables on caregiver depression. Given the significant gender effects found in earlier analyses, separate regressions were done for males and females. First, three sociodemographic variables (caregiver age, income adequacy, and number of people in household) were entered. Next, patient status variables (ADL and IADL assistance, and frequency of problem behaviors) were entered. Finally, conditioning variables were entered (number of people helping with patient care, prior relationship quality, satisfaction with social contacts, perceived social support, and negative social support). Self-rated health was not included in these analyses because such measures are often confounded with depression. Household income was also excluded because 5% of the participants either refused or were unable to give this information.

For males, 65% of the variance in depression was explained at Time 1. Variables accounting for the majority of explained variance were income adequacy (22%), number of people in household (6%), amount of IADL assistance provided (10%), satisfaction with social contacts (6%), quality of prior relationship (6%), and number of problem behaviors (6%). Age, ADL, number of helpers, perceived social support, and negative social support were not statistically significant. In sum, men were more likely to be depressed if they (a) perceived their incomes to be less adequate, (b) had fewer people in their household, (c) encountered more problem behaviors and provided more instrumental support to the patient, (d) were less satisfied with their social contacts, and (e) rated their prior relationship with the patient more negatively. The pattern of results for males was essentially identical at Time 3, although the significance levels were lower because of the smaller sample size.

For females at Time 1, only two variables, satisfaction with social contacts and perceived social support, were significantly related to depression (each accounting for 7% of the variance) in the regression analysis. Moreover, all 11 variables combined explained only 24% of the variance in depression. Similar results were obtained at Time 3.

Table 6.3
Changes in Predictor and Outcome Variables by Gender

	Males		Females	
Variable	*Time 1*	*Time 3*	*Time 1*	*Time 3*
Depression	8.35	9.54	14.10	12.41
Income category	5.58	5.67	5.50	5.38
Income adequacy	3.03	3.26	3.20	3.30
Number in household	1.39	1.37	2.07	1.74**
ADL assistance provided	4.45	7.39**	4.29	5.57*
IADL assistance provided	24.11	26.84	22.09	23.42
Problem behaviors	56.33	66.47**	59.76	66.38**
Number helping with care	0.71	0.71	0.94	0.73
Satisfaction with social contacts	10.47	10.24	9.81	10.29
Perceived social support	4.89	5.84*	4.88	4.81
Negative social support	3.11	2.82	3.66	3.07
Objective health	2.32	2.32	2.26	2.64*
Subjective health	2.16	2.35	2.57	2.68

*Time 1 to Time 3 change significant at $p < .05$.
**Time 1 to Time 3 change significant at $p < .01$.

Changes in Predictor and Outcome Variables, Time 1 to Time 3

For individuals continuing in the caregiving role at Time 3, repeated-measures ANOVAs were calculated for males and females separately. As shown in Table 6.3, both males and females reported significant increases in the amount of ADL assistance provided ($Fs = 6.86, p < .01$, and $3.95, p < .04$, respectively) and in the number of problem behaviors exhibited by patients ($Fs = 12.72, p < .001$, and $8.61, p < .004$, respectively). Males also reported a decrease in the amount of perceived social support, $F(1, 37) = 4.42, p < .04$. Women reported a significant decrease in the number of people living in their household, $F(1, 90) = 11.29, p < .001$. Women also reported a significant decline in objective health, $F(1, 91) = 5.17, p < .03$.

Although mean levels of depression did not change reliably from Time 1 to Time 3, it is possible that significant changes occurred at the individual level. In order to investigate correlates of change, we calculated a difference score by subtracting Time 1 depression scores from Time 3 depression scores. These derived values were then regressed onto change scores for income adequacy, number of people in household, ADL, IADL, problem behaviors, number of people helping with patient care, satisfaction with social contacts, perceived social support, negative social support, objective health, and subjective health. For females, all change variables together accounted for 29% of the change in depression variance with the most important contributions being made by changes in number of people in household (7%), IADL (4%), problem behaviors (10%), and satisfaction with social contacts (4%). Women who experienced increases in depression reported increases in IADL provided and in patient problem behaviors, decreases in number of people living in their household, and decreases in satisfaction with social contacts. Of course, a complementary interpretation of these relationships can be made as well. That is, a reduction in IADL and problem behaviors, increased number of people in the household, and greater satisfaction with social contacts were associated with improved emotional state. For males, a similar pattern of results was observed, but it was statistically nonsignificant (perhaps as a result of the small sample size of this group, $n = 34$).

Becoming More or Less Depressed Over Time

A third approach to the analysis of change over time was more qualitative in nature. All participants (including those who were no longer acting as caregivers) for whom data were available at Time 1 and Time 3 ($N = 145$) were divided into three groups: (a) Individuals who improved by more than one standard deviation were classified as the *positive change group* (mean change = −16.0); (b) individuals who became more depressed by at least one standard deviation were classified as the *negative change group* (mean change = 12.0); and (c) individuals who met neither of these criteria were classified as the *little change group* (mean change = 0.3). The rationale for this particular classification system was to identify individuals who exhibited clinically significant changes and then attempt to identify why they changed. Although dividing the total sample into equal thirds would have improved the statistical power, it would have diluted the meaningfulness of the changes examined.

Characteristics of the three groups are summarized in Table 6.4. It should be noted that the level of depression at Time 1 for the positive

Table 6.4
Level of Depression, Gender, Kinship, and Patient Status by Depression Change (Time 1 to Time 3) Groups

Variable	Positive change (n = 21)	Little change (n = 107)	Negative change (n = 17)
Depression			
Time 1*	25.38	10.15	11.12
Time 3*	9.43	10.43	23.24
Females (%)**	86	69	71
Kinship (%)			
Daughters	48	40	24
Wives	19	23	41
Husbands	10	18	18
Sons	5	12	12
Other	19	6	6
Patient status at Time 3 (%)			
In community	76	72	71
Institutionalized	14	13	18
Deceased	10	15	12

$*p < .001; **p < .06.$

change (less depressed) group was significantly higher than either of the other two groups, $F(2, 142) = 34.13$, $p < .0001$. At Time 3, the negative change (more depressed) group was significantly more depressed than either of the other two groups, $F(2, 146) = 21.79$, $p < .0001$. Given the classification system used, these differences in depression levels might be expected.

However, other differences emerged as well. The positive change group had a higher proportion of females ($z = 1.88$, $p < .06$) than the little change group. Although not statistically significant, it appears that daughters were likely to become less depressed and wives were likely to become more depressed. Interestingly, neither death nor institutionalization of the patient appeared to have a significant impact on care-giver depression.

We also examined Time 1 correlates of changes in depression within groups. A conservative significance criterion of $p < .01$ was adopted to control for Type I error. Results are shown in Table 6.5. In the positive change (less depressed) group, the magnitude of decrease in depression was related to more people living in caregivers' homes at Time 1 and

Table 6.5
Correlates of Time 1 Measures with Time 1 to Time 3
Change in Depression by Depression Change Groups

Variable	Positive change (n = 21)	Little change (n = 107)	Negative change (n = 17)
Patient variables			
MMS	.30	−.11	.08
Problem behavior	−.40	−.10	.38
ADL assistance	−.09	−.11	.09
IADL assistance	−.02	−.07	.22
Caregiver variables			
Gender	.06	.16	.10
Age	−.09	.01	.06
Household income	−.18	−.01	.02
Income adequacy (higher values = less adequate)	.01	−.07	.72*
Objective health	−.16	−.10	.24
Subjective health	.10	−.16	.13
Number of people who help care for patient	−.52*	−.01	−.05
Number of people living in caregiver's home	−.61*	−.09	.16
Satisfaction with social contacts	−.16	−.04	−.24
Perceived social support	.30	.03	.15
Negative social support	.20	−.11	.61*
Prior relationship quality	.04	.10	−.35

*$p < .01$.

more people who helped in caring for the patient at Time 1. Within the negative change (more depressed) group, the change in depression was significantly related to negative social support and (lack of) income adequacy.

Positive Aspects of Caregiving

In an open-ended question, all caregivers were asked whether the patient's illness had any purpose or positive meaning. Approximately 47% and 42% of study participants responded affirmatively to this question at Time 1 and Time 3, respectively, with 51% of the women and 38% of the men indicating they found purpose or positive meaning at Time 1. Responses were content analyzed and categorized into eight thematic categories.

Most commonly, caregivers indicated feeling good about themselves because of the patience, compassion, courage, and strength the illness brought out in them (31%). The second most common type of response involved feeling appreciated (15%). This was followed by increased closeness to the patient (14%), increased awareness of one's own health (13%), and increased closeness to family and friends (12%). Change in personal values (7%), increased knowledge (5%), and spiritual meaning or growth (2%) were mentioned less frequently.

Attempts to link types of positive meaning responses to levels of depression or changes in depression yielded no systematic effects. The only suggestive finding in these data was that persons who became much more depressed over time appeared to be more likely to attribute positive meaning to the illness at both measurement points (50% at Time 1 and 57% at Time 3) than individuals who became less depressed (39% at Time 1 and 33% at Time 3) or those who showed no change in depression (47% at Time 1 and 39% at Time 3).

Discussion

The major findings of this study can be briefly summarized as follows. Caregivers were predominantly females who were mostly middle-aged daughters or wives of the patients. These women were substantially more depressed than the men in our sample. Although such gender differences in depressive symptoms are also found in non-caregiving populations, the magnitude of differences found in this study was greater than general population gender differences (Williamson & Schulz, in press).

For the total group of caregivers, the level of depression was related in the expected direction to (a) patient variables (amount of instrumental assistance provided and frequency of problem behaviors exhibited by the patient) and (b) social network variables (number of people in the household, perceived social support, satisfaction with social contacts, and negative social support). These data are consistent with findings reported in other caregiving studies showing that the worse the patient's condition and the lower the support received from others, the higher the level of caregiver depression.

The patient's condition declined over the 18-month period encompassed by these data. As expected, given the nature of AD, patients became less able to care for themselves, more cognitively impaired, and exhibited more problem behaviors. However, even though patient functioning declined significantly, mean levels of caregiver depression did not increase significantly. Correlates of change in depression were similar to cross-sectional correlates of depression. Specifically, increases in patient problem behaviors, decreases in social support, and decreases in satisfaction with social contacts were associated with increases in caregiver depression.

Focusing on persons who exhibited extreme changes in depression over time, three groups emerged. One was made up largely of daughters and other female kin (not wives) who became depressed relatively early in the caregiving process but improved substantially over the 18-month period. These individuals were unique in that they had competing family role responsibilities and received higher levels of support from others in their household for caregiving tasks. The suggestive picture that emerges from these data is that these individuals took on the caregiving role even though they had other primary responsibilities, became overwhelmed relatively early by the multiple demands placed on them, monitored and recognized their decreased capacity to function, and obtained help from other family members in caring for the disabled patient.

The second group became more depressed over time and consisted primarily of patients' wives whose primary role responsibility was the welfare of the spouse. We can speculate that, because their energies were focused on one as opposed to multiple primary commitments and because of greater attachment to the patient, their tolerance for caregiving was higher and they became depressed later in the caregiving process. At Time 3, these individuals reached depression levels similar to those of the previous group at Time 1.

The third and largest group exhibited little change in depression over 18 months. These individuals were similar in this respect to other caregiving populations in the postacute phase of the illness. To the extent that depressive symptomatology is an indicator of adjustment to the caregiving role, they adapted relatively well.

Alzheimer's Coping and Stress-Coping Models

It is both a strength and a weakness of existing stress-coping models that all the findings described above can reasonably be accounted for by such models. The models' generality and flexibility encompass almost any empirical data. However, precisely because of this inclusiveness, they provide little guidance about specific variables likely to be important at specific points in time. For example, these models tell us little about differences between short-term versus long-term adjustment to stress.

Finally, one can raise questions about the adequacy of a model whose relevant variables account for only a small proportion of outcome variance (as was the case for women caregivers in our study). A possible response would be to focus on inadequacies of the research effort, but it is also possible that the model fails to incorporate important relevant variables. In sum, stress-coping models clearly provide a starting point for research efforts such as these, but they are limited in their ability to make sense of complex longitudinal data.

Temporal Response Models

An alternative to the stress-coping approach is to focus on changing responses of caregivers over time. Researchers have identified three different models that may characterize the temporal impact of patient decline on caregivers (Haley & Pardo, 1989; Townsend, Noelker, Deimling, & Bass, 1989). The *wear-and-tear* hypothesis states that both dementia patients and their caregivers experience progressive deterioration in functioning as the patient declines. An opposing perspective, the *adaptation* hypothesis, claims that caregivers either stabilize or improve over time. According to this view, the demands of caregiving may provide opportunities for psychological growth. A third alternative, the *trait* hypothesis, maintains that level of caregiver functioning remains relatively stable over time, despite patient decline, because of preexisting coping skills and resources.

The wear-and-tear and adaptation hypotheses were recently tested in a study of adult children caregivers of impaired elderly parents (Townsend et al., 1989). Caregiver mental health was assessed twice, with 14 months between assessment points. Although there was considerable individual variability in psychological adaptation over time, improvement was more common than deterioration at both the individual and aggregate level. Thus these data tend to support an adaptation model.

Our own data also appear to be consistent with such a model. At the aggregate level, there was little change in depression for men and women at the three measurement points examined. Indeed, women exhibited a significant decline in depression from Time 2 to Time 3, although it should be noted that their mean level of depression was still considerably higher than age-based gender norms.

At the individual level, caregivers exhibited oscillating patterns of depressive symptomatology over time. Cycles of increasing depression were followed by cycles of decreasing depression, suggesting that caregivers utilized whatever resources were available to deal with the changing problems confronting them. The stability of this pattern, its clinical significance, and its underlying causes are important questions to pursue in future research.

Practical Implications

Data such as those reported in this chapter provide information that can be used to identify individuals who are potentially vulnerable to experiencing adverse effects as a result of caring for a family member with AD. Taken together, these findings suggest that caregivers who evidence initial symptoms of depression and do not have resources to draw on (e.g., social support, sufficient income to purchase help with caregiving tasks) may be especially vulnerable. This observation makes salient the value of low-cost, readily available respite care services and points out caregivers for whom such services may be particularly important.

However, a variety of additional factors may influence caregiver adaptation. In our own work, analyses focused on other portions of this data set have revealed that symptoms of depression were also related to the strategies caregivers employed in coping with specific situations (Williamson & Schulz, 1990a). For example, among those who found dealing with the patient's memory deficits difficult, participating in relaxing activities and accepting that nothing could be done to solve the problem were related to less depression. Such strategies as wishing the problem would go away, trying to see it in a different light, and keeping feelings to oneself were associated with increased symptoms of depression. These results suggest that, particularly when the patient is severely cognitively impaired, interventions aimed at helping caregivers accept the reality of the situation may be useful, as may services that allow caregivers time and resources for relaxation.

In addition to the large number of variables that appear to influence caregiver outcomes, we have recently reported some evidence indicating that variables may interact in complex ways (Williamson & Schulz, in press). Specifically, we found that "communal orientation" (a dispositional tendency to give and receive help in interpersonal relationships) interacted with caregiver gender and closeness of the relationship that existed between caregiver and patient prior to the AD onset. Individuals high in communal orientation were less depressed than those low in communal orientation, and those who felt close to the patient prior to illness experienced fewer feelings of caregiving burden. Examining men and women separately, however, revealed two groups whose mean CES-D scores were high enough to put them at risk for clinical depression: (a) men low in communal orientation who had not been close to the patient, and (b) women low in communal orientation who indicated having had a close relationship with the patient.

As with the data reported in this chapter, these results may help in identifying specific groups of individuals likely to experience high levels of depressive symptomatology as a result of caring for an AD patient. Moreover, there was also a suggestion in additional analyses (Williamson & Schulz, 1990b) that the caregiver's communal orientation and prior relationship closeness between the caregiver and recipient may have implications for patient outcomes as well. Specifically, caregivers reporting a close prior relationship tended to be less likely to place their patient in an institution, and patients with caregivers high in communal orientation were somewhat less likely to die over the course of our study.

We emphasize that these results are far from conclusive. However, they do suggest the intriguing possibility that variables that are easy and inexpensive to measure may turn out to be good predictors of caregiver distress and, possibly, of an individual's suitability for providing care.

References

Barnes, R. E., Raskind, M. A., Scott, R., & Murphy, C. (1981). Problems of families caring for Alzheimer patients: Use of a support group. *Journal of the American Geriatric Society, 29*, 80-85.

Berkman, L. F., Berkman, C. S., Kasl, S. V., Freeman, D. H., Leo, L., Ostfeld, A. M., Cornoni-Huntley, J., & Brody, J. A. (1986). Depressive symptoms in relation to physical health and functioning in the elderly. *American Journal of Epidemiology, 124*, 372-388.

Biegel, D. E., Sales, E., & Schulz, R. (1991). *Family caregiving in chronic illness.* Newbury Park, CA: Sage.

Center fot the Study of Aging and Human Development. (1978). *Multidimensional functional assessment, the OARS methodology: A manual* (2nd ed.). (1978). Durham, NC: Duke University.

Cohen, D., & Eisdorfer, C. (1988). Depression in family members caring for a relative with Alzheimer's disease. *Journal of the American Geriatric Society, 36*, 885-889.

Cohen, S., Mermelstein, R., Kamarck, T., & Hoberman, H. M. (1985). Measuring the functional components of social support. In I. G. Sarason & B. R. Sarason (Eds.), *Social support: Theory, research, and application* (pp. 73-94). The Hague, The Netherlands: Martinus Nijhoff.

Cohler, B., Groves, L., Borden, L., & Lazarus, L. (1989). Caring for family members with Alzheimer's disease. In E. Light & B. Lebowitz (Eds.), *Alzheimer's disease treatment and family stress: Directions for research* (pp. 50-105). Washington, DC: National Institute of Mental Health.

Evans, D. A., Funkenstein, H. H., Albert, M. S., Scherr, P. A., Cook, N. R., Chown, M. J., Hebert, L. E., Hennekens, C. H., & Taylor, J. O. (1989). Prevalence of Alzheimer's disease in a community population of older persons. *Journal of the American Medical Association, 262*, 2551-2556.

Folstein, M. F., Folstein, S., & McHugh, P. R. (1975). "Mini-Mental State": A practical method for grading the cognitive state of patients for the clinician. *Journal of Psychiatric Research, 12*, 189-198.

George, L. (1980). *Role transitions in later life.* Monterey, CA: Brooks/Cole.

George, L. K., & Gwyther, L. P. (1986). Caregiver well-being: A multidimensional examination of family caregivers of demented adults. *The Gerontologist, 26*, 253-259.

Gurland, B. J., Copeland, J., Kuriansky, J., Kelleher, M., Sharpe, L., & Dean, L. (1983). *The mind and mood of aging.* London: Croom Helm.

Haley, W. E., Levine, E. G., Brown, S. L., & Bartolucci, A. A. (1987). Stress, appraisal, coping, and social support as predictors of adaptational outcome among dementia caregivers. *Psychology and Aging, 4*, 323-330.

Haley, W. E., Levine, E. G., Brown, S. L., Berry, J. W., & Hughes, G. H. (1987). Psychological, social, and health consequences of caring for a relative with senile dementia. *Journal of the American Geriatric Society, 35*, 405-411.

Haley, W. E., & Pardo, K. M. (1989). Relationship of severity of dementia to caregiving stressors. *Psychology and Aging, 4*, 389-392.

House, J. (1974). Occupational stress and coronary heart disease: A review and theoretical integration. *Journal of Health and Social Behavior, 15*, 12-27.

Kiecolt-Glaser, J. K., Glaser, R., Shuttleworth, E. E., Dyer, C. S., Ogrocki, P., & Speicher, C. E. (1987). Chronic stress and immunity in family caregivers of Alzheimer's disease patients. *Psychosomatic Medicine, 49,* 523-535.

Mace, N. L., & Rabins, P. V. (1981). *The 36-hour day.* Baltimore, MD: Johns Hopkins University Press.

McKahn, D., Drachman, D., Folstein, M., Katzman, R., Price, D., & Standlan, E. M. (1984). Clinical diagnosis of Alzheimer's disease: Report of the NINCDS-ADRDA Work Group under the auspices of the Department of Health and Human Services Task Force on Alzheimer's Disease. *Neurology, 34,* 939-944.

Montgomery, R. J. V., Stull, D. E., & Borgatta, E. F. (1985). Measurement and the analysis of burden. *Research on Aging, 7,* 137-152.

Morycz, R. K. (1985). Caregiving strain and the desire to institutionalize family members with Alzheimer's disease. *Research on Aging, 7,* 329-361.

Pruchno, R. A., & Potashnik, S. L. (1989). Caregiving spouses: Physical and mental health in perspective. *Journal of the American Geriatric Society, 37,* 697-705.

Rabins, P. V., Mace, N. L., & Lucas, M. J. (1982). The impact of dementia on the family. *Journal of the American Medical Association, 248,* 333-335.

Radloff, L. (1977). The CES-D Scale: A self-report depression scale for research in the general population. *Applied Psychological Measurement, 1,* 385-401.

Schulz, R., Tompkins, C. A., & Rau, M. T. (1988). A longitudinal study of the psychosocial impact of stroke on primary support persons. *Psychology and Aging, 3,* 131-141.

Schulz, R., Tompkins, C. A., Wood, D., & Decker, S. (1987). The social psychology of caregiving: Physical and psychological costs of providing support to the disabled. *Journal of Applied Social Psychology, 17,* 401-428.

Schulz, R., Visintainer, P., & Williamson, G. M. (in press). Psychiatric and physical morbidity effects of caregiving. *Journals of Gerontology: Psychological Sciences.*

Skinner, H. A., Steinhauer, P. D., & Santa-Barbara, J. (1983). The Family Assessment Measure. *Canadian Journal of Community Mental Health, 2,* 91-105.

Stone, R., Cafferata, G. L., & Sangl, J. (1987). Caregivers of the frail elderly: A national profile. *Gerontologist, 27,* 616-626.

Townsend, A., Noelker, L., Deimling, G. T., & Bass, D. M. (1989). Longitudinal impact of interhousehold caregiving on adult children's mental health. *Psychology and Aging, 4,* 393-401.

Williamson, G. M., & Schulz, R. (1990a). *Coping with Alzheimer's disease caregiving: A longitudinal study.* Unpublished manuscript, University of Pittsburgh.

Williamson, G. M., & Schulz, R. (1990b). [Family caregivers of Alzheimer's patients]. Unpublished data, University of Pittsburgh.

Williamson, G. M., & Schulz, R. (in press). Relationship orientation, quality of prior relationship, and distress among caregivers of Alzheimer's patients. *Psychology and Aging.*

Zarit, S. H., Reever, K. E., & Bach-Peterson, J. (1980). Relatives of the impaired aged: Correlates of feelings of burden. *The Gerontologist, 20,* 649-655.

7

Understanding Living Kidney Donation: A Behavioral Decision-Making Perspective

EUGENE BORGIDA
CYNTHIA CONNER
LAURIE MANTEUFEL

D uring the past three decades, clinical renal transplantation has entered the medical mainstream. Improved surgical techniques, new immunosuppressive drugs, and more advanced tissue-matching capabilities have all contributed to this state of affairs (Bay & Hebert, 1987; Suranyi & Hall, 1990). It is clear that organ transplantation improves the lives of people with otherwise terminal illnesses or seriously diminished quality of life. For example, longitudinal data from the University of Minnesota Hospitals, presented in Table 7.1, show that impressive patient survival and graft survival rates

---

AUTHORS' NOTE: Research reported in this chapter was supported by the National Institutes of Health Grant No. 5PO DK13083-23 to Eugene Borgida. The authors are grateful to Brian Kojetin for his statistical consultation, and to Sonja Lengnick, Susan Zeeveld, and Brian Kojetin for their helpful comments on an earlier version of this chapter.

Table 7.1
Survival Rates (in Percentages) According to
Donor Source of all Kidney Transplants
at the University of Minnesota: 1963-1989

Category[a]	No. of cases	1 year percentage Patient[b]	1 year percentage Graft[c]	3 year percentage Patient	3 year percentage Graft	5 year percentage Patient	5 year percentage Graft
HLA identical	351	96	94	94	92	89	87
Close relatives	1106	91	81	83	73	78	65
Distant relatives	69	91	73	81	62	79	58
Living unrelated	19	75	72	75	72	75	72
Cadaver	1373	83	70	73	60	66	51
Total	2918						

NOTE: This table is adapted from Matas et al. (1989).
a. HLA (Human Leukocyte Antigen) Identical = zero HLA mismatch and mixed lymphocyte culture is nonresponsive; Close relatives = parents, siblings, and offspring; Distant relatives = grandparents, aunts, uncles, and cousins; Living unrelated = spouse and close friend; Cadaver = brain-dead donor.
b. Patient = surviving transplant recipient.
c. Graft = functioning kidney, no patient dialysis.

have been realized for living kidney donation (Elick, Sutherland, Gillingham, & Najarian, 1989). Unfortunately, each year, the number of candidates for kidney transplantation increases and the waiting lists for solid organs grow longer (Levenson & Olbrisch, 1987; Perkins, 1987). As of August, 1989, the national patient waiting list maintained by the United Network for Organ Sharing (UNOS) contained more than 18,000 names, including 15,457 people waiting for a kidney transplant.[1] Estimates suggest that between one third to one half of patients on these organ transplantation waiting lists die before a transplantable cadaveric organ can be found.[2]

The growing shortage of organs is partly the result of increasing demand attributable to the success of transplantation. Exacerbating the problem, however, is the inefficiency of the organ procurement system. Each year, for example, only a fraction of brain-dead eligible organ donors actually give their organs for transplantation. The reasons for this lack of success are unclear. The organ procurement problem, however, has directed considerable attention to donations from living persons as an alternative to cadaveric donation. "Living donation," as it is called, raises a host of interesting and relatively unexplored social psychological issues (Borgida, Simmons, Conner, & Lombard, 1990; House & Thompson, 1988; Smith et al., 1986).

This chapter focuses on a subset of these issues, particularly those that pertain to the behavioral decision making of prospective living kidney donors. Most psychological research on living kidney donation has focused on genetically related donors such as parents, siblings, children, uncles, and aunts, because in the past genetically related donation offered the best prognosis for transplantation recipients. Over the last decade, transplant centers have expressed increasing interest in the use of living donors who are genetically unrelated to the recipient but emotionally involved with the recipient (e.g., spouses, co-workers, close friends, stepparents, and in-laws). Some transplant centers, such as the one at the University of Minnesota Hospitals, have been accepting genetically unrelated living donors for kidney transplantation in addition to genetically related donors (e.g., Spital, 1989; Spital & Spital, 1987). To date, however, very few studies have systematically examined the decision making of these living donors.

The senior author's longstanding research interests in the nature of psychologically involving and consequential decisions (e.g., Borgida & Howard-Pitney, 1983; Harkness, DeBono, & Borgida, 1985; Howard-Pitney, Borgida, & Omoto, 1986; Omoto & Borgida, 1988) drew our research group to examine behavioral decision making in this domain. Our questions do not constitute standard fare for social psychological research on altruism (see Batson, 1990, for a review). Rather, the research discussed in this chapter examines several questions about the nature of kidney donor decision making. Are these altruistic decisions made effortlessly and instantaneously, as has been suggested previously (Simmons, Marine, & Simmons, 1977), or do they reflect considerable deliberation, intent, and cognitive effort? Is it the case, for example, that the living donation decision is quite different than "ordinary" decision making? If so, then are such involving and consequential decisions made with considerable deliberation? Sherman and Fazio (1983), for example, have suggested that highly consequential behaviors are more likely to prompt a deliberative and reasoned analysis than are less consequential behaviors.

As we illustrate in this chapter, theory and research in social psychology can provide a substantive foundation for carefully examining these questions. In particular, Ajzen's (1985) theory of planned behavior represents a pertinent theoretical framework for empirically examining the influence of attitudes, salient referents, and perceptions of control on the decision-making process. Such an application not only can contribute to theory development in social psychology, but ultimately should be able to generate some practical insights into the nature of kidney donation that will be useful to transplant centers.

Previous Psychological Research on Living Kidney Donation

During the past 20 years, the vast majority of kidney transplantation research has been generated by the medical community, and the available research literature not surprisingly focuses more on the medical than the psychological aspects of kidney donation (e.g., Dunn, Nylander, Richie, Johnson, MacDonnell, & Sawyers, 1986). For example, a great deal has been written regarding the survival rates of cadaver- versus living-related grafts (e.g., Kountz, Perkins, Payne, & Belzer, 1970; Matas et al., 1989; Sutherland, 1985), the use of donor-specific blood transfusion techniques (e.g., Belzer, Kalayoglu, & Sollinger, 1987; Reding et al., 1987), and the steadily rising success rates obtained as immunosuppressive drug therapy is fine-tuned (e.g., Kumar, White, Samhan, & Abouna, 1987; Wood & Lemaire, 1985). The extant psychological literature on kidney donation primarily focuses on the posttransplant psychological and emotional adjustment of the *recipient*, with fewer studies examining the living kidney *donor's* psychological adjustment or decision making (Chambers, 1982; Christensen, Holman, Turner, & Slaughter, 1989; Hirvas, Enckell, Kuhlback, & Pasternack, 1980; Muslin, 1971; Sharma & Enoch, 1987; Viederman, 1975).

The first section of this chapter briefly reviews the few psychological studies on living kidney donors, and then discusses the equally few behavioral decision making studies on living kidney donation. An overview of the relevant social psychological theory—Ajzen's (1985) theory of planned behavior—is then provided, followed by a presentation of new research examining variables that may predict an individual's intention to donate a kidney.

Early Psychological Studies

Kemph (1966) may have been the first to direct attention to the posttransplant psychological responses of the living kidney donor (cited in Abram & Buchanan, 1976-1977, p. 155). He reported on the psychiatric evaluations of seven living donors who were related to the recipients. Taking a psychodynamic perspective, Kemph observed, "Although all donors were consciously altruistic, there was considerable unconscious resentment toward the recipient" (p. 1274). He concluded that brief posttransplant psychotherapy was warranted for the living donor to address this "unconscious resentment," as well as any other short-term, negative psychological reactions.

A second account, also concerning the potential mental health risks for living related kidney donors, was published by Cramond, Court, Higgins, Knight, and Lawrence (1967). They reviewed the screening protocol used in a then-experimental transplant program in South Australia. Based on psychological and psychiatric interviews and assessments with 25 prospective living kidney donors, further recommendations for pretransplant psychological screening were made. Cramond et al. provided specific, qualitative case studies, illustrating the complexities in living related donor selection and foreshadowing some of the current ethical controversies. Although they strongly advocated the use of blood-relatives as donors, they nevertheless observed that these same blood relative family members were "the very people who will have the most ambivalent and complex attitudes toward the patient" (Cramond et al., 1967, p. 1214).

Behavioral Decision-Making Studies

Eisendrath, Guttmann, and Murray (1969) published perhaps the first study to examine the specific nature of the behavioral decision-making process of living kidney donors. Twenty-five prospective donors were interviewed by both a medical internist and a psychiatrist. Based on the qualitative pretransplant interviews, the authors concluded: "In most instances, no real decision-making problem existed for the donor" (p. 245). From a follow-up questionnaire sent to 57 willing but unselected donors, Eisendrath et al. reported that answers to such questions as "How did you decide to donate your kidney?" consistently reflected the respondents' perception that the decision was simply a matter of having been "called" and that no conscious or deliberative decision-making process was involved (p. 245). However, both the small sample size and the qualitative nature of the data limit the generalizability of the reported findings.

Fellner (1976-1977) conducted an investigation that directly examined the donation decision-making processes of prospective living kidney donors. Both posttransplant interviews and questionnaire data led the author to conclude that the decision making of donors (and nondonors) was "unconflicted, voluntary, immediate and/or instantaneous" (p. 141), and that both groups reported positive psychological benefits. In addition, Fellner also reported from a follow-up study that the immediate, positive psychological benefits to the donors were sustained across time. The exceptions were cases of unsuccessful transplants. Although Fellner's analysis was one of the first to examine the decision dynamics associated with living kidney donation, it should be noted that the samples were drawn from different sources and were merged together over the years. Therefore, although this procedure resulted in a large sample, the data were not based on a scientifically representative sample of donors.

The first systematic empirical research on living genetically related kidney donors was conducted by Simmons et al. (1977). The psychological reactions of both living related donors and nondonors were examined and three different decision-making models were proposed and assessed. The first was a moral, or *instantaneous*, decision-making model, which assumes no deliberation or weighing of costs and benefits that would be associated with donation; the donor immediately and spontaneously volunteers to donate. The second was a rational model of *deliberation*, in which the potential donor examines the action, evaluates it, and seeks relevant information in order to make a donation decision. The third model was a *postponement* or stepwise model. In this approach, individuals consciously avoid making a decision and instead engage in a series of small predecision steps; only later do they find themselves inextricably locked into the donation process.

Simmons et al.'s decision-making data were based on four questionnaire items for posttransplant donors and qualitative interviews with prospective donors at the blood-testing stage. Based on the four questionnaire items, Simmons et al. reported that the great majority of these donors (88%) said they first considered donation as soon as they found out about the need for a kidney. Over three fourths claimed they knew right away that they would definitely donate if given the opportunity. In addition, 73% perceived their donation decision as not at all hard (e.g., "Spontaneous—it was no decision"). In other words, a voluntary, spontaneous, and immediate or "snap" decision with little or no deliberation was reported by almost three fourths of these donors.

Interestingly, Simmons et al. suggest that the term *decision* is a misnomer in this specific behavioral domain because of the immediacy with which the donors said they "knew" they would definitely donate. This characterization was bolstered by interviewing other involved family members. These family member interviews were coded by two independent raters in terms of the three decision models, and interrater reliability was very high (agreement was reached in 107 of 113 cases). Simmons et al. found that donor decision making was consistent with the instantaneous model in 62% of the cases, whereas 25% of the donors seemed to fit the deliberative model and 5% were classified into the postponement category. The remaining 8% were uncodable as a result of either unreliability or lack of required information.

Although Simmons et al. argued that the same finding for both the actual donors and for blood-tested relatives lends greater support to their conclusions about instantaneous decision making, several methodological questions arise. The data were gathered posttransplant for one subsample and at the blood-testing stage for the other subsample; thus the combined sample tapped two very different points along the donation decision-making path. Moreover, the perceptions of donors may have been somewhat biased because of their posttransplant status. In other words, their self-reported "snap" decisions may reflect socially desirable postdecision rationalizations. On the other hand, in light of the apparent immediacy of the decision making, it is possible that the two subsamples were more alike than different, and that the data were not affected by response bias. In fact, Simmons et al. (1977) report that by the blood-testing stage, 57% of these individuals had "already definitely decided to donate and had informed the family of this fact" (p. 247).

Sadler, Davison, Carroll, and Kountz (1971) published a study on the behavioral decision making of living *unrelated* donors. Their study was both prospective and retrospective. The prospective donors ($n = 8$) were administered a battery of psychodynamic and psychometric tests and were interviewed for a minimum of 10 hours. Members of the retrospective group ($n = 10$) were administered the MMPI and interviewed for no less than 3 hours. As in previous studies, Sadler et al. (1971) reported that on the basis of their data the most "universal" finding was that the donation decision was immediate (p. 88). Specifically, 15 of the 18 donors claimed they made their decision within 12 hours of hearing of the need for a kidney.

This view of the donor decision-making process as voluntary, spontaneous, and instantaneous has subsequently been corroborated by other studies. Steinberg, Levy, and Radvila (1981) examined kidney rejection in the recipient as a function of various psychological factors. The study's sample included 26 kidney transplant donors and recipients at New York's Downstate Medical Center; qualitative interviews were conducted with 25 living related donors and 1 unrelated donor. Consistent with the Simmons et al. (1977) findings, the investigators reported that all but three donors "spontaneously volunteered." "Unconscious guilt" was suggested as the explanation for this generosity on the part of these 23 donors (Steinberg et al., 1981, p. 190). Unfortunately, no interview protocol or coding scheme was reported in order to gain a more complete understanding of the nature of spontaneous volunteering.

A second study supporting the "snap" behavioral decision making of donors was conducted by Higgerson and Bulechek (1982). This study both explored the broad psychosocial dimensions of kidney donation and specifically investigated donor decision making, using the three models described by Simmons et al. (1977). Higgerson and Bulechek interviewed 27 living related donors using a semistructured interview protocol (also based on Simmons et al.). They concluded that 22 of the 27 donors (81%) "knew right away that they would donate" and therefore made instantaneous decisions, whereas 5 of the donors were classified as using the deliberation model and none were classified as having used the postponement model.

Consistent with prior work, a third study conducted by Smith et al. (1986) found that 70% of the kidney donors studied "volunteered to donate without having been solicited" (p. 225). This large multicenter study examined various dimensions of living related kidney donation and was based on questionnaire data obtained from 536 related donors. The study was designed to examine a broad range of donation-related issues. The key finding from this study for our purposes involved decision making and the donor-recipient relationship: The closer the donor-recipient relationship, the more likely that the potential donor engaged in spontaneous decision making.

Based on their phenomenological investigation, Fellner and Marshall (1970, 1981; Marshall & Fellner, 1976-1977) proposed that the living kidney donor's decision-making process involves three systems: medical selection, donor self-selection, and the family system of selection. Fellner and Marshall pointed out that although the medical selection process assumes that the donor's decision is not made until the potential donor has passed a series of medical tests (e.g., blood testing, histocompatibility testing, and a physical work-up assessing general physical health and renal functioning), many donors reported that they "immediately" and "instantaneously" decided to donate when donation was first broached with them—*prior* to medical selection. Based on their donor interviews, Fellner and Marshall (1981) observed that "the immediacy of the decision making with regard to donorship often contrasts markedly with the usual way in which the person makes other important decisions" (p. 354). They further questioned donors about this tendency and were unequivocally told that the living donation decision was a "rather special situation and could not be compared to ordinary decision making" (p. 354).

The third and final system conceptualized by Fellner and Marshall is the family system of donor selection. They suggested that a complex, idiosyncratic family selection process occurs before the family ever identifies potential, individual donors to the medical system for evaluation. Although this multisystem approach to the living donor decision process illustrates the complexities involved in becoming a kidney donor, the approach has only generated descriptive and retrospective insights into the behavioral decision making of living donors. The next section of the chapter discusses the theory-guided approach that we have used to generate empirical insights into the behavioral decision process of living kidney donors.

Applying the Theory of Planned Behavior
to Kidney Donation

The theory of planned behavior and its predecessor, the theory of reasoned action, are particularly appropriate for enriching our understanding of decision making in the behavioral domain of kidney donation. This section of the chapter explains how this theoretical orientation enables us to examine the extent to which the behavioral decision-making process is more or less deliberative, and to determine empirically the role of normative and attitudinal factors. The theory of reasoned action (Ajzen & Fishbein, 1980; Fishbein & Ajzen, 1975) has been successfully applied to the prediction of intention and behavior in such diverse areas as students' class attendance, problem drinking, weight loss (Schifter & Ajzen, 1985), voting behavior, and blood donation (see Ajzen, 1988, 1989, for reviews). According to the theory of reasoned action, the best predictor of a specific behavior is the *intention* to perform that behavior (e.g., Bagozzi & Yi, 1989; Granberg & Holmberg, 1990). The stronger a person's intention and behavioral motivation toward enacting a specific behavior, the greater the likelihood that the behavior actually will be performed (Ajzen & Madden, 1986; Sheppard, Hartwick, & Warshaw, 1988).

The theory of reasoned action specifies that an individual's intention to perform a behavior is predicted by two independent components (Burnkrant & Page, 1988; Miller & Grush, 1986). One of the determinants of intention is *attitude toward the behavior*, which refers to an individual's favorable or unfavorable evaluation of the specific act or behavior. Attitude toward the behavior in turn reflects the set of salient *behavioral beliefs* about the likely consequences of the behavior involved. These beliefs, weighted by the person's evaluation of each consequence, are expected to be strongly related to an evaluative measure of attitude toward the behavior.

The other predictor of intention is the normative component, *subjective norm*, defined as the perceived social pressure an individual feels to perform or not to perform the behavior. *Normative beliefs* are the underlying determinants of the subjective norm measure. These are beliefs about what various important reference groups or individuals want the person to do. Normative beliefs, weighted by the motivation to comply with the given group or individual, are expected to be strongly related to the overall subjective norm measure. Thus a person's attitude toward the behavior and subjective norm are the two key determinants of his or her behavioral intention, with intention being the primary determinant of actual behavior (see Figure 7.1). According to the theory of reasoned action, any other external variables, such as personality variables, affect toward more general attitude objects, or

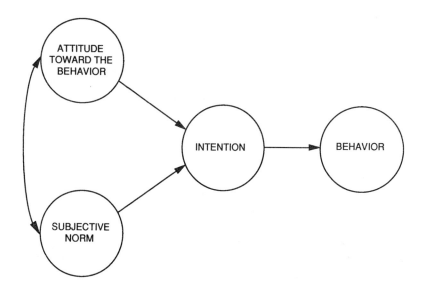

Figure 7.1. Theory of Reasoned Action

demographics, are assumed to have only indirect effects on behavior (acting through the attitude or subjective norm components).

Various assumptions must be met for the theory of reasoned action to predict behavior adequately. First, all components of the model must be measured at the same level of specificity. Second, the predicted relationship between behavioral intention and behavior presumes that there is a minimal time interval between the measurement of behavioral intention and the measurement of behavior. As the time interval increases, the stability of behavioral intention as a predictor of behavior is assumed to diminish and the predictive role of other components of the model, like attitude, increases (Bentler & Speckart, 1979; Harrison, Thompson, & Rodgers, 1985). A third assumption specifies that the behavior must be under the person's volitional control.

However, many factors, both internal and external to the individual, can reduce a person's perception of control over the intended behavior. If the performance of the behavior is contingent on the availability of certain personal resources or opportunities, performance then involves some degree of uncertainty. The theory of reasoned action does not appear to generalize to those situations where this assumption is violated and where there is *variation* in volitional control. Behaviors that have addictive, habitual properties or behaviors that entail considerable affect, for example, tend to be behaviors for which there is variation in volitional control (Bentler & Speckart, 1979; Manstead, Proffitt, & Smart, 1983; Schlegel, d'Avernas, Zanna, & Manske, 1989).

The *theory of planned behavior*, proposed by Ajzen (1988) as an extension of the theory of reasoned action, provides a predictive framework for a broader class of behaviors, including behaviors that involve greater variability in volitional control. This more generalized model includes three components. As in the theory of reasoned action, there are the attitudinal and normative components. The third predictive component, which is unique to the theory of planned behavior, is *perceived behavioral control*. This component represents an estimate of the perceived ease or difficulty of performing the specific behavior, based on a person's past experiences and anticipated obstacles. Self-efficacy beliefs about the presence or absence of necessary resources and opportunities (indirect perceived behavioral control) are assumed to determine direct perceived behavioral control.

By including an estimate of the individual's perceived control over the specific behavior, the theory of planned behavior allows for improved predictions of intentions and behavior (e.g., McCaul, O'Neill, & Glasgow, 1988; see also Fishbein & Stasson, 1990). Figure 7.2 illustrates the two versions of Ajzen's theory of planned behavior. The first version includes a solid line indicating an association between perceived behavioral control and intention, which is not mediated by attitude or subjective norm. The second version of the theory of planned behavior includes the dotted line, representing the possibility of a direct predictive link between perceived behavioral control and behavior. Thus perceived behavioral control may influence and predict behavior indirectly through intentions, or it may be a direct predictor of behavior. The direct link between perceived control and behavior, however, is expected only if individuals have *actual* control over the target behavior.

In studying living unrelated and related kidney donors, we have applied the theory of planned behavior to examine and predict donation intentions and behavior. Because kidney donation is a behavioral domain in which there is variation in volitional control (i.e., various factors beyond a person's control can affect the likelihood of donation), we expected that the inclusion of a measure of perceived behavioral

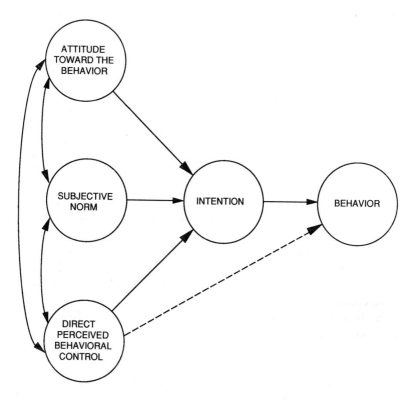

Figure 7.2. Theory of Planned Behavior

control would increase the theory's predictive power. A second and equally important consideration when applying the planned behavior model to kidney donation concerns the nature of the choice behavior involved. Behavioral choice in this context is characterized by how consequential the action is for another person, for one's self, *and* for one's relationship with that other person. Thus, although some other behaviors studied from this theoretical perspective have been personally involving and consequential, a characteristic that distinguishes kidney donation is the extent to which the donor-recipient relationship is embedded within a prospective donor's behavioral motivation to enact the particular behavior. The evaluative strength of behavioral intention, in other words, is bolstered by the commitment and attachment to another person who is in need of (perhaps immediate) assistance. Bagozzi and Yi (1989), for example, have suggested that behavioral intentions based on this kind of commitment should be well formed and, therefore, should be more likely to mediate the effects of attitudes on behavior. Others have suggested that behavioral intention will be a more stable predictor of behavior, even over longer time intervals, if intention is based on self-identity (Granberg & Holmberg, 1990) or a salient role identity (Charng, Piliavin, & Callero, 1988). Kidney donation therefore represents a behavioral choice domain wherein behavioral intention should play an important predictive and explanatory role, and it would be expected to do so even if the time interval assumption of the theory is strained or violated.

To summarize, in our research on kidney donor decision making, we expected that perceived behavioral control would add to the predictive and explanatory power of the theory of planned behavior, thus providing further empirical support for the model's generalizability. By implication, we viewed the theory of reasoned action as a less satisfactory theoretical framework for understanding and predicting kidney donor decision making. A second focus of our research is on the stability of behavioral intention and behavioral motivation as a predictor of actual behavior. In the behavioral choice context of kidney donation, we expected that behavioral intention would reflect the strength of the donor-recipient relationship and therefore would be a stable and strong predictor of the donation decision over time. An overview of our methodological approach and findings is presented next.

Methodological Approach

Table 7.2 profiles the demographic characteristics of our sample of genetically related and emotionally related potential donors from throughout the United States who contacted the University of Minnesota Transplant Center and expressed at least minimal interest (i.e., an inquiry for further information) in donating a kidney to a family member, spouse, or friend. This sample included individuals who decided not to donate, those who were motivated to donate but who were ruled out for a variety of reasons beyond their control, and those who subsequently decided to donate a kidney. It may be seen in Table 7.2 that our donor sample was rather heterogeneous with regard to a number of

Table 7.2
Profile of Living Donor Project Sample (*N* = 201)

Variable	*n*	%
Age:		
Mean = 40 years		
Range = 16 to 72		
Gender		
Female	113	56
Male	88	44
Race		
White	193	96
American Indian	5	3
Black	3	2
Asian	0	0
Marital status		
Married	140	70
Never married	30	15
Divorced	21	10
Separated	4	2
Long-term, unmarried	5	2
Widowed	1	1
Family income		
Less than $15,000	39	20
$15,000-$25,000	42	22
$25,000-$40,000	55	28
Greater than $40,000	51	26
Religion		
Protestant	89	45
Catholic	64	32
Other	18	9
Jewish	4	2
No preference	24	12
Donor status		
Related	147	73
Unrelated	54	27
Education		
Less than high school	15	8
High school graduate	55	27
Some college	43	21
College graduate	35	17
Postgraduate degree	18	9
Region of country		
Minnesota	85	42
Other	116	58

NOTE: Deviations from *N* = 201 represent missing data.

background variables (age, gender, race, marital status, income, religion, and education). Moreover, almost three fourths of the donors in the sample were genetically related donors, and well over half of all donors lived outside of Minnesota.

An extensive research questionnaire was sent to all potential and prospective donors immediately after they expressed their interest in the possibility of donation. Over a 13-month period ending in March 1990, the response rate for prospective related donors was 75% ($n = 146$), and for unrelated donors it was 68% ($n = 55$). Each component of the theory of planned behavior was operationalized in our pretransplant survey. A principle axis factor analysis with varimax rotation was conducted on each of the three sets of variables—behavioral beliefs, normative beliefs, and attitude-toward-donating measures. The factors extracted from these analyses were then used in our subsequent data analyses.

Table 7.3 contains the subset of items that were used to test the reasoned action and planned behavior models. The seven semantic differentials that loaded on the first factor were used to measure attitude toward donation. For example, the respondents evaluated items like, "My donating a kidney to X is important/unimportant." The behavioral belief section of the questionnaire asked a series of 10 questions that represented the various outcomes or consequences of donating a kidney (e.g., "If I donate, my donating a kidney to X will make me feel better about myself."). Prospective donors also were asked to evaluate the same series of outcome statements (i.e., the behavioral beliefs) on 7-point scales that ranged from *extremely good* to *extremely bad.*

Another series of questions focused on assessment of the individual's subjective norms and the degree of their influence with regard to donation. To this end, donors rated statements such as "X (the potential recipient) thinks I should donate a kidney to him/her." The questionnaire also assessed the subject's motivation to comply with each such normative belief expectation—for example, "Generally speaking, how much do you want to do what X thinks you should do?"

Perceived behavioral control was measured both directly and indirectly by having respondents estimate the extent to which they expected to donate and whether they anticipated any obstacles to donation. For example, one direct measure of perceived behavioral control was, "For me to donate a kidney to X is easy/difficult." An indirect measure of perceived behavioral control that was selected empirically was, "Do

Table 7.3
Questionnaire Items Used to Test
Theory of Planned Behavior

Attitude toward donating (alpha = .83)
satisfying/not satisfying; caring/uncaring; important/unimportant; worthless/valuable; good/bad; logical/not logical; selfish/unselfish.

Behavioral beliefs (alpha = .75)
If I donate, my donating a kidney to X will make me feel better about myself.
If I donate, my donating a kidney to X will allow X and me to spend more time together.
If I donate, my donating a kidney to X will improve X's quality of life.
If I donate, my donating a kidney to X will allow X to be more self-sufficient.
If I donate, my donating a kidney to X will prolong X's life.
If I donate, my donating a kidney to X will allow X to spend more time with family.
If I donate, my donating a kidney to X will improve X's outlook on life.
If I donate, my donating a kidney to X will result in a closer personal relationship between X and me.
If I donate, my donating a kidney to X will help others who are considering donation.
If I donate, my donating a kidney to X will make me feel more satisfied with my life.

Subjective norm
Most people who are important to me think I should donate a kidney to X.

Normative beliefs (alpha = .92)
X thinks I should donate a kidney to him/her.
My parents think I should donate a kidney to X.
My brothers and sisters think I should donate a kidney to X.
My relatives think I should donate a kidney to X.
X's parents think I should donate a kidney to X.
X's brothers and sisters think I should donate a kidney to X.
X's relatives think I should donate a kidney to X.

Behavioral intention (alpha = .90)
I intend to donate a kidney to X.
I will try to donate a kidney to X.
I will make an effort to donate a kidney to X.
I expect that I will donate a kidney to X.

Direct perceived behavioral control (alpha = .72)
For me to donate a kidney to X is: easy/difficult
If I wanted to, I could easily donate a kidney to X: likely/unlikely

Indirect perceived behavioral control (alpha = .73)
Do you have concerns about the impact of the donation decision on your family? (many concerns/no concerns)

(continued)

Table 7.3
Questionnaire Items Used to Test
Theory of Planned Behavior (Continued)

Do you have any personal problems that could interfere with your donating a kidney to
  X? (many personal problems/no personal problems)
Are you employed in a job that could interfere with your donating a kidney to X?
  (definitely yes/definitely no)
Can you think of any upcoming events in your life that might conflict or prevent your
  donating a kidney to X? (many events/no events)

Behavior

Transplanted	$n = 38$
Attempted to transplant	$n = 14$[a]
Decided not to transplant	$n = 102$
Status not determined	$n = 47$

NOTE: Attitude items were assessed along a 7-point semantic differential scale. Behavioral beliefs, normative beliefs, subjective norm, and behavioral intention were all assessed along a 7-point scale ranging from *extremely likely* to *extremely unlikely,* with the exception of behavioral intention Item 2 which ranged from *very much* to *not at all.* Direct perceived behavioral control was also measured on a 7-point scale ranging from *easy* to *difficult* for Item 1 and from *extremely likely* to *extremely unlikely* for Item 2. Alpha reliability coefficients are indicated in parentheses.
a. "Attempted to transplant" refers to potential donors whose transplant center computer medical records indicated they had not been medically ruled out, and who clearly stated they intended to donate and/or were simply waiting to donate (e.g., transplant had already been, or was in the process of being, scheduled).

you have any personal problems that could interfere with your donating
a kidney to X?"

Behavioral intention was measured by four statements concerning
the likelihood of donation for that individual (e.g., "I intend to donate
a kidney to X"). Finally, behavior was assessed by an examination of
hospital and transplant center computer files. Prospective donors were
classified as having transplanted, being motivated to transplant but still
awaiting the opportunity, or not having transplanted.

Results: Is Kidney Donation
Reasoned Action or Planned Behavior?

The first set of hypotheses to examine in any application of the
theory of planned behavior involves the underlying empirical assump-

tions of the model. We found strong support for these assumptions based on our analysis of the combined related and unrelated donor sample. First, the set of salient behavioral beliefs, multiplicatively weighted by outcome evaluations, was adequately correlated with the attitude-toward-donating measure ($r = .58$). Second, the set of normative beliefs, weighted by the appropriate motivations to comply, was strongly related to the overall subjective norm measure ($r = .71$). Third, as expected by the planned behavior model, perceptions of direct behavioral control over donation were reliably correlated with the underlying set of indirect control beliefs ($r = .51$). All of these correlations were significant beyond the $p < .0001$ level. Finally, no external variables were reliably related to behavioral intention or behavior—donor status, income, gender, age, employment, current mood, level of altruism, or level of self-esteem did not influence behavior when behavioral intention was controlled. In addition, none of these external variables influenced behavioral intention when attitude, subjective norm, and perceived behavioral control were controlled.

The next phase of the analysis examined the applicability of the theory of reasoned action and the theory of planned behavior to predicting actual kidney donation over time. Figures 7.3 and 7.4 present the results of a series of hierarchical regression analyses that examined the adequacy of these two theoretical approaches. First, it may be seen in Figure 7.3 that the strongest predictor of behavior, consistent with the theory of reasoned action, was behavioral intention (standardized beta $= .33, p = .0002$). Although only attitude toward donating was a reliable predictor of behavioral intention (standardized beta $= .38, p < .0001$), neither attitude nor subjective norm *directly* influenced actual donation behavior. These findings are based on a dichotomous measure of the behavior of interest (i.e., transplanted versus no transplantation). Moreover, the pattern of findings reported here, and in Figures 7.3 and 7.4, was identical when the behavior was treated as a trichotomous measure (i.e., behavior, attempted behavior, no behavior).

Second, the predictive strength of behavioral intention also emerged in testing the theory of planned behavior. As shown in Figure 7.4, behavioral intention again was the strongest predictor of donation behavior (standardized beta $= .41, p < .0001$). Interestingly, there was a marginally significant tendency for perceived behavioral control to influence behavior, independent of intention (standardized beta $= -.17$, $p < .10$). Those biologically related and emotionally involved donors who felt that they had more psychological control over kidney donation

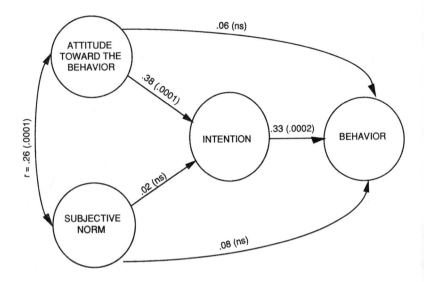

Figure 7.3. Test of the Reasoned Action Model: Total Sample

actually tended to be marginally *less* likely to donate a kidney to the person in need. With regard to the determinants of behavioral motivation, attitude also predicted intention (standardized beta = .16, $p < .02$) in the planned behavior model, but perceived behavioral control was over three times more important as a predictor of behavioral intention than attitude (standardized beta = .52, $p < .0001$). Finally, for the planned behavior model, as with the reasoned action model, normative influences did not play a role in predicting either behavioral intention or behavior.

Table 7.4 provides a fuller account of these findings. For the prediction of behavioral intention, the inclusion of perceived behavioral control in the theory of planned behavior more than doubled the amount of variance accounted for compared to the theory of reasoned action (R^2 = .37 and .15, respectively). For the prediction of behavior, the theory of planned behavior again significantly increased the amount of variance accounted for compared to the reasoned action model (R^2 = .16 and .14, respectively).

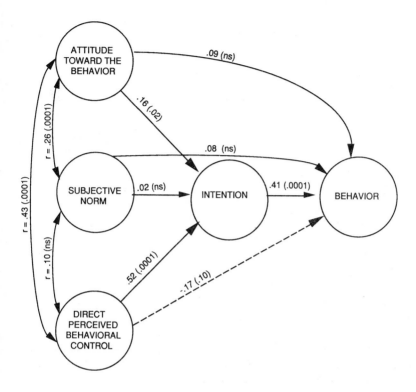

Figure 7.4. Test of the Planned Behavior Model: Total Sample

Conclusions

These findings provide strong empirical support for our hypotheses. First of all, the basic theoretical assumptions of both the reasoned action and planned behavior models were met in this behavioral domain. Behavioral beliefs were reliably related to attitude toward donating; normative beliefs were strongly correlated with the overall subjective norm measure; indirect control beliefs were related to direct perceived behavioral control; and external variables were not reliably related to intention or behavior in either model. Taken together, these

Table 7.4
Results of Hierarchical Regressions: Reasoned Action Versus Planned Behavior Models

Step and predictor variable	r	beta	R	R^2
Prediction of intentions				
Step 1—Theory of reasoned action				
Attitude	.39	.38***		
Subjective norm	.12	.02	.39	.15
Step 2—Theory of planned behavior				
Attitude	.39	.16**		
Subjective norm	.12	.02		
Perceived behavioral control	.59	.52***	.61	.37
Prediction of behavior				
Step 1—Theory of reasoned action				
Intention	.36	.33***	.37	.14
Step 2—Theory of planned behavior				
Intention	.36	.41***		
Perceived behavioral control	.13	−.17*	.40	.16

NOTE: R^2 changes between steps are statistically significant.
*$p = .10$; **$p < .02$; ***$p < .0002$.

results clearly support the applicability of both models to predicting and understanding behavioral decision making in the kidney donation domain.

It was proposed earlier in this chapter that the theory of planned behavior represents a more generalizable model than the theory of reasoned action and that the planned behavior model would improve our understanding of the behavioral decision making of prospective kidney donors. The results from the combined sample strongly supported this view. As expected, the inclusion of perceived behavioral control in the planned behavior model significantly increased the amount of variance accounted for—in behavioral intention *and* in behavior—over and above the reasoned action model. Given that donors in the sample did not have full control over whether they donated a kidney, our finding that the influence of perceived behavioral control on actual behavior was mediated through behavioral intention makes considerable theoretical (and intuitive) sense.

These findings also provided strong support for the robustness of the models even despite violation of the time-interval assumption associated with the planned behavior and reasoned action models. Behavioral intention was a stable predictor over a considerable time interval, and no other theoretical components directly influenced actual behavior over time. In contrast to other applications of the reasoned action approach (e.g., Bentler & Speckart, 1979; Manstead et al., 1983), affect—as captured by our attitude measure—did not directly influence behavior in this behavioral domain.

Generalizability Across Behavioral Domains

Several caveats concerning generalizability are in order. It must be kept in mind that the research presented in this chapter was conducted at only one hospital's transplant center. Although the donor sample was indeed geographically diverse, transplant centers nevertheless have sufficiently different professional practices and philosophies about living donation that it would be important to conduct comparable research at other transplant centers to bolster the generalizability of these findings.

A more important and interesting question to entertain is whether our findings on the decision-making process generalize across diverse behavioral domains—that is, whether decision making in this context is somehow qualitatively different from other donation decisions because living kidney donation is a "special situation," as some of Fellner and Marshall's (1981) donors reported. There have been a number of studies that have investigated the experience of, and attitudes toward, blood donation (Piliavin, 1990). Charng et al. (1988), for example, were interested in understanding and predicting blood donation as a repeated behavior. They hypothesized that an internalized blood-donor role identity developed with repeated experience, and that it would have a more direct influence on behavioral intentions and behavior than would attitudes or subjective norms. For first-time blood donors, however, they predicted that attitude toward blood donation and subjective norms would be the primary predictors of behavioral intention, and intention, in turn, would be the primary predictor of behavior.

The Charng et al. study was based on a sample of 658 blood donors who walked into one of four midwestern blood donation centers over a seven-month period. This sample was interviewed at the time of donation and completed a mail questionnaire that included measures of behavioral intention, attitude, subjective norms, blood donor identity, and other related variables. Follow-up interviews, questionnaires, and records at the donation centers were the source of additional data. Although not all the components of the theory of reasoned action were included in the questionnaire, the results were generally consistent with the reasoned action model. Attitudes and subjective norms predicted behavioral intention as expected. Current donation behavior, however, was *directly* predicted by both intention and subjective norms. The addition of role identity variables also reliably improved the prediction of behavioral intention.

An internal analysis by Charng et al. also examined the applicability of the theory of reasoned action as a function of different stages of blood donation experience. Donors were divided into four groups based on the number of times they had donated: those who donated once, twice, three or four times, and five or more times. The researchers suggested that because role identities require experience over time to develop, the addition of role identity variables to the theory of reasoned action should improve prediction only for the more experienced donors. Their findings generally supported these predictions. For first-time donors, it was found that attitude toward donation was the most important factor in predicting behavioral intention. As expected, role identity variables did not improve these predictions. The results also indicated that the attitude-intention relationship was strongest for first-time donors and that attitudes of first-time donors were significantly different from those of more experienced donors. With increasing experience in blood donation, attitude was less important in predicting behavioral intention. According to Charng et al., their results support the notion that with increasing experience an internalized role identity becomes a more important influence on intention, and attitudes and subjective norms decrease in importance as determinants of intention.

These findings as well as other research on blood donation have some interesting implications for evaluating the generalizability of our research on kidney donor decision making. Because kidney donation is a behavior that individuals can choose to perform only once, individuals will not have had prior experience in kidney donation and will not have well-developed role identities associated with being a kidney donor. Though potentially beneficial for predicting repeated behaviors, role identity variables should be less important for the prediction of single behaviors like kidney donation. Furthermore, research by Breckler and Wiggins (1989a, 1989b) on blood donation suggests that emotional factors should be more likely to play an important role in the prediction of a first-time donation behavior. Especially because kidney donation is much more personally involving and risky than blood donation, affect—unmediated by behavioral intention—would be expected to influence the prediction of kidney donation. Finally, first-time blood donation requires comparatively fewer resources and opportunity barriers than kidney donation. As a result, perceived behavioral control should be less influential in the prediction of blood donation but more influential in the prediction of kidney donation.

The results presented in this chapter indeed provide support for the importance of perceived behavioral control in predicting and understanding donor decision making, but the findings did not support an unmediated role for affect (i.e., attitude toward the behavior). Behavioral intention, and not attitude, proved to be the strongest predictor of actual behavior over time. Contrary to previous claims based on retrospective data that donor decision making was immediate and instantaneous, we found strong evidence for what Fazio (1990) calls a *deliberative processing mode* among donors who are considering kidney donation. Such a mode of processing emphasizes the extent to which certain social behaviors are relatively more reasoned and deliberate. Both the theory of reasoned action and the theory of planned behavior reflect more deliberative processing to the extent that behavioral intention plays a central role in predicting the course of action.

Understanding that the behavioral decision making of kidney donors may entail a more careful, reasoned analysis than previously believed should prove quite useful to transplant center personnel as living donation becomes an even more frequent approach to solving the organ procurement problem in this country. There has been a long-standing concern in the organ transplantation community that informed consent is problematic if donor decisions are spontaneous, irrational, overly influenced by peer pressure, and generally insensitive to the risks and costs associated with donation. However, a key message of the present chapter is that such concerns about prospective kidney donors do not appear to be empirically well-founded.

Notes

1. American Council on Transplantation, U.S. Transplant Statistics Sheet, December, 1988.

2. U.S. Department of Health and Human Services, "Organ Transplantation: Issues and Recommendations," Report of the Task Force on Organ Transplantation, April, 1986.

References

Abram, H. S., & Buchanan, D. C. (1976-1977). The gift of life: A review of the psychological aspects of kidney transplantation. *International Journal of Psychiatry in Medicine, 7*(2), 153-164.

Ajzen, I. (1985). From intentions to actions: A theory of planned behavior. In J. Kuhl & J. Beckman (Eds.), *Action-control: From cognition to behavior* (pp. 11-39). Heidelberg, Germany: Springer.

Ajzen, I. (1988). *Attitudes, personality, and behavior.* Homewood, IL: Dorsey.

Ajzen, I. (1989). Attitude structure and behavior. In A. R. Pratkanis, S. J. Breckler, & A. G. Greenwald (Eds.), *Attitude structure and function* (pp. 241-274). Hillsdale, NJ: Lawrence Erlbaum.

Ajzen, I., & Fishbein, M. (1980). *Understanding attitudes and predicting social behavior.* Englewood Cliffs, NJ: Prentice-Hall.

Ajzen, I., & Madden, T. (1986). Prediction of goal-directed behavior: Attitudes, intentions, and perceived behavioral control. *Journal of Experimental Social Psychology, 22*, 453-474.

Bagozzi, R. P., & Yi, Y. (1989). The degree of intention formation as a moderator of the attitude-behavior relationship. *Social Psychology Quarterly, 52*, 266-279.

Batson, C. D. (1990). How social an animal? The human capacity for caring. *American Psychologist, 45*, 336-346.

Bay, W. H., & Hebert, L. A. (1987). The living donor in kidney transplantation. *Annals of Internal Medicine, 106*, 719-727.

Belzer, F. O., Kalayoglu, M., & Sollinger, H. W. (1987). Donor-specific transfusion in living-unrelated renal donor-recipient combinations. *International Journal of Transplantation Proceedings, 19*(1), 1514-1515.

Bentler, P. M., & Speckart, G. (1979). Models of attitude-behavior relations. *Psychological Review, 86*, 452-464.

Borgida, E., & Howard-Pitney, B. (1983). Personal involvement and the robustness of perceptual salience effects. *Journal of Personality and Social Psychology, 45*, 560-570.

Borgida, E., Simmons, R. G., Conner, C., & Lombard, K. (1990). The Minnesota living donor studies: Implications for organ procurement. In J. Shanteau & R. J. Harris (Eds.), *Organ donation and transplantation: Psychological and behavioral factors* (pp. 108-121). Washington, DC: American Psychological Association.

Breckler, S. J., & Wiggins, E. C. (1989a). Affect versus evaluation in the structure of attitudes. *Journal of Experimental Social Psychology, 25*, 253-271.

Breckler, S. J., & Wiggins, E. C. (1989b). *The experience of donating blood: Motivations, emotions, and attitudes.* Unpublished manuscript, Johns Hopkins University, Baltimore.

Burnkrant, R. E., & Page, T. J., Jr. (1988). The structure and antecedents of the normative and attitudinal components of Fishbein's theory of reasoned action. *Journal of Experimental Social Psychology, 24*, 66-87.

Chambers, M. (1982). Psychological aspects of renal transplantation. *Psychiatry in Medicine, 12*(3), 1982-1983.

Charng, H., Piliavin, J. A., & Callero, P. L. (1988). Role identity and reasoned action in the prediction of repeated behavior. *Social Psychology Quarterly, 51*, 303-317.

Christensen, A. J., Holman, J. M., Turner, C. W., & Slaughter, J. R. (1989). Quality of life in end-stage renal disease: Influence of renal transplantation. *Clinical Transplantation, 3*, 46-53.

Cramond, W. A., Court, J. H., Higgins, B. A., Knight, P. R., & Lawrence, J. R. (1967). Psychological screening of potential donors in a renal homotransplantation programme. *British Journal of Psychiatry, 113*, 1213-1221.

Dunn, J. F., Nylander, W. A., Richie, R. E., Johnson, H. K., MacDonaell, R. C., & Sawyers, J. L. (1986). Living related kidney donors. *Annals of Surgery, 203*(6), 637-643.

Eisendrath, R. M., Guttmann, R. D., & Murray, J. E. (1969, August). Psychologic considerations in the selection of kidney transplant donors. *Surgery, Gynecology, & Obstetrics, 129*, 243-248.

Elick, B. A., Sutherland, D. E. R., Gillingham, K., & Najarian, J. S. (1989, September). *Use of distant relatives and living unrelated donors: A strategy to increase the application of kidney transplantation to treat chronic renal failure.* Paper presented at the meeting of the International Transplantation Conference, Minneapolis, MN.

Fazio, R. H. (1990). Multiple processes by which attitudes guide behavior: The MODE model as an integrative framework. In M. P. Zanna (Ed.), *Advances in experimental social psychology* (Vol. 23, pp. 75-109). New York: Academic Press.

Fellner, C. H. (1976-1977). Renal transplantation and the living donor: Decision and consequences. *Psychotherapy and Psychosomatics, 27*, 139-143.

Fellner, C. H., & Marshall, J. R. (1970). Kidney donors. In J. Macaulay & L. Berkowitz (Eds.), *Altruism and helping behavior* (pp. 269-279). New York: Academic Press.

Fellner, C. H., & Marshall, J. R. (1981). Kidney donors revisited. In J. P. Rushton & R. M. Sorrentino (Eds.), *Altruism and helping behavior: Social, personality, and developmental perspectives* (pp. 351-365). Hillsdale, NJ: Lawrence Erlbaum.

Fishbein, M., & Ajzen, I. (1975). *Belief, attitude, intention, and behavior.* Reading, MA: Addison-Wesley.

Fishbein, M., & Stasson, M. (1990). The role of desires, self-predictions, and perceived control in the prediction of training session attendance. *Journal of Applied Social Psychology, 20*(3), 173-198.

Granberg, D., & Holmberg, S. (1990). The intention-behavior relationship among U.S. and Swedish voters. *Social Psychology Quarterly, 53*, 44-54.

Harkness, A. R., DeBono, K. G., & Borgida, E. (1985). Personal involvement and strategies for making contingency judgments: A stake in the dating game makes a difference. *Journal of Personality and Social Psychology, 49*, 22-32.

Harrison, W., Thompson, V. D., & Rodgers, J. L. (1985). Robustness and sufficiency of the theory of reasoned action in longitudinal prediction. *Basic and Applied Social Psychology, 6*(1), 25-40.

Higgerson, A. B., & Bulechek, G. M. (1982). A descriptive study concerning the psychosocial dimensions of living related kidney donation. *American Association of Nephrology Nurses and Technicians, Vol 2*, pp. 27-31.

Hirvas, J., Enckell, M., Kuhlback, B., & Pasternack, A. (1980). Psychological and social problems encountered in active treatment of chronic uraemia. *Acta Medica Scandinavia, 208*, 285-287.

House, R. M., & Thompson, T. L. (1988). Psychiatric aspects of organ transplantation. *Journal of the American Medical Association, 260*, 535-539.

Howard-Pitney, B., Borgida, E., & Omoto, A. M. (1986). Personal involvement: An examination of processing differences. *Social Cognition, 4*, 39-57.

Kemph, J. P. (1966). Renal failure, artificial kidney, and kidney transplant. *American Journal of Psychiatry, 122*, 1270-1274.

Kountz, S. L., Perkins, H. A., Payne, R., & Belzer, F. O. (1970). Kidney transplants using living unrelated donors. *Transplantation Proceedings, 2*(3), 427-429.

Kumar, M. S. A., White, A. G., Samhan, M., & Abouna, G. M. (1987). Nonrelated living donors for renal transplantation. *Transplantation Proceedings, 19*(1), 1516-1517.

Levenson, J. L., & Olbrisch, M. E. (1987). Shortage of donor organs and long waits: New sources of stress for transplant patients. *Psychosomatics, 28*, 399-403.

Manstead, A. S. R., Proffitt, C., & Smart, J. L. (1983). Predicting and understanding mothers' infant-feeding intentions and behavior: Testing the theory of reasoned action. *Journal of Personality and Social Psychology, 44*, 657-671.

Marshall, J. R., & Fellner, C. H. (1976-1977). Kidney donors revisited. *American Journal of Psychiatry, 134*(5), 575-576.

Matas, A. J., Sutherland, D. E. R., Payne, W. D., Dunn, D. L., Perry, E., & Najarian, J. S. (1989). Approaches to living donor renal transplantation. *Minnesota Medicine, 72*, 589-592.

McCaul, K. D., O'Neill, H. K., & Glasgow, R. E. (1988). Predicting the performance of dental hygiene behaviors: An examination of the Fishbein and Ajzen model and self-efficacy expectations. *Journal of Applied Social Psychology, 18*, 114-128.

Miller, L. E., & Grush, J. E. (1986). Individual differences in attitudinal versus normative determination of behavior. *Journal of Experimental Social Psychology, 22*, 190-202.

Muslin, H. (1971). On acquiring a kidney. *American Journal of Psychiatry, 127*(9), 105-108.

Omoto, A. M., & Borgida, E. (1988). Guess who might be coming to dinner? Personal involvement and racial stereotyping. *Journal of Experimental Social Psychology, 24*, 571-593.

Perkins, K. A. (1987). The shortage of cadaver donor organs for transplantation: Can psychology help? *American Psychologist, 42*, 921-929.

Piliavin, J. A. (1990). Role identity and organ donation: Some suggestions based on blood donation research. In J. Shanteau & R. J. Harris (Eds.), *Organ donation and transplantation: Psychological and behavioral factors* (pp. 150-158). Washington, DC: American Psychological Association.

Reding, R., Squifflet, J. P., Pirson, Y., Jamart, J., De Bruyere, M., Moriau, M., Latinne, D., Carlier, M., & Alexandre, G. P. J. (1987). Living-related and unrelated donor kidney transplantation: Comparison between ABO-compatible and incompatible grafts. *Transplantation Proceedings, 19*(1), 1511-1513.

Sadler, H. H., Davison, L., Carroll, C., & Kountz, S. L. (1971). The living, genetically unrelated, kidney donor. *Seminars in Psychiatry, 3*(1), 86-101.

Schifter, D. B., & Ajzen, I. (1985). Intention, perceived control, and weight loss: An application of the theory of planned behavior. *Journal of Personality and Social Psychology, 49*, 843-851.

Schlegel, R. P., d'Avernas, J. R., Zanna, M. P., & Manske, S. R. (1989). *Problem drinking: A problem for the theory of reasoned action.* Unpublished manuscript, University of Waterloo, Toronto.

Sharma, V. K., & Enoch, M. D. (1987). Psychological sequelae of kidney donation. A 5-10 year follow up study. *Acta Psychiatrica Scandinavia, 75*, 264-267.

Sheppard, B. H., Hartwick, J., & Warshaw, P. R. (1988). A theory of reasoned action: A meta-analysis of past research with recommendations for modifications and future research. *Journal of Consumer Research, 15*, 325-343.

Sherman, S. J., & Fazio, R. H. (1983). Parallels between attitudes and traits as predictors of behavior. *Journal of Personality, 51*, 308-345.

Simmons, R. G., Marine, S. K., & Simmons, R. L. (1977). *Gift of life: The effect of organ transplantation on individual, family, and societal dynamics.* New Brunswick, NJ: Transaction Books.

Smith, M. D., Kappell, D. F., Province, M. A., Hong, B. A., Robson, A. M., Dutton, S., Guzman, T., Hoff, J., Shelton, L., Cameron, E., Emerson, W., Glass, N. R., Hopkins, J., & Peterson, C. (1986). Living-related kidney donors: A multicenter study of donor education, socioeconomic adjustment, and rehabilitation. *American Journal of Kidney Diseases, 8*(4), 223-233.

Spital, A. (1989). Unconventional living kidney donors' attitudes and use among transplant centers. *Transplantation, 48*(2), 243-248.

Spital, A., & Spital, M. (1987). Kidney donation: Reflections. *American Journal of Nephrology, 7*, 49-54.

Steinberg, J., Levy, N. B., & Radvila, A. (1981). Psychological factors affecting acceptance or rejection of kidney transplants. In N. B. Levy (Ed.), *Psychological factors in hemodialysis and renal transplantation* (pp. 185-193). New York: Plenum.

Suranyi, M. G., & Hall, B. M. (1990). Current status of renal transplantation. *Western Journal of Medicine, 152*, 687-696.

Sutherland, D. E. R. (1985). Living related donors should be used whenever possible. *Transplantation Proceedings, 17*(1), 1503-1509.

Viederman, M. (1975). Psychogenic factors in kidney transplant rejection: A case study. *American Journal of Psychiatry, 132*(9), 957-959.

Wood, A. J., & Lemaire, M. (1985). Pharmacologic aspects of cyclosporine therapy: Pharmacokinetics. *Transplantation Proceedings, 17*(Suppl. 1, 4), 27-31.

8

Who Helps and Why?
The Psychology of
AIDS Volunteerism

MARK SNYDER
ALLEN M. OMOTO

C ountless generations of Sunday school
students (and others familiar with
the curriculum) will recognize the
following parable:

> A man was going down from Jerusalem to Jericho, and he fell among
> robbers, who stripped him and beat him, and departed, leaving him half
> dead. Now by chance a priest was going down the road; and when he saw
> him he passed by on the other side. So likewise a Levite, when he came
> to the place and saw him, passed by on the other side. But a Samaritan,
> as he journeyed, came to where he was; and when he saw him, he had

AUTHORS' NOTE: Preparation of this chapter and the research on which it is based have
been supported by grants from the American Foundation for AIDS Research. Portions of
this chapter were written while Mark Snyder was a Fellow at the Center for Advanced
Study in the Behavioral Sciences, supported in part by a fellowship from the James
McKeen Cattell Fund.

We acknowledge and appreciate the cooperation of the Minnesota AIDS Project
(Minneapolis, Minnesota) and the Good Samaritan Project (Kansas City, Missouri), as
well as the substantial contributions of Stephen Asche and James Berghuis to this
research.

213

compassion, and went to him and bound his wounds, pouring on oil and wine; then he set him on his own beast and brought him to an inn, and took care of him. And the next day he took out two dennarii and gave them to the innkeeper, saying, "Take care of him; and whatever you spend, I will repay you when I come back." (Luke 10:29-37, RSV)

This, of course, is the story of the Good Samaritan. We begin our chapter with this parable because it raises a central question of *who* helps others in the real world. The general question is: Who chooses to help people—like the assault victim in the parable—who are alone, in dire straits, and shunned by others? In particular, why do some people do as the Samaritan did, and engage in sustained helpfulness and make a continuing commitment to the ongoing care and well-being of those in need? Our specific research question is: Who volunteers to help people with AIDS (referred to as PWAs) and, relatedly, why do these helpers engage in their Samaritan acts?

To set the stage for answering this question, this chapter first provides a brief overview of our program of research on AIDS volunteerism, with special emphasis on people's perceptions of and motivations for AIDS volunteer work. Next, it presents data that speak to questions of who helps PWAs and why. Finally, we place our research in the broader tradition of "action research" (Lewin, 1946, 1947) and consider potential connections between basic theory and research in social psychology and practical concerns related to the AIDS epidemic.

AIDS in Contemporary Society

There is no doubt that AIDS extracts huge economic, medical, and psychological tolls from those struck by the disease, from their loved ones and associates, and from society at large. In 1981, the Centers for Disease Control reported the first case of what would come to be known as AIDS. Now, less than a decade later, there are already over 130,000 confirmed cases of AIDS in the United States alone ("AIDSWEEK," 1990), and an estimated 1.5 million Americans are infected with the HIV virus that is thought to cause AIDS (Morin, 1988). Up to 99% of these infected individuals are expected to develop AIDS (Lui, Darrow, & Rutherford, 1988), leading to projections that by the end of 1991 there will be a cumulative total of nearly 500,000 cases of AIDS in the

United States ("Report," 1989). AIDS is also no longer a disease restricted to certain "high risk" groups (Morgan & Curran, 1986); indeed, researchers at the federal Centers for Disease Control project that AIDS will be the fifth leading cause of death among all U.S. women of childbearing age by 1991 ("AIDS Leading Killer," 1990). Thus, with neither a vaccine nor a cure for AIDS on the horizon (even the most optimistic projections predict the end of the century as the date for development of a vaccine against AIDS; "AIDS Conferees Hopeful on Vaccine," 1990), the full impact of AIDS—as devastating and profound as it already has been—has yet to be felt, and it will touch all segments of the population.

AIDS, it should be recognized, is more than a medical crisis, and has had profound social, legal, and political ramifications. Society has responded to the AIDS epidemic on a number of fronts and in a variety of ways, both medical and nonmedical. Not only have new medical treatments and drugs been developed in response to AIDS, but also AIDS-related issues have been the focus of legislative activities, religious and ethical debates, community education and public health campaigns, and media and popular culture presentations. Understanding AIDS therefore involves understanding not just its medical aspects but also its psychological, social, and societal effects.

An increasingly critical component of society's response to AIDS has been the development of community-based grass-roots organizations that recruit, train, assign, and supervise volunteers who assist with the care of PWAs and with AIDS public-education efforts. For example, some volunteers help PWAs with their household chores; some provide emotional and social support as "buddies" to PWAs; others staff AIDS hotlines providing information, counseling, and referral services; still others volunteer for speaking, educational, and public-information assignments. Indeed, it has been observed that "one of the most remarkable and heartening byproducts of the HIV epidemic has been the development of grass-roots organizations [of volunteers] dedicated to serving the needs of people with AIDS" (Fineberg, 1989, p. 117). AIDS volunteerism clearly is a testimonial to human kindness and to the power of communities of "ordinary people" to unite and organize in response to extraordinary events.

AIDS volunteerism not only benefits the recipients of services, but also may provide rewards for those who donate their time and energy. Volunteerism promotes a sense of community spirit and civic solidarity. Volunteering offers tangible evidence to people that they live in a kind and gentle culture in which people choose to "give something back" to society. AIDS volunteers themselves have a great deal to say about their experiences and the benefits of volunteerism. Almost without exception, their narrative accounts reveal that volunteers find their work to be psychologically moving and powerful; many claim that it has substantially and irrevocably changed their lives (Omoto & Snyder, 1989a). Volunteers report, for example, that their work "makes me feel good all over," "gives me purpose in life," and that they feel they are "making a difference as an AIDS buddy." Through their work, moreover, many volunteers believe that they are "gaining an awareness of other people's overwhelming problems and unfulfilled needs."

Volunteer work may also reward its givers with new skills, feelings of helpfulness, heightened self-esteem, and new friendships (e.g., King, Walder, & Pavey, 1970; Scheibe, 1965). Ironically, though, in the specific case of AIDS, volunteers may find themselves being punished for their good deeds. That is, others may stigmatize and avoid them because of stereotyped beliefs and prejudicial attitudes associated with AIDS and PWAs (e.g., Herek & Glunt, 1988). In fact, active volunteers often suggest that many of their associates respond differently to them after learning about their involvement as volunteers.

Finally, it should be noted that volunteerism offers direct benefits to society, as volunteers donate many and valuable services. For example, in Seattle, AIDS volunteers provided over 70,000 hours of services just in the year 1987 (General Accounting Office, 1989). These services translate into tangible monetary savings. In San Francisco, it has been estimated that when volunteer services are utilized, the cost of care for a PWA drops from roughly $150,000 per year to less than $40,000, for a savings of over two thirds (National AIDS Network, personal communication, July 11, 1989).

Applied and Theoretical Aspects of AIDS Volunteerism

In our research, we are working to understand the social and psychological aspects of volunteerism. We seek not only to find out who volunteers and why, but also to explore the consequences of volunteering for volunteers themselves, for the recipients of their efforts, and for society at large. The research is guided both by applied concerns regarding the role of volunteers in society's response to AIDS and by theoretical concerns with the nature of helping relationships and the social phenomenon of volunteerism.

At an *applied* level, by all accounts the number of AIDS cases will only increase in the years ahead as many of the millions of people already infected with the HIV virus actually develop AIDS and related illnesses. In addition, as medical advances extend the life expectancy of PWAs, more and more people will be living with AIDS (and living longer with AIDS). In fact, life expectancy after an AIDS diagnosis is over 50% longer now than it was at the beginning of the epidemic (Lemp, Payne, Neal, Temelso, & Rutherford, 1990), and it is estimated that 11% of those diagnosed with AIDS are now living longer than three years ("HIV: Longer Life," 1990). As society and an already greatly burdened health care system struggle to care for an increasing number of PWAs who are living longer, then, one can expect an escalating demand for the benefits and services provided by AIDS volunteers. These volunteers will also be taxed by this increasing reliance on them, however, as many will experience weariness and distress from repeatedly confronting the sorrow of AIDS. Eventually, volunteers may experience battle fatigue and burnout from watching people with AIDS suffer and eventually die (e.g., "Noble Experiment," 1990). In fact, there are already troubling indications that, in some communities, the supply of volunteers is falling short of the demand for their services (e.g., "Volunteering Drops," 1990).

At a *theoretical* level, studying AIDS volunteerism may be highly informative about the nature of helping behavior and about human relationships more generally. The study of helping behavior has long been a central area of research in personality and social psychology, with researchers attracted to it both because of its obvious social relevance and because it speaks to the issue of whether or not there is an intrinsically altruistic side to human nature (Batson, 1990).

Generally speaking, volunteer efforts and volunteer organizations constitute intriguing social phenomena of helping in the real world. For not only do people help in AIDS organizations, but citizens volunteer themselves in providing companionship to the elderly, health care to the sick, tutoring to the illiterate, and counseling to the troubled. Volunteer activity is quite prevalent in American society. According to the most recent Gallup Poll on the subject, 80 million American adults engaged in some form of volunteerism in 1987, with 21 million giving five or more hours per week to volunteer work (Independent Sector, 1988). By at least one estimate, there were almost 10,000 people actively involved as AIDS volunteers in the United States in 1989 (National AIDS Network, personal communication, March 7, 1990). What is common to all of these volunteer acts is that they are prosocial in nature and involve people devoting substantial amounts of their time and energy to aiding and benefiting others, often giving of themselves for extended periods of time.

Studying AIDS volunteerism provides an arena for examining *sustained*, *planned*, and *potentially costly* helping behavior. As such, it stands in contrast to much of the social psychological literature on helping, which has focused on situations in which potential helpers encounter unexpected opportunities to help that may also require quick decisions about whether or not to offer assistance (the classic example being the "bystander intervention" situation; Latané & Darley, 1970). The helping that occurs in such situations typically is confined to relatively brief and limited periods of time and to acts that are not particularly costly or risky, and that usually entail no future contact between the helper and the recipient.

In volunteerism, however, people have sought out opportunities to help others, rather than simply reacting to situations that have confronted them. Instead of being pressed to make quick decisions about whether or not to offer assistance, people may have deliberated for considerable amounts of time about whether or not to become a volunteer, the extent of their involvement, and the degree to which particular volunteer opportunities fit with their own personal patterns of needs, goals, and motivations. And, instead of limited and relatively low-cost assistance, many types of volunteer work involve commitment to an ongoing helping relationship that is of relatively long duration and involves considerable personal sacrifice in time, energy, emotional and psychological resources, and even financial expense (for a review of psychological research on volunteerism, see Clary & Snyder, 1991).

AIDS volunteerism embodies each of these features; AIDS volunteers have made deliberate decisions to engage in sustained helpfulness that is characterized by a continuing commitment to the recipient's care and well-being. Like the Good Samaritan of the parable, they have gone beyond offering immediate help and instead made long-term investments in the well-being of another person. Thus they provide an excellent opportunity to investigate the dynamics of sustained ongoing

Table 8.1
Stages of the Volunteer Process

Level of analyses	Antecedents	Experiences	Consequences
Individual volunteer	Personality Demographics Personal history Motivations Psychological functions	Relationship development	Satisfaction Commitment Increased knowledge Attitude change
Broader social influences	Recruitment of volunteers	Effects on PWAs Treatment process	Social diffusion Public education

helping relationships. Perhaps because of the relatively recent emergence of AIDS volunteerism, there is very little in the way of a published literature, and what little of it there is tends to focus on reports of the development of volunteer programs (Arno, 1988; Dumont, 1989; Lopez & Getzel, 1987; for an exception, see Williams, 1988). Nevertheless, we believe that, in studying AIDS volunteerism, we have isolated a socially significant laboratory in which to extend, evaluate, refine, and apply psychological theories of individual and social behavior. The benefits of this research should be an increased understanding of AIDS volunteerism, to be sure, but also a greater understanding of prosocial action and of helping relationships.

In recognition of volunteerism as sustained, ongoing, and potentially costly helping behavior, we have developed a conceptual model that identifies three stages of the *volunteer process*. As shown in Table 8.1, this model (which guides our program of research) specifies the psychological and behavioral features associated with each stage and the social, organizational, and societal contexts in which they occur. In the specific case of AIDS volunteerism, the first stage involves *antecedents* of volunteerism, and addresses the questions of who volunteers and why. The second stage concerns *experiences* of volunteers and the PWAs they work with, and the effects of AIDS volunteerism on the general treatment and coping processes. The third stage focuses on *consequences* of volunteerism and looks at changes in attitudes, knowledge, and behavior that occur in volunteers themselves, in the members of their immediate social networks, and in society at large. At each stage, psychological theories and the evidence of basic research are helping us frame research questions, the answers to which in turn should have implications for applied issues. To illustrate, let us focus on the antecedents stage of the AIDS volunteer process and consider the motivations behind volunteering, and the implications of these motivations for what transpires in voluntary helping relationships.

A Functional Approach to AIDS Volunteerism

For all prospective volunteers, there are many costs associated with volunteerism and formidable barriers that may keep them from getting involved in it. In the specific case of AIDS, not only are there limits of time and energy, but also fear of AIDS and death, and concerns about stigmatization. What, then, motivates some people to volunteer to help PWAs, to staff AIDS hotlines, or be "buddies" for PWAs? Who are the Good Samaritans when it comes to PWAs?

As Kurt Lewin, father of the "action research" tradition in the social sciences, suggested many years ago, "there is nothing so practical as a good theory" (Lewin, 1951, p. 169). In our research on AIDS volunteerism, we have taken this dictum to heart, as well as associated prescriptions that "we must infuse the field of applied social psychology with theory—and good theory at that" (Mark & Bryant, 1984, p. 247). To answer the questions of who volunteers and why they volunteer, we have adopted a *functional approach* to understanding the antecedents of AIDS volunteerism. We are extending psychological theories that suggest that people may engage in what appear to be the same behaviors for very different motivational reasons and to serve quite different psychological functions. This type of approach may hold great promise for unraveling the complex web of personal and social motivations that serve as the foundations of volunteer activity.

Functional Approaches

In personality and social psychology, functional approaches are most strongly identified with theories of attitudes and persuasion. To answer the question, "Of what use to people are their attitudes?", functional theorists argue that attitudes help people meet needs, execute plans, and achieve goals. Functional theorists further propose that the same attitudes may serve very different psychological functions for different people (Herek, 1987; Katz, 1960; Smith, Bruner, & White, 1956; Snyder & DeBono, 1987, 1989). For example, in the case of prejudice, one person's negative attitudes toward minorities may reflect the fact that others in the community hold such attitudes; this person's prejudices are serving the function of allowing him or her to fit into important social groups and to interact smoothly with others. But another person's equally negative and hostile prejudices may derive from anxieties and uncertainties about his or her self-worth, concerns that are alleviated by downward social comparison (Wills, 1981) and the derogation of others; this person's prejudices are serving the function of protecting him or her from accepting unpleasant truths about the self.

One of the key elements of a functional approach, and one of the primary reasons that it has utility beyond the field of attitudes, is its explicit concern with motivation. Specifically, the central assertion that the same attitude may serve different functions for different people can be broadened to include the possibility that virtually any pattern of thoughts, feelings, and actions that shares the same surface features may actually reflect very different motivational processes and may be serving different psychological functions for different individuals. Broadly defined in this way, a functional approach constitutes an explicit emphasis on the motivational and purposive agendas that guide and direct individuals and that may provide foundations for diverse social phenomena (for elaboration, see Snyder, 1988).

The logic of a functional approach is readily applicable to understanding the antecedents of volunteerism. Acts of volunteerism that appear to be quite similar on the surface may reflect markedly different underlying motivational processes; that is, they may be serving different psychological functions. Thus a functional approach brings into sharp focus the second question in the title of this chapter: Why do people help?

The specific case of AIDS volunteerism can illustrate the set of functions that has been identified with some regularity in diverse theoretical treatments of attitudes (e.g., Katz, 1960; Smith et al., 1956). The act of volunteering may for one person serve a *social* function, reflecting the normative influences of friends and significant others who are AIDS volunteers, or the desire to make friends and solidify certain social ties through volunteering. For another person, the same act of volunteering may flow from underlying values that prescribe altruistic contributions to society, thereby serving what may be termed a *value-expressive* function. For yet another person, volunteering may serve a *knowledge* function, providing a sense of understanding and information about AIDS and what it does to people. And, in still other cases, volunteering may serve a *defensive* or protective function, helping people to cope with personal fears of AIDS, illness, and death.

These distinctions have several implications. If, in fact, volunteering serves different functions for different people, then it follows that volunteer organizations may do well to consider targeting their recruitment efforts at the particular motivations of selected sets of potential volunteers. For example, people struggling with their own fears, anxieties, and uncertainties about AIDS may be indifferent to recruitment appeals that stress societal obligations to help the needy. Rather, they may be stirred to action if the recruitment appeal makes clear how AIDS volunteer work provides opportunities for working through precisely the fears and anxieties that grip them.

In addition, a functional analysis has implications for understanding why some volunteers continue to donate their time and services, whereas others do not. A persistent frustration in volunteer programs is the high rate of attrition (i.e., dropout) of their volunteers. As difficult as it may be to recruit volunteers, it is sometimes even more difficult to ensure their continued participation and service. One source of attrition may be a failure of volunteer programs to attend to the psychological functions served by volunteerism. That is, AIDS volunteers whose personal needs and motivations are being adequately fulfilled by their experiences should be more likely than those whose purposes for volunteering are not being addressed to be effective volunteers, to be satisfied with their work, and to plan to continue their service.

As this analysis suggests, therefore, the applied concerns of effective volunteer recruitment and retention may be profitably addressed with tools borrowed from basic theory and research on motivational functions. However, the street connecting these applied and basic aspects of AIDS volunteerism is doubtless two-way. The possibility exists, for example, that volunteering might serve psychological functions and purposes not anticipated by existing theory. Thus research in this applied domain may ultimately contribute to the further development and evolution of basic theory. Similarly, in our research on the other stages of the volunteer process, we are trying to map the two-way street that connects basic theory and research and applied work on societally-relevant issues (see Omoto & Snyder, 1990).

Investigating the Volunteer Process

In our program of research on AIDS volunteerism, we are conducting coordinated cross-sectional and longitudinal field studies coupled with experiments carried out in the laboratory. In these investigations, moreover, we are sampling from diverse subject populations, including people actually working as AIDS volunteers, individuals in training to become AIDS volunteers, volunteers for non-AIDS causes, and non-volunteers as well.

In one study, for example, we have conducted a national survey of currently active AIDS volunteers, assessing their personality, demographic, and experiential characteristics, and using open-ended and structured items to ascertain their motivations for their service. In an extended longitudinal study, additionally, we are tracking new volunteers over the entire course of their service as a "buddy" or "ally," as they provide emotional support and living assistance to PWAs. In this long-term study, we are examining the same people at all stages of the volunteer process and, therefore, will be able to examine causal relations more systematically both within and between stages. Finally, we are also conducting a series of laboratory experiments and intervention studies, each relevant to one or more stages of the volunteer process.

What have we found? Specifically, what do we know at this point about who volunteers and why? Because much of our research is still in progress, what follows is a preliminary and selective illustration of some of the motivational foundations of volunteerism.

Perceptions of AIDS Volunteer Work

We began our research with two studies of people's perceptions of AIDS volunteerism and of AIDS volunteers (Omoto & Snyder, 1989b). We chose this point of departure because the decision to become involved in AIDS volunteer work, as much as it may intrinsically invoke humanitarian values and altruistic concerns, may also be very much influenced by factors such as stereotyped beliefs and prejudicial attitudes toward AIDS, people with AIDS, and people potentially at risk for AIDS. For this reason, the prospect of providing emotional support and companionship to a terminally ill person may take on a very different meaning when that person is afflicted with AIDS than when that person suffers from, say, terminal cancer. It seems reasonable to expect that these different meanings will influence not only *who* volunteers, but the *reasons* why individuals would choose to donate their time and energy.

In this investigation of people's perceptions of volunteer work, 135 undergraduates anonymously reported on the extent to which they thought different factors would make them more or less likely to volunteer to provide emotional support and practical assistance to a terminally ill patient. Participants were then randomly assigned to read about volunteer work with a cancer patient or a PWA, work that included providing "emotional support and companionship through regular home and hospital visits, as well as telephone contact." Even though the volunteer activities and responsibilities were described in absolutely identical terms in the two conditions, students felt that they had many more good reasons (i.e., reasons that made them *more* likely to serve as a volunteer, such as general personal gains, humanitarian values, and community responsibility) to volunteer to help a patient with cancer than one who had AIDS—and they foresaw more potential barriers to doing AIDS volunteer work (i.e., reasons that made them *less* likely to volunteer, such as prejudice and fear), all Fs > 4.35 and all ps < .05. Clearly, the results of this experiment suggest that AIDS volunteer work is perceived by some to be a very "different" kind of volunteer activity.

Consistent with a functional approach to volunteerism, then, quite different reasons and motivations are required for the very same acts depending on who will be the recipient. This finding was reinforced by a companion study in which 39 volunteers from non-AIDS organizations (that is, people with histories of donating their time and energy to helping others) were questioned about their reasons for engaging in their current work and the reasons they saw as being important for doing AIDS-related volunteer work (Omoto & Snyder, 1989b). The results of this study revealed that active volunteers claimed rather pragmatic and *selfish* reasons (such as résumé building, feeling good about oneself, and gaining experience) for their current work. But when it came to doing AIDS volunteer work, they cited different and distinctly altruistic and *selfless* reasons (such as an obligation to help others in need) as critical in decisions to help. In other words, these "Samaritans" said they would require *different* reasons for engaging in AIDS volunteer work than for their current volunteer work, and these were reasons that entailed concern for rather remote rewards that may be unlikely to motivate many people.

Motivations for Becoming an AIDS Volunteer

Thus, even those who volunteer for non-AIDS work perceive AIDS volunteerism to be a "special" form of volunteer activity, one requiring unique motivations for its engagement and one that might serve psychological functions quite different than other forms of volunteer work. But what about the motivations of AIDS volunteers themselves? In another study, we conducted a short-term longitudinal investigation of 81 people going through AIDS volunteer training (Omoto & Berghuis, 1990). This study involved a community-based volunteer organization in Kansas City, Missouri, and focused intensively on community residents immediately before and after they took part in a 2½-day AIDS volunteer training program. Of particular concern were people's initial motivations and intentions for training, as well as their reactions to training and their subsequent decisions to volunteer or not.

This study revealed a diverse set of primary reasons for going through AIDS volunteer training. The two types of reasons that consistently received the highest mean ratings from these volunteers in training were those that revolved around knowledge concerns (e.g., wanting to learn more about how to prevent AIDS) and those that concerned humanitarian values (e.g., concern for PWAs), suggesting the possibility that, in functional terms, AIDS volunteer work could serve knowledge and value expressive functions for them. These reasons were also systematically related to people's reactions to training. To the extent that people were motivated by either knowledge or value-expressive reasons, for example, they were generally satisfied with their training experiences (all $rs > .25$ and all $ps < .05$).

As expected, however, a more specific question about the extent to which training had allowed volunteers to express their personal values, convictions, and beliefs proved relevant only to trainees who had enlisted for value-expressive reasons ($r = .19$, $p < .07$) and not to volunteers who espoused knowledge concerns ($r = .09$, ns). Similarly, knowledge reasons were related to the extent to which volunteers felt that training had increased their knowledge about the gay community ($r = .24$, $p < .05$), whereas value reasons were not ($r = .12$, ns). Thus, it seems that motivations for AIDS volunteer training differ between people, and they also apparently predict participants' reactions to training and perhaps even the dimensions along which they assess their subsequent volunteer experiences.

In a more systematic attempt to address the motivational foundations of AIDS volunteerism, we conducted an extensive questionnaire survey of 116 currently active AIDS volunteers at a community-based volunteer organization in Minneapolis, Minnesota. AIDS volunteers in this study filled out a confidential questionnaire about themselves, their backgrounds, and their experiences as volunteers. This survey included sections assessing their demographic characteristics, their involvement in past and current volunteer activity, and standard psychological measures of potentially relevant personality attributes (e.g., self-esteem, empathic tendencies, nurturance, death anxiety, need for social recognition, and concerns about social responsibility). The survey also contained items relevant to developing a structured self-report inventory for assessing motivations for AIDS volunteer work.

The simple question of who volunteers to do AIDS-related work actually has a very complex answer. The volunteers were a diverse group, with considerable variability in their backgrounds and experiences as volunteers, and running the gamut on the measures of personality (see Omoto & Snyder, 1990). In terms of demographics, these volunteers ranged in age from 20 to 66 years, with a median age of 35. Sixty-four percent (64%) of them were males, 36% females; 60% defined themselves as exclusively or predominantly homosexual, 34% as exclusively or predominantly heterosexual, and the remaining 6% claimed to be bisexual. Rural (35%) and urban (32%) backgrounds were fairly equally represented in this group, as were income levels (ranging from less than $10,000 to over $100,000 annually). Collectively, and interestingly, these respondents were highly educated, with 91% having attended at least some college and 67% having earned a college degree. Finally, these volunteers had served anywhere from 2 to 42 months, and devoted approximately 4 hours per week on their volunteer tasks.

In spite of the diversity of their backgrounds, of course, all of these individuals shared something in common—they were all donating their time as AIDS volunteers. But did they share a common motivation for volunteering, and did volunteer work serve a common function for them? To assess their motivations, these volunteers rated how important each one of a set of different reasons was for their AIDS volunteer work. Included in this set were items designed to tap each of the motivations suggested by previous theorizing on psychological functions (i.e., the value expressive, knowledge, social, and defensive functions), as well as motivations thought to be particularly relevant to AIDS volunteer work (e.g., concern for the communities particularly affected by AIDS, knowing someone who has AIDS). In constructing a motivation inventory, factor analytic techniques were employed, and they revealed five distinguishable sets of motivations for AIDS volunteer work, each one reliably measured by five different items (alphas > .74).

Of the five motivational functions obtained, some partially overlap with those specified by prior theory on psychological functions and some do not. The first set of motivations for doing AIDS volunteer work involved *community concern*, reflecting people's sense of obligation to or concern about a community or social grouping (e.g., "because of my concern and worry about the gay community," "to help members of the gay community"). The second set of motivations invoked considerations related to personal *values* (e.g., "because of my humanitarian obligation to help others," "because people should do something about issues that are important to them"). The third set of motivations was characterized as relevant to concerns about *understanding* (e.g., "to learn about how people cope with AIDS," "to deal with my personal fears and anxiety about AIDS"). The fourth set of motivations was labeled *personal development* and centered on issues of personal growth (e.g., "to challenge myself and test my skills," "to gain experience dealing with emotionally difficult topics"). Finally, the fifth category of motivations concerned *esteem enhancement* and included considerations about current voids or deficits in one's life (e.g., "to feel better about myself," "to feel less lonely").

This inventory, as rough as it yet may be, has made possible a more thorough analysis of the psychological functions of AIDS volunteerism, including directly addressing the question of why people volunteer. In spite of what appears to be a commonality of purpose in being a volunteer, the data show striking individual-to-individual variability in which motivations are most and least important to volunteers. Some indication of the diversity of motivations behind AIDS volunteerism is provided by the information presented in Figure 8.1, which displays the percentage of volunteers choosing each of the five categories of

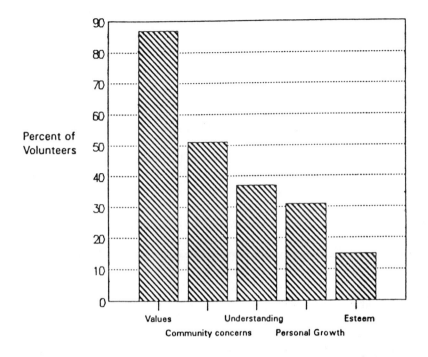

Figure 8.1. Percentage of Volunteers Choosing Each Type of Reason

reasons for volunteering. This state of affairs is, of course, anticipated by a functional approach, which emphasizes that different people may possess different motivations for engaging in the same acts of volunteerism.

In attempting to understand these motivations, it is informative to view them against the backdrop of global personality dispositions. For instance, AIDS volunteer work, by its very nature, should provide excellent opportunities for expressing values central to nurturing, empathetic, and socially responsible personalities. In fact, AIDS volunteers who were motivated in their work by *value* concerns (as frequently represented as these motivations are among volunteers; see Figure 8.1) also scored relatively high on measures of nurturance, empathy, and social responsibility (all $rs > .41$ and all $ps < .001$). To the extent that volunteers have nurturing dispositions, easily feel empathy for others, and think that people should take action on social issues, their work as volunteers may allow them to express these aspects of themselves.

As another example, AIDS volunteer work may provide numerous opportunities for people to work on unresolved internal conflicts about their self-worth, their social regard, and their mortality. And, in point of fact, *esteem enhancement* motivations were associated with volunteer perceptions of having little social support ($r = .23$, $p < .01$) and were also related to relatively low self-esteem, high need for social recognition, and high death anxiety (all $rs > .19$ and all $ps < .05$). It appears that these people may be doing AIDS volunteer work to feel less lonely, to feel better about themselves, or to cope with their personal fears and anxieties about AIDS and death. Overall, these esteem enhancement motivations tended to be relatively less frequent among AIDS volunteers (as indicated, for example, in Figure 8.1), but it nevertheless seems possible to identify subsets of people for whom, by virtue of features of their personalities, such motivations seem to be particularly central in their volunteer activities.

Motivations for Continuing as an AIDS Volunteer

Just as motivations for volunteering may be traced backward to differences in personality, the preceding analysis also implies that they may foreshadow certain volunteer outcomes. Consider, for example, the specific types of work that volunteers choose to do and some of the differences between people who choose to work directly with PWAs (e.g., as a buddy or providing in-home care and assistance) and those who make decisions to work in other capacities (e.g., staffing the phone lines, doing general office work, or joining a speakers' bureau). We found that people who chose to work as buddies scored higher on motivations revolving around a concern for others, and incorporating feelings of compassion and empathy for PWAs and a desire to learn how to help PWAs, than did people who took on other volunteer assignments (all $ts > 2.15$ and all $ps < .05$). Motivations for volunteering that are more selfish and that involve primarily esteem enhancement (wanting to feel better about oneself) and perhaps cravings for recognition and social reward, by contrast, were more characteristic of volunteers who did *not* have direct or extensive contact with PWAs than they were of those who worked as buddies (all $ts > 1.80$ and all $ps < .05$).

Returning to our conceptual framework, it appears that the influence of psychological and motivational functions may extend well beyond the antecedents of volunteerism, and into the experiences and consequences stages of the volunteer process. In fact, the particular motivations that lead people to become volunteers may subsequently interact with their experiences so as to influence their ultimate effectiveness as volunteers, their satisfaction with their work, or even the length of time that they remain active. For that matter, people may develop very different reasons for staying involved in AIDS volunteer work than they had for getting started with it in the first place. The volunteer who enlisted for esteem enhancement or community concern reasons, for example, may derive little satisfaction from being assigned the solitary task of stuffing and licking envelopes, and may decide to quit the organization as soon as social convention will allow. Similarly, volunteer work that is performed primarily for knowledge or understanding reasons may wear thin fairly quickly, for volunteers may become well-informed about AIDS relatively early—perhaps even as a result of training. Rather than continuing in the organization, then, these volunteers may turn their attention and energy to other challenges, causes, and questions, or they may decide that remaining active in the organization is a good way to fulfill value motivations that have become salient.

To examine some of these possibilities, we recontacted the volunteers who had completed the extensive questionnaire approximately 1 year after the first survey, successfully reaching 78% of them. As part of this follow-up, volunteers were asked whether or not they were still active in the AIDS volunteer organization and about their satisfaction and complaints with their experiences. A year after the first contact, approximately one half of this group of AIDS volunteers was still active. There were no differential rates of attrition between men and women, nor between volunteers who had chosen to work as buddies and those who had donated their time and energy in other capacities. Hence, we moved on to examine the psychological and motivational characteristics of these people.

In focusing on the quitters, it was somewhat surprising that they reported their volunteer experiences to have been satisfying overall and that they were still personally committed to the purposes and philosophy of their AIDS organization. In fact, their levels of satisfaction and commitment were comparable to people who were persevering in their work (all ts < 1.41, ns). Quitters were apparently particularly affected, however, by the *costs* of volunteer work. That is, even though they had found their AIDS work satisfying and rewarding, they claimed that volunteering was taking up too much of their time and, importantly, that it caused them to feel embarrassed, stigmatized, or uncomfortable. Quitters claimed these costs to be much greater and more severe than continuing volunteers (all ts > 2.3 and all ps < .05). The negative repercussions and *not* the benefits or rewards of their work, then, distinguished quitters from the volunteers who continued to serve.

Beyond these post hoc characterizations, however, a key question was whether we could have predicted who would continue and who would drop out from our first contact a year earlier. For example, were there certain people or personalities who were more likely to stay with the organization and others who were more likely to drop out? Or, as suggested by our conceptual model, were certain psychological functions and motivations associated with continued participation and others more strongly related to attrition?

In addressing these issues, the results showed that the initial measures were successful at predicting which volunteers would persevere and which ones would quit. However, it was *not* the measures of global personality dispositions that proved to be strongly related to these decisions about continued involvement. Quitters, in general, scored no higher or lower than those who remained active in the organization on measures of empathy, nurturance, social responsibility, self-esteem, death anxiety, and need for social recognition.

Rather, people's initial reasons for volunteering, or the measures of psychological *functions*, successfully predicted volunteer attrition and longevity of service. Regression analyses were conducted in which the measures of volunteer motivation were separately utilized along with measures of satisfaction, psychological cost, and job assignment in predicting attrition and length of service. To the extent that people espoused esteem enhancement or personal development reasons for their work (rather than community concern, values, or understanding motivations), they were more likely still to be active volunteers at the 1-year followup (all Fs > 2.60 and all ps < .05). Relatedly, in comparable analyses for predicting the total length of time that volunteers served, the esteem enhancement motivations and the reasons tapping understanding proved valuable. Volunteers who enlisted with the AIDS organization to fill voids in their own lives and to understand AIDS better remained active longer than volunteers who joined in attempts to fulfill other psychological motivations and functions (Fs = 2.05, 2.47, repectively; and ps < .10, .06, respectively).

Thus continuing volunteers could be distinguished from quitters not so much by their community concern and humanitarian values, as one might expect, but by their more "selfish" desires to feel good about themselves and to learn about AIDS. These selfish reasons, as noted previously, are also characteristic of volunteers active in non-AIDS causes (Omoto & Snyder, 1989b). Taken together, these findings suggest that volunteer organizations might profit from attending to the psychological benefits that volunteers themselves derive from their work as one key to promoting their continued service as volunteers. The good (and perhaps romantic) intentions related to humanitarian concern may not be strong enough to sustain volunteers who are faced with the tough realities of working with PWAs.

Summary

These studies of AIDS volunteerism have revealed no simple answers to the questions of who volunteers to help PWAs and why these individuals engage in their helpful acts. AIDS volunteers cannot easily and conveniently be characterized in terms of demographic characteristics or personality traits, nor are their reasons for volunteering marked by a single theme. AIDS volunteerism is perceived quite differently from other types of volunteer work, and this perception is even held by people who are known to possess Samaritan tendencies. Consistent with a functional approach, the reasons that AIDS volunteers report for going through training and doing volunteer work indicate a diversity of underlying motivations. There is at least one common thread woven throughout these studies, however; namely that humanitarian and value-based concerns seem to figure prominently in people's *initial* decisions to pursue AIDS-related volunteer work. Importantly, though, a 1-year followup of actual volunteers revealed that these motivations are relatively unimportant in accounting for *continuing* volunteer service, at least as compared to more personal and selfish reasons. Although these results are only preliminary, they nevertheless seem to have clear and important implications for AIDS organizations attempting to recruit new volunteers most effectively and to structure their subsequent training and work experiences.

Basic Research and Practical Problems

In concluding, we would like to address explicitly an issue to which all of our research speaks: the relation between basic research and practical problems. Although our research is simultaneously basic *and* applied in nature, it most strongly attests to the utility of basic theory and research in guiding the study of issues of importance and concern to society. In this chapter, we have focused on the antecedents stage of the volunteer process (i.e., who helps, and why, in these real-world voluntary helping relationships), but in our work on the other stages of the volunteer process we are similarly building connections between basic theory and research and applied issues related to society's response to AIDS (Omoto & Snyder, 1990).

At the experiences stage, we are concerned with the in-service experiences of volunteers and the PWAs with whom they work. Of particular importance here are the relationships that develop between volunteers and PWAs, and the implications of these relationships for their participants. Individuals who are diagnosed with AIDS often lose much of their social support, with friends, families, and lovers shunning them (Ferrara, 1984; Triplet & Sugarman, 1987). Ironically, social support may actually help insulate people against the effects of many stressors and diseases (e.g., Cohen & Wills, 1985; Suls, 1982). Quite possibly, volunteers can and do serve as significant sources of social support for PWAs. In this stage, therefore, we are investigating volunteer-PWA relationships to determine the forms they take and the implications of the different forms.

Using basic theory and research on personal relationships and the stages through which they move (e.g., Altman & Taylor, 1973; Berscheid, Snyder, & Omoto, 1989a, 1989b; Kelley et al., 1983; Levinger & Huesmann, 1980) as a starting point, we are quantifying and tracking the patterns of interaction between AIDS volunteers and PWAs, and trying to analyze the special features and development of their relationships. In particular, we seek to probe the implications of some of the "special" features of volunteer-PWA relationships. These relationships take place against a backdrop of stigma and chronic illness, and they tend to be asymmetrical in terms of physical capabilities and the expectations of the psychological investments to be made. Also, until a cure for AIDS is found, both participants know from the outset just how the relationship most certainly will end. (Some of these features, it should be pointed out, are also evident in relationships in other contexts, such as hospice care and some foster homes.) In addition, we are examining linkages between features of volunteer-PWA relationships and the affective and evaluative experiences of volunteers and the psychological functioning of PWAs.

At the consequences stage, we are addressing the consequences of volunteerism—for AIDS volunteer organizations and their programs, for AIDS volunteers personally, for volunteers' social networks, and for society at large. At this stage, therefore, we are examining the consequences of AIDS volunteerism for volunteers' personal attitudes, fears, knowledge, and actions. Psychological theories of how new behaviors change old attitudes and subsequent actions (Bem, 1967; Festinger, 1957) provide every reason to expect that, as a result of working in AIDS organizations, volunteers should develop more favorable attitudes toward PWAs, have decreased fear and increased knowledge about AIDS, become more likely to practice safe-sex behaviors, and be more likely to engage in AIDS-related activism (e.g., monetary donations, lobbying). We also expect experienced volunteers to have increased self-esteem and greater feelings of self-efficacy (Bandura, 1986) in comparison to new volunteers. In addition, we are attempting to identify volunteers most at risk for burnout (Maslach, 1982; Pines & Aronson, 1981) and to devise ways to combat it.

With respect to broader consequences, we are exploring the possibility of having AIDS volunteers educate nonvolunteers and fight "AIDS hysteria" (negative, fearful, prejudicial attitudes based on scant or incorrect information; Herek & Glunt, 1988; Omoto & Morier, 1988). Psychological research has demonstrated that "social diffusion," or hearing acquaintances talk about firsthand experiences, can be an effective method of information dissemination and persuasion (Costanzo, Archer, Aronson, & Pettigrew, 1986; Darley & Beniger, 1981). It seems reasonable to expect that, as AIDS volunteers become better informed and less fearful about AIDS and PWAs, they may talk about their experiences in ways that encourage other people to reassess their own beliefs, attitudes, and behaviors. In other words, AIDS volunteers may set in motion a "domino effect," in which changes in their attitudes and behaviors reverberate throughout the social system. It seems likely that AIDS volunteers, by virtue of their experiences, are particularly credible sources of AIDS-related information and may be able to contribute directly to the social diffusion of knowledge and changes in attitudes and behaviors.

Clearly, then, at each stage of the volunteer process, the intertwining of applied and theoretical concerns is evident. This intertwining is squarely in the rich social science tradition of action research (Lewin, 1946, 1947; Sanford, 1970). In this enterprise, basic and applied research are linked in a reciprocal relation in which they can and should mutually inform and enrich each other. Action research can take many forms, for the term is used to refer to research oriented toward social problems, research together with social action, and research as a part of social action (Festinger, 1989). There is nevertheless an important element common to all forms of action research: the commitment to research as an integral component of social action.

In fact, four partially overlapping and mutually compatible varieties of action research have been distinguished (Chein, Cook, & Harding, 1948), each of which is exemplified to some degree in our program of research. *Diagnostic* action research involves analyzing a current situation and formulating a plan of action aimed at solving the problems in that situation; our descriptive surveys are clearly relevant to this form of action research. *Participant* action research, the second type, stresses that those who will ultimately effect and be affected by social change should be included in the research process from the very beginning. Consistent with this form of action research, we have ventured into the real world and developed amicable working relationships with several volunteer organizations, informed and refined our research plan through extensive interviews with the staff at these agencies, and agreed to share our results with them and their volunteers.

Third, *empirical* action research focuses on collecting data relevant to the action or intervention that has been implemented and its corresponding effects; some of our studies of AIDS volunteers, the PWAs with whom they work, and their social networks are relevant here, particularly our ongoing longitudinal study of new volunteers. Finally, *experimental* action research seeks to identify the most effective techniques for social change through controlled study of the comparative effectiveness of alternative actions. In this regard, we are conducting laboratory tests and intervention studies that should have clear potential to contribute most to this form of action research.

Our work conveys another important element of action research, namely, the reciprocities and the permeable boundaries that exist between basic and applied research and between theory and application. Not only can answers to applied questions profitably be built on foundations provided by basic research, but theories themselves can be further developed and advanced by research on practical problems conducted in applied contexts (for a related perspective, see the discussion of substantive theorizing in Wicker, 1989). In a sense, we have been taking advantage of "the best of both worlds" by testing hypotheses derived from basic theory and research in naturally occurring contexts and settings (McGuire, 1969), although we are also remaining open to the implications of our real-world findings for the theories with which we started.

Such an approach, we believe, offers many potential benefits for developing theory and research domains. First, through our research we hope to gain a fuller understanding of the nature of prosocial action, particularly as it occurs in ongoing, sustained, and voluntary helping relationships. In addition, functional theories have been in a state of near hibernation for decades now; our work may help not only to rejuvenate them, but to further develop and extend them into global, integrative, and powerful theories of personal and social motivation (see also Snyder, 1988). Finally, the implications of our research for applied concerns may contribute to increasing the effectiveness of volunteer efforts in combating AIDS and in alleviating the suffering of PWAs and their loved ones.

In all likelihood, the AIDS epidemic will only intensify and worsen in the years ahead; so, too, will the need for the contributions of theory-based research relevant to all facets of AIDS. It has been said that a society is judged by how well it responds in times of need. Clearly, the age of AIDS is, and will continue to be, a time of great need, and a time of helping and being helped in the real world. AIDS presents not only a medical crisis but also a broader challenge to individuals (whether or not they are good Samaritans) and to society. In this vein, we believe that our research constitutes one example of how basic and applied research in psychology can become an integral part of society's collective response to AIDS.

References

AIDS conferees hopeful on vaccine. (1990, June 23). *San Francisco Examiner,* p. A1.

AIDS leading killer of young black women in N.Y., N.J. (1990, July 11). *Minneapolis Star Tribune*, p. 7A.

AIDSWEEK. (1990, June 3). *San Francisco Examiner*, p. A4.

Altman, I., & Taylor, D. A. (1973). *Social penetration: The development of interpersonal relationships.* New York: Holt, Rinehart & Winston.

Arno, P. S. (1988). The nonprofit sector's response to the AIDS epidemic: Community-based services in San Francisco. *American Journal of Public Health, 76,* 1325-1330.

Bandura, A. (1986). *Social foundations of thought and action: A social cognitive theory.* Englewood Cliffs, NJ: Prentice-Hall.

Batson, C. D. (1990). How social an animal? The human capacity for caring. *American Psychologist, 45,* 336-346.

Bem, D. J. (1967). Self-perception: An alternative interpretation of cognitive dissonance phenomena. *Psychological Review, 74,* 183-200.

Berscheid, E., Snyder, M., & Omoto, A. M. (1989a). Issues in studying close relationships: Conceptualizing and measuring closeness. In C. Hendrick (Ed.), *Review of personality and social psychology* (Vol. 10, pp. 63-91). Newbury Park, CA: Sage.

Berscheid, E., Snyder, M., & Omoto, A. M. (1989b). The Relationship Closeness Inventory: Assessing the closeness of interpersonal relationships. *Journal of Personality and Social Psychology, 57,* 792-807.

Centers for Disease Control. (1981, June 5). Pneumocystis pneumonia—Los Angeles. *Morbidity and Mortality Weekly Report*, pp. 250-252.

Chein, I., Cook, S. W., & Harding, J. (1948). The field of action research. *American Psychologist, 3,* 43-50.

Clary, E. G., & Snyder, M. (1991). A functional analysis of altruism and prosocial behavior: The case of volunteerism. In M. S. Clark (Ed.), *Review of personality and social psychology* (Vol. 12, pp. 119-148). Newbury Park, CA: Sage.

Cohen, S., & Wills, T. A. (1985). Stress, social support, and the buffering hypothesis. *Psychological Bulletin, 98,* 310-357.

Costanzo, M., Archer, D., Aronson, E., & Pettigrew, T. (1986). Energy conservation behavior: The difficult path from information to action. *American Psychologist, 41,* 521-528.

Darley, J. M., & Beniger, J. R. (1981). Diffusion of energy-conserving innovation. *Journal of Social Issues, 37*(1), 150-171.

Dumont, J. A. (1989). Volunteer visitors for patients with AIDS. *Journal of Volunteer Administration, 8,* 3-8.

Ferrara, A. J. (1984). My personal experience with AIDS. *American Psychologist, 39,* 1285-1287.

Festinger, L. (1957). *A theory of cognitive dissonance.* Stanford, CA: Stanford University Press.

Festinger, L. (1989). Looking backward. In S. Schachter & M. S. Gazzaniga (Eds.), *Extending psychological frontiers: Selected works of Leon Festinger* (pp. 547-566). New York: Russell Sage.

Fineberg, H. V. (1989). The social dimensions of AIDS. In J. Piel (Ed.), *The science of AIDS: Readings from* Scientific American (pp. 111-121). San Francisco: Freeman.

General Accounting Office. (1989). *AIDS: Delivering and financing health services in five communities* (Report No. 89-120 to Congressional Committees, Human Resources Division). Washington, DC: Author.

Herek, G. M. (1987). Can functions be measured?: A new perspective on the functional approach to attitudes. *Social Psychology Quarterly, 50,* 285-303.

Herek, G. M., & Glunt, E. K. (1988). An epidemic of stigma: Public reaction to AIDS. *American Psychologist, 43,* 886-891.

HIV: Longer life before AIDS begins. (1990, March 18). *San Francisco Examiner,* p. A5.

Independent Sector. (1988). *Giving and volunteering in the United States: Findings from a national survey.* Washington, DC: Author.

Katz, D. (1960). The functional approach to the study of attitudes. *Public Opinion Quarterly, 24,* 163-204.

Kelley, H. H., Berscheid, E., Christensen, A., Harvey, J., Huston, T. L., Levinger, G., McClintock, E., Peplau, L. A., & Peterson, D. R. (1983). *Close relationships.* New York: Freeman.

King, M., Walder, L., & Pavey, S. (1970). Personality change as a function of volunteer experience in a psychiatric hospital. *Journal of Consulting and Clinical Psychology, 35,* 423-425.

Latané, B., & Darley, J. M. (1970). *The unresponsive bystander: Why doesn't he help?* New York: Appleton-Century-Crofts.

Lemp, G. F., Payne, S. F., Neal, D., Temelso, T., & Rutherford, G. W. (1990). Survival trends for patients with AIDS. *Journal of the American Medical Association, 263,* 402-406.

Levinger, G., & Huesmann, L. R. (1980). An "incremental exchange" perspective on the pair relationship: Interpersonal reward and level of involvement. In K. J. Gergen, M. S. Greenberg, & R. H. Willis (Eds.), *Social exchange: Advances in theory and research.* New York: Plenum.

Lewin, K. (1946). Action research and minority problems. *Journal of Social Issues, 2,* 34-46.

Lewin, K. (1947). Group decision and social change. In T. M. Newcomb & E. L. Hartley (Eds.), *Readings in social psychology* (pp. 330-344). New York: Holt, Rinehart, & Winston.

Lewin, K. (1951). *Field theory in social science* (D. Cartwright, Ed.). New York: Harper & Row.

Lopez, D., & Getzel, G. S. (1987). Strategies for volunteers caring for persons with AIDS. *Social Casework, 68,* 47-53.

Lui, K., Darrow, W., & Rutherford, G. W. (1988). A model-based estimate of the mean incubation period for AIDS in homosexual men. *Science, 240,* 1333-1335.

Mark, M. M., & Bryant, F. B. (1984). Potential pitfalls of a more applied social psychology: Review and recommendations. *Basic and Applied Social Psychology, 5,* 231-253.

Maslach, C. (1982). *Burnout, the cost of caring.* Englewood Cliffs, NJ: Prentice-Hall.

McGuire, W. J. (1969). Theory-oriented research in natural settings: The best of both worlds for social psychology. In M. Sherif & C. W. Sherif (Eds.), *Interdisciplinary relationships in the social sciences* (pp. 21-51). Hawthorne, NY: Aldine.

Morgan, W. M., & Curran, J. W. (1986). Acquired immunodeficiency syndrome: Current and future trends. *Public Health Reports, 101,* 459-465.

Morin, S. F. (1988). AIDS: The challenge to psychology. *American Psychologist, 43,* 838-842.

Noble experiment: Volunteers' distress cripples huge effort to provide AIDS care. (1990, March 12). *Wall Street Journal,* p. A1.

Omoto, A. M., & Berghuis, J. (1990). *The training of AIDS volunteers: Determinants of communication apprehension.* Unpublished manuscript, University of Kansas, Lawrence.

Omoto, A. M., & Morier, D. (1988). *Fear as a source of information: Perceptions of AIDS.* Unpublished manuscript, University of Kansas, Lawrence.

Omoto, A. M., & Snyder, M. (1989a). [AIDS volunteers' narrative accounts of their experiences]. Unpublished raw data.

Omoto, A. M., & Snyder, M. (1989b, May). *Volunteering to work with people with cancer or AIDS: Differences between me and you.* Paper presented at the meeting of the Midwestern Psychological Association, Chicago, IL.

Omoto, A. M., & Snyder, M. (1990). Basic research in action: Volunteerism and society's response to AIDS. *Personality and Social Psychology Bulletin, 16,* 152-165.

Pines, A. M., & Aronson, E. (1981). *Burnout: From tedium to personal growth.* New York: Free Press.

Report: AIDS estimate low. (1989, June 26). *Lawrence Journal-World,* p. 2A.

Sanford, N. (1970). Whatever happened to action research? *Journal of Social Issues, 26*(4), 3-23.

Scheibe, K. E. (1965). College students spend eight weeks in mental hospital: A case report. *Psychotherapy: Theory, Research, and Practice, 2,* 117-120.

Smith, M. B., Bruner, J. S., & White, R. W. (1956). *Opinions and personality.* New York: John Wiley.

Snyder, M. (1988, August). *Needs and goals, plans and motives: The new "new look" in personality and social psychology.* Invited address presented at the meeting of the American Psychological Association, Atlanta, GA.

Snyder, M., & DeBono, K. G. (1987). A functional approach to attitudes and persuasion. In M. P. Zanna, J. M. Olson, & C. P. Herman (Eds.), *Social influence: The Ontario symposium* (Vol. 5, pp. 107-125). Hillsdale, NJ: Lawrence Erlbaum.

Snyder, M., & DeBono, K. G. (1989). Understanding the functions of attitudes: Lessons from personality and social behavior. In A. R. Pratkanis, S. J. Breckler, & A. G. Greenwald (Eds.), *Attitude structure and function* (pp. 339-359). Hillsdale, NJ: Lawrence Erlbaum.

Suls, J. (1982). Social support, interpersonal relations, and health: Benefits and liabilities. In G. S. Saunders & J. Suls (Eds.), *Social psychology of health and illness* (pp. 255-277). Hillsdale, NJ: Lawrence Erlbaum.

Triplet, R. G., & Sugarman, D. B. (1987). Reactions to AIDS victims: Ambiguity breeds contempt. *Personality and Social Psychology Bulletin, 13,* 265-274.

Volunteering drops as AIDS cases rise. (1990, June 20). *San Jose Mercury News,* p. 1A.

Wicker, A. W. (1989). Substantive theorizing. *American Journal of Community Psychology, 17,* 531-547.

Williams, M. J. (1988). Gay men as "buddies" to persons living with AIDS and ARC. *Smith College Studies in Social Work, 59,* 38-52.

Wills, T. A. (1981). Downward comparison principles in social psychology. *Psychological Bulletin, 90,* 245-271.

Author Index

Subject Index

About the Authors

DAVID E. BIEGEL is the Henry L. Zucker Professor of Social Work Practice and Co-Director, Practice Demonstration Program, Mandel School of Applied Social Sciences, Case Western Reserve University. He received his Ph.D. in social work from the School of Social Work and Community Planning, University of Maryland at Baltimore. He has been involved in research over the past 15 years pertaining to factors affecting the delivery of services to hard-to-reach population groups and the relationship between informal and formal care.

DAVID E. BLASBAND received his Ph.D. in clinical psychology from UCLA in 1990. He is currently a staff psychologist at the University of California, San Diego, where he also serves on the university's AIDS Task Force. His past research includes studies of child abuse and of close relationships of gay and bisexual men.

EUGENE BORGIDA is Professor of Psychology and Adjunct Professor of Law and Political Science at the University of Minnesota. He received his Ph.D. in psychology from the University of Michigan and joined the faculty at Minnesota in 1976. He is director of the social psychology doctoral program and associate editor of the *Journal of Personality and Social Psychology: Attitudes and Social Cognition.* His research interests focus on the nature of human inference and decision making in a variety of social, political, and legal contexts.

CYNTHIA CONNER is a doctoral student in the counseling psychology program at the University of Minnesota. She received her B.A. in psychology and biology from St. Olaf College in 1983. Her research interests include decision making, coping strategies used in chronic illness, control, commitment, and compliance. She is currently examining some of these issues with regard to kidney transplant patients as well as with epileptic patients and their families.

CHRISTINE DUNKEL-SCHETTER received her Ph.D. in social psychology from Northwestern University. For nearly 10 years she has taught at UCLA, where she is Associate Professor of Psychology, a member of the faculty in the social psychology program, and codirector of the health psychology program. Her research in social psychology concerns helping and social support processes, social reactions to victims, and commitment. Her research in health psychology concerns stress, coping, and social support processes as they operate in chronic illness, particularly cancer, and in women's reproductive health, specifically stress in pregnancy and adjustment to infertility.

LAWRENCE G. FEINSTEIN received his Ph.D. in social psychology in 1988 from UCLA, with an emphasis in health psychology. He is directing an outpatient weight management and health promotion program in Temecula, California, and is in private practice. His past research includes published papers on Type A behavior and coronary heart disease.

TRACY BENNETT HERBERT received her master's degree from the University of Guelph in Canada and is currently a doctoral candidate at UCLA in social psychology with a concentration in health psychology. For several years, she has been involved in theoretical and empirical work on social support and coping with stress. Her current research is in psychoneuroimmunology, focusing on the effects of behavioral and dispositional factors on immune functioning.

LAURIE MANTEUFEL is a doctoral student in social psychology at the University of Minnesota. She received her B.A. (summa cum laude) in psychology from the University of Minnesota in 1990. Her research interests include the relationship between attitudes and behavior—particularly the processes by which attitudes guide behavior. She is also interested in the interface between social psychology and law and is investigating the social psychological effects of electronic media coverage of courtroom trials.

LOUIS MEDVENE is Assistant Professor of Psychology at the Claremont Graduate School. He was a community organizer with the National Welfare Rights Organization, earned an M.S. in community organization from Columbia University's School of Social Work, and received his Ph.D. in social and organizational psychology from

Columbia in 1983. He has been a postdoctoral fellow at Yale's Institute for Social and Policy Studies, as well as a lecturer and research psychologist at UCLA where he worked with the California Self-Help Center. His research interests are in helping relationships, with a focus on voluntary relationships in mental health.

RICHARD K. MORYCZ is Associate Professor of Psychiatry, Medicine, and Social Work at the University of Pittsburgh. He is also Program Director of the Benedum Geriatric Center, Clinical Administrator of the Geriatric Psychiatry and Behavioral Neurology Module at Western Psychiatric Institute and Clinic, and Geriatric Health Services Program Director at the University of Pittsburgh School of Medicine. His experience in the field of aging includes clinical work, teaching, administration, and research, with numerous publications focusing on family caregiver burden.

ALLEN M. OMOTO received his B.A. from Kalamazoo College and his Ph.D. from the University of Minnesota, and has been Assistant Professor of Psychology at the University of Kansas since 1988. His primary research interests include interpersonal relationships, the social and psychological aspects of volunteerism, and stereotyping and prejudice. He has also been actively involved in community-based responses to the AIDS epidemic.

STUART OSKAMP is Professor of Psychology at Claremont Graduate School. He received his Ph.D. from Stanford University and has had visiting appointments at the University of Michigan, University of Bristol, London School of Economics and Political Science, University of New South Wales, and University of Hawaii. His main research interests are in the areas of attitudes and attitude change, behavioral aspects of energy and resource conservation, and social issues and public policy. His books include *Attitudes and Opinions* and *Applied Social Psychology*. He is a past president of the APA Division of Population and Environmental Psychology and is editor of the *Journal of Social Issues*.

JENNIFER S. PITTS is a graduate student in social psychology at the Claremont Graduate School. She has a bachelor's degree in behavioral sciences from California State Polytechnic University at Pomona, and a master's degree in experimental psychology from California State

University at Fullerton. Her research interests include psychological aspects of cancer and its treatment, doctor-patient communication, and patient involvement in medical decision making.

RICHARD SCHULZ is Professor of Psychiatry and Director of Gerontology at the University of Pittsburgh. He received his Ph.D. from Duke University in 1974. He has published extensively on topics relevant to aging, illness, institutionalization, and informal caregiving. Recent books include *Adult Development and Aging* (1988, with R. Ewen) and *Family Caregiving: Theory, Practice, and Policy* (1991, with D. Biegel and E. Sales). Current research interests are physical illness and depression in the elderly, home care for cancer patients receiving radiation therapy, and adjustment to limb amputation among the elderly.

MARK SNYDER is Professor of Psychology at the University of Minnesota, where he has been a member of the faculty since 1972. He received his B.A. from McGill University and his Ph.D. from Stanford University. His research interests include theoretical and empirical issues associated with the motivational foundations of individual and social behavior, and the applications of basic theory and research in personality and social psychology to practical problems confronting society. In 1992, he will serve as president of the Society for Personality and Social Psychology (APA Division 8). He has authored the book *Public Appearance/Private Realities: The Psychology of Self-Monitoring*.

SHIRLYNN SPACAPAN is Associate Professor of Psychology at Harvey Mudd College and at the Claremont Graduate School. She received her Ph.D. from the University of Oregon in 1982, where she taught for two years before moving to Claremont. She is currently studying topics at the interface of environmental psychology and organizational behavior such as perceived control in the workplace and workplace design. Recently, she was a Haynes Foundation Faculty Fellow for her work on the social psychology of aging.

SUZANNE C. THOMPSON is Associate Professor of Psychology at Pomona College. She received her Ph.D. in social psychology in 1983 from the University of California, Los Angeles. Her current research interests include styles of caregiving, doctor-patient communication, and interventions to encourage conservation.

GAIL M. WILLIAMSON is Assistant Professor of Psychology at the University of Georgia in Athens. She received her Ph.D. from Carnegie Mellon University in 1989 and was a postdoctoral fellow in gerontology at the University Center for Social and Urban Research, University of Pittsburgh. Her research interests are in social psychological aspects of aging, with emphasis on determinants of caregiver stress and adaptation. Currently, she is studying psychosocial factors involved in adjustment to limb amputation among the elderly.

THOMAS ASHBY WILLS is Associate Professor of Psychology, Epidemiology and Social Medicine at the Ferkauf Graduate School of Psychology and the Albert Einstein College of Medicine. His research interests are in help-seeking and social support, social comparison theory, stress and coping processes, and adolescent substance use. He is associate editor of the *Journal of Social and Clinical Psychology* and serves as consulting editor for the *American Journal of Community Psychology, Health Psychology,* and the *Journal of Personality and Social Psychology.*

Notes